Contents

The prices and rates listed in this guidebook were confirmed at press time. We recommend, however, that you call establishments before traveling to obtain current information.

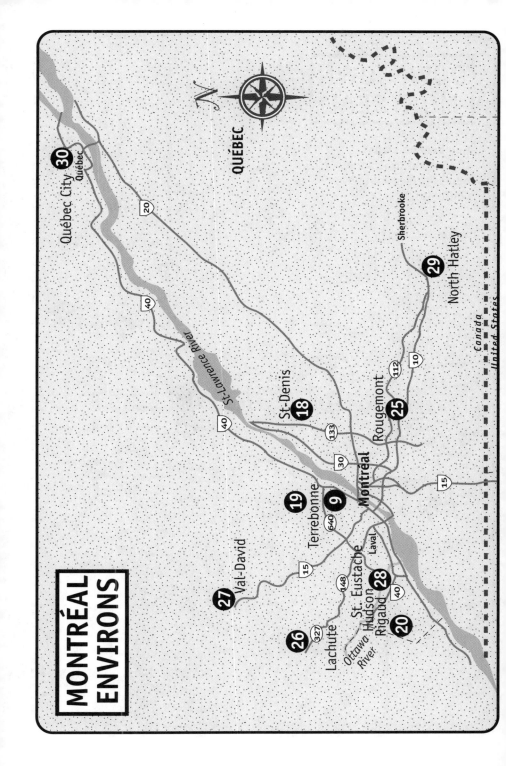

MONTRÉAL ENVIRONS

QUÉBEC

Québec City
Québec
30

Sherbrooke
29
North Hatley

Canada
United States

St-Denis
18

Rougemont
25

Montréal

Terrebonne
19
9

Val-David
27

Lachute
26

St. Eustache
Hudson
Rigaud
Laval
28
20

Ottawa River

St-Lawrence River

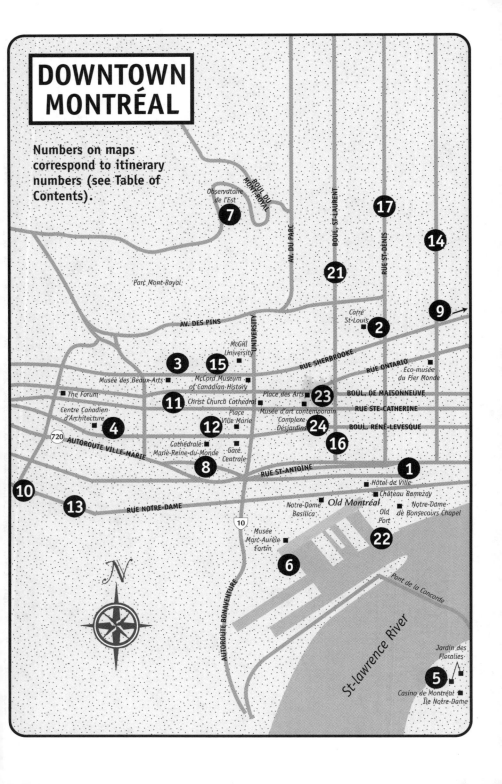

ROMANTIC DAYS AND NIGHTS® SERIES

Romantic Days and Nights®

IN MONTRÉAL

Romantic Diversions
in and around the City

SECOND EDITION

by Linda Kay

The Globe Pequot Press

GUILFORD, CONNECTICUT

To Bernard Rivest,

who showed me the town all those years ago

Text design and cover and interior illustrations by M.A. Dubé
Maps by Mary Ballachino
Spot Art by www.ArToday.com

Romantic Days and Nights is a registered trademark of The Globe Pequot Press.

Library of Congress Cataloging-in-Publication Data

Kay, Linda (Linda Merry)
    Romantic days and nights in Montréal : romantic diversions in and around
    the city / by Linda Kay. — 2nd ed.
        p.   cm. — (Romantic days and nights series)
    Includes index.
    ISBN 0-7627-0471-3
    1. Montréal (Québec) Guidebooks. I. Title. II. Series.
F1054.5.M83K38   1999
917.14'27044—dc21   99-33346
                                                     CIP

Manufactured in the United States of America
Second Edition/First Printing

Acknowledgments

MY PROFOUND THANKS to the guides who shared their expertise and their romantic notions: my safety net Gilles Bengle; Roselyne Hébert; Suzanne Bonin; Dinu Bumbaru; Eric Schifi, and Johanne Leduc. My boundless gratitude, as well, to my husband, Bernard Rivest, for helping to land this bird gently; and to my daughter, Emily Isabel, for her patience—and her hugs.

Introduction

I FELL IN LOVE WITH MONTRÉAL AT THE SAME TIME that I fell in love with a Montréaler. It happened in deepest *hiver* (the French word for winter still makes me shiver), when a Montréaler I met on vacation in Mexico invited me to his city for the weekend. I arrived during an unseasonable warm spell in February. The roads were dry, and I didn't even need boots.

My Montréaler surprised me the following morning by securing a small plane and a pilot, who swept us up over the city landmarks for a bird's-eye view of the arching tower at the Olympic Stadium, the space-age geodesic dome designed for Expo '67, and the imposing steel cross on Mont-Royal.

Talk about romantic.

Saturday night we walked for hours along boisterous rue Ste-Catherine as cruisers in hot cars inched down the strip begging for attention. We paused outside hockey's temple, The Forum, and peeked in sundry boutiques. As midnight approached, we were caught in a snow squall and dashed into a café for shelter and hot chocolate.

Talk about romantic.

That summer we toured historic Old Montréal, where I convinced my Montréaler to have his portrait sketched by a street artist in Place Jacques-Cartier. We climbed a narrow staircase to the watchtower in a church for a privileged view of the waterfront. We drove east and visited the walled city of Québec.

Talk about romantic.

Since my initial visit to La Belle Province fifteen Februarys ago, much has changed in my life—romantically speaking. I married that Montréaler. I'm now a wife, a mother, and a suburban dweller who drives a van. Not the stuff of romance. But every so often the van heads for the city, and the same sights that sparked my passion reignite. I fall for Montréal again.

In sharing with you the city that charmed and seduced me, I've divided the itineraries in this book to reflect characteristics that jumped out at me the first time I saw Montréal: these are physical, spiritual, historical, and emotional.

First off, Montréal surprises visitors with its physical characteristics. Few realize that the city is surrounded on all sides by water and that in the middle of this island sits a mountain.

As for Montréal's spiritual characteristics, Mark Twain said after visiting the city in the 1880s that you couldn't throw a brick here without breaking a church window. He wasn't exaggerating much. Montréal was founded by a band of French settlers in 1642 for the very purpose of converting the native American Indians to Christianity. The role religion played is obvious even today. Just look at the 83-foot cross on the mountain.

North Americans looking for romance are above all smitten by the city's historical side and the mix of old and new. History seems to permeate every walk, every vista, every outing. As for Montréal's emotional character, you find it in the blend of antiquity, physical beauty, and continental charm. Both ancient and *au courant*, the largest French-speaking city in the world after Paris makes you believe you have been transported to Europe without crossing an ocean.

What makes Montréal an even more appealing romantic destination now is the current Canadian exchange rate: for every $1.00 (U.S.) spent, visitors get roughly $1.40 (Canadian) in return. That means prices for a hotel room or a restaurant meal in Montréal cost more than a third less in U.S. dollars, so you can eat, sleep, and play on a grand scale without blowing the budget.

The best source for general information about Montréal—métro maps, tours, guidebooks, and such—are the two Infotouriste centers (514–873–2015; 800–363–7777) located downtown (1001 Dorchester Square) or in Old Montréal (174 rue Notre-Dame Est). Both centers carry the same information, and the staff is personable and bilingual in each office. Better yet, by calling the toll-free number before your trip, you can have information sent to your home to make planning easier. I strongly suggest you request the Montréal Tourist Guide, a treasure trove of information that is updated annually by the Greater Montréal Convention and Tourism Bureau. It will become your bible. And be sure to phone ahead before you venture to a museum, club, or restaurant listed in the guide or in this book, particularly since many places curtail their schedules in the off-season or simply change their hours of operation.

Here are five points to keep in mind as you use this guide:
1. All prices are in Canadian dollars. Meal prices are based on cost per

person before taxes, drinks, and tip, and are rated inexpensive (under $20), moderate (under $40), or expensive ($40 and more). If you deviate from the itinerary, swapping a dinner spot for a lunch spot, for instance, please call ahead to make certain the restaurant is open. Many restaurants close for lunch on weekends; some don't open for lunch at all, and still others close for dinner.

2. A word about taxes. Canada's federal sales tax is 7 percent; Québec adds an additional 7.5 percent on goods and services. Tourists, however, get a federal sales tax rebate on lodging and on most items purchased but not used in Québec. You must fill out forms (available at border crossings, hotels, and shops) and submit them, with original receipts, within a year of purchase. Details are contained in a brochure entitled "GST Rebate for Visitors" published by Revenue Canada, Customs and Excise. Tourists also get a rebate on the Québec provincial sales tax on items of $50 or more. Do save your receipts. My cousins didn't and were bemoaning the fact after they bought a beautiful Inuit sculpture here—and missed out on a hefty tax refund.

3. Navigating the island is a breeze on the métro. Built for Expo '67, the world's fair that put Montréal on the map, it's an absolute miracle in North American transport—clean, efficient, and enjoyable. At many stations, you'll find paintings, stained glass, or murals. At transfer points, you'll hear buskers play music ranging in quality from helplessly out-of-tune to symphonic quality. One day I heard two young classical violinists, dressed in white tie and tails, play for commuters at Lionel-Groulx station. If you're going to be using the métro quite a bit, it's best to purchase tickets six at a time and thereby derive a discount. Or consider buying a Tourist Card at one of the Infotouriste centers mentioned earlier. The Tourist Card allows you to travel by bus or métro all day for $4.00—or for $10.00 on three consecutive days. The métro opens at 5:30 A.M. and closes at 1:00 A.M. Trains run every three to ten minutes—and bicycles are allowed on the first car between 10:00 A.M. and 3:00 P.M. and after 7:00 P.M. on weekdays (outside commuter hours) and all day Saturday and Sunday.

4. Since getting around is simple on the métro, feel free to substitute hotels and inns from one itinerary to another. I've indicated the métro stop nearest each hotel recommended, so if a particular lodging sounds wonderful to you but it's not paired with the itinerary

you like, go for it. It won't be difficult to access your resting place.

5. Montréal is filled with B&Bs you won't find in any guidebook. Their owners may live in a heritage home and rent out rooms discreetly to help underwrite the cost of purchase or renovation. I've seen no-name B&Bs in a Victorian mansion and in a former convent converted to a condominium. To access these special places, which are often extremely romantic and huge bargains besides, call Bed & Breakfast Downtown Network (514–289–9749; 800–267–5180), one of the most reputable location services in town. Given advance notice, Bob and Mariko Finkelstein can tailor the residence to your chosen itinerary. A similar service is run by Hébergement Touristique du Plateau Mont-Royal (514–597–0166 or 800–597–0597; be sure to ask for operator 28), which has a stable of fifteen private lodgings in the Plateau area. Marian Kahn, founder of the Bed & Breakfast `a Montréal reservation service (514–738–9410), has a stable of about fifty rooms in all price ranges, mostly on the west side of town. You may have to share a bathroom in these places, but many couples find that the ambience of the residence and the low cost more than compensate for that compromise.

La ville d'amour awaits. Dépêchez-vous.

Montréal's Bests

MOST ROMANTIC RESTAURANTS IN MONTRÉAL

Laloux (250 avenue des Pins Est), 124
Le Club des Pins (156 avenue Laurier Ouest), 129
Le Passe-Partout (3857 boulevard Décarie), 41
Les Caprices de Nicolas (2072 rue Drummond), 94
Ritz Garden (for lunch and brunch, 1228 rue Sherbrooke Ouest), 25

MOST ROMANTIC RESTAURANTS OUT-OF-TOWN

Café de la Terrasse (1 rue des Carrierès in Québec City), 238
Clementine (398 chemin Main in Hudson), 223
Edelweiss (3050 chemin Doncaster in Val-David), 217
Le Champagne (1000 rue du Rivage in St-Antoine-sur-Richelieu), 154
Laurie Raphael (117 Dalhousie in Québec City), 240

MOST ROMANTIC LODGINGS IN MONTRÉAL

Auberge du Vieux Port (97 rue de la Commune Est), 56
Auberge Les Passants du Sans Soucy (171 rue St-Paul Ouest), 91
Aux Portes de la nuit (3496 avenue Laval), 36
Hotel Vogue (1425 rue de la Montagne), 99
La Maison Pierre du Calvet (405 rue Bonsecours), 4

MOST ROMANTIC LODGINGS OUT-OF-TOWN

Auberge Hatley (325 Virgin Road in North Hatley), 228
Hotel du Lac Carling (Route 327 Nord in Pine Hill), 210
La Maison de Bavière (1470 chemin de la Rivière in Val-David), 215
Le Château Frontenac (1 rue des Carrières in Québec City), 236
Manoir Hovey (575 Hovey Road in North Hatley), 232

BEST KEPT SECRETS (HUSH-HUSH)

Hôtel de Ville (275 rue Notre-Dame Est), for its swanky art deco interior, 7
Jardin des Floralies (Île Notre-Dame), where you can stroll or bike through
gardens designed by artisans around the world, 56
Mont-Royal Cemetery (chemin de la Forêt), a burial ground designed
to be a paradise on earth, 65
Pointe-aux-Prairies regional park (12980 boulevard Gouin Est),
where you can bike or hike through exquisite swampland, 86
Westmount Greenhouse (corner rue Sherbrooke Ouest and Landsdowne),
a tiny tropical setting in the city, 68

SHOPPING MUSTS

Galerie Le Chariot for native art (446 Place Jacques-Cartier), 7, 42
Le Petit Musée for fine antiques (1494 rue Sherbrooke Ouest), 121, 133
Le Sieur Duluth for designer hats (4107 rue St-Denis), 150
Lili-les-Bains for designer bathing suits for women
(1336 rue Notre-Dame Ouest), 148
Ogilvy for men's and women's clothing (1307 rue Ste-Catherine
Ouest), 29, 51, 99
Vermeil for blown glass (90 rue Prince), 148

ROMANTIC REFRESHERS

Dessert at Le Daphne (3803 rue St-Denis), 125
Drinks in the courtyard at Le Jardin Nelson (406 Places Jacques-Cartier), 6
French fries at Frite Alors (433 rue Rachel), 46
Tea at Ambiance Tea Room (1874 rue Notre-Dame Ouest), 119
Truffles at Divine Chocolatier (1454 rue Drummond), 139

BEST PLACES TO KISS

Bench in Parc Drolet (avenue Mont-Royal and rue Drolet), 18
Lookout at Chalet du Mont-Royal (Parc du Mont-Royal), 70
Lighthouse perch at Pavillon des Marais (12300 boulevard Gouin Est), 87
Observatory at Chemin du Belvédère (chemin Belvédère in Westmount), 67
Parapet atop Notre-Dame de Bonsecours Chapel (400 rue St-Paul Est), 4

MOST ROMANTIC PLACE TO MAKE A TOAST

La Sila restaurant's dark and sultry interior (2040 rue St-Denis), 22, 101
Le Jardin Nelson's leafy outdoor courtyard (406 Places Jacques-Cartier), 6
Restaurant 737's lofty perch above the city (1 Place Ville Marie), 102
Vignoble des Pins' airy tasting room (136 Grand Sabrevois, Sabrevois), 103
Cidrerie Michel Jodoin's backyard picnic table (1130 rang Petite-Caroline in Rougemont), 205

SPLENDID SPIRITUAL RESPITES

Cathédrale Marie-Reine-du-Monde (425 rue de la Cathédrale), 110
Église de la Visitation (1847 boulevard Gouin Est), 83
Notre-Dame Basilica (116 rue Notre-Dame Ouest), 9, 78, 147
Notre-Dame de Bonsecours Chapel (400 rue St-Paul Est), 4
Notre-Dame-de-Lourdes (430 rue Ste-Catherine Est), 21

BEST STROLLS IN MONTRÉAL

Botanical Garden (hundreds of species of flowers and trees), 47, 145
Carré St. Louis (prettiest square in the city), 20, 41
Golden Square Mile (historic district in Centre Ville), 23–31
Parc Lafontaine (180 shady acres in the Plateau), 18
Rue St-Denis (shopping district in the Plateau), 23, 178
Rue St-Paul (heart of Old Montreal), 6
Sault-au-Recollet (historic district in Montréal North), 81

BEST FIRST-DATE VENUES

Botanical Garden exhibition greenhouses: year-round exotic natural beauty, (4101 rue Sherbrooke Est), 47, 145
Cidrerie et Verger Denis Charbonneau: apple-picking and picnicking (576 rang de la Montagne in Mont-St-Gregoire), 203
Comedy Nest: laughter and love (Nouvel Hotel, 1740 boulevard René-Levesque Ouest), 182
Finnegan's Market: antiquing (775 chemin Main in Hudson), 220
Mont-Royal: climb it and make a picnic, 63–71
Mount Stephen Club: brunch in an old-world setting (1440 rue Drummond), 138
Office National du Film du Canada: screen foreign films (1564 rue St-Denis), 20
Sucrerie de la Montagne: an authentic taste of Québec life, food, and music (300 rang St-Georges in Rigaud), 163

Heart
and Soul

Like a Rock
OLD MONTRÉAL

LD MONTRÉAL IS THE SOUL OF THE CITY, its spiritual heart, a dazzling display of antiquity that will captivate both of you. Amble arm in arm down the narrow, cobblestone streets and retrace Montréal's beginnings. Imagine a band of rugged settlers leaving La Rochelle, France, in 1641, wintering in Québec City, then landing on the shores of the St-Lawrence River in May of 1642, naming the colony they founded Ville-Marie—or city of Mary. Led by Paul de Chomedey, sieur de Maisonneuve, the colonists were acting on religious impulse—they wanted to convert the native American Indians to Christianity.

That spiritual ardor comes through clearly in Old Montréal even centuries later. It's hard to believe now that the neighborhood was rescued from the clutches of decay only thirty years ago. Business, commerce, and the population had gradually abandoned Old Montréal for greener pastures downtown, but in the 1960s, people started moving back and reclaiming their heritage, and business and government joined forces in a formidable restoration campaign. To me, Old Montréal today is a secular cathedral, where you can cherish the worldly, adore the divine—and worship each other.

PRACTICAL NOTES: Cobblestones are hard on the feet, and sore feet are not conducive to romance. Make sure to pack comfortable walking shoes on this trip—or boots, of course, if you come in winter. The itinerary can be used any time of year. Casual clothing is fine for most of the itinerary, but some restaurants do not allow shorts, jeans, or sneakers in the evening.

Romance AT A GLANCE

♦ Enter **La Maison Pierre du Calvet** (405 rue Bonsecours; 514– 282–1725), an exquisite heritage home from the 1700s that has been converted into an inn. Once you've taken in its beauty, walk across the street to humble **Notre-Dame de Bonsecours** (the Sailor's Church), climbing to the parapet on top for a breathtaking view of the St-Lawrence River and the city.

♦ Walk along ancient cobblestone streets in Old Montréal, envisioning life centuries ago, stopping at **Galerie Le Chariot** (446 Place Jacques-Cartier; 514–875–4994), where you can browse for hours through the largest collection of Inuit art in Canada.

♦ Dine on the intimate terrasse (weather permitting) at the elegant **La Marée** (404 Place Jacques-Cartier; 514–861–8126) for a ringside seat on the mimes and musicians who perform in the square at night. For another performance, stroll down to club **l'Air du Temps** (194 rue St-Paul Ouest; 514–842–2003) to hear live jazz.

DAY ONE: morning

Alight from either cab or car at **La Maison Pierre du Calvet** (405 rue Bonsecours; 514–282–1725; station Champ-de-Mars; $165 to $225 double occupancy, breakfast included), and you're standing at the most extraordinary corner in the entire city of Montréal—and the one most popular with film crews, who prize the union of antiquity and spirituality here and the majesterial view of the St-Lawrence River in the background. La Maison Pierre du Calvet, with its thick stone walls, heavy chimneys, and French windows, is the oldest home in the city open for public accommodation. Directly across the street stands the unpretentious **Notre-Dame de Bonsecours Chapel** (at 400 rue St-Paul Est; open Tuesday to Sunday, 10:00 A.M. to 6:00 P.M.), with its burnished gold statue of mother and child placed just above the red painted wood door. Experience the mystery for a moment, then enter La Maison and feast on history.

Inside, La Maison is a masterpiece of antiquity lovingly contrived by owner Gaetan Trottier, who can trace his family back almost as far as the first settlers. The will of his ancestor, who arrived in Ville Marie in 1646, was witnessed by Paul de Chomedey, sieur de

Maisonneuve, founder of the colony. Trottier's parents once ran one of Montréal's finest restaurants, Les Filles du Roi, which attracted notables like Princess Grace of Monaco, Sophia Loren, and Mick Jagger. When the restaurant closed in 1992, Trottier decided it would be a shame to keep the space to himself. The Trottier family had already bought the home next door, whose first owner was merchant Pierre Calvet, a Huguenot from France who supported the American Revolution and met Benjamin Franklin here in 1775. Trottier annexed the former Calvet home to his family's shuttered restaurant and opened La Maison Pierre du Calvet in 1994.

Nine bedrooms are here, all with canopy beds and old-world touches like low, beamed ceilings, wood-planked floors, Louis XVI chairs, and porcelain washbowls. The furnishings, many of them family heirlooms, are an eclectic mix of French and British design and reflect Trottier's desire to acknowledge the role both cultures had in building Montréal. This explains the burgundy leather couches and the mounted caribou head in the living room—status symbols of the wealthy English living in the Golden Square Mile in the 1800s.

There's much to see (including paintings done by Trottier himself) at La Maison, but it must wait. Old Montréal beckons. After you have settled your belongings in your room, step out the door of the inn and explore rue Bonsecours, one of the oldest in Montréal. To get the best perspective on the quartier, cross the street to Notre Dame de Bonsecours Chapel (400 rue St-Paul Est). Not only is the modest church a favorite spiritual respite, but its tower provides one of the best perches for viewing the city and the St-Lawrence River. Construction of the church was begun in 1657, but the current building is the product of a twenty-year renovation begun in the 1880s—and renovation still proceeds today. In fact, frescoes believed to be painted in 1886 were recently discovered under a canvas spread across the vaulted dome of the chapel.

Notice the model ships hanging from the ceiling. At one time, fleets of these miniature boats hung in the chapel, offered by sailors and travelers as thanks for safe passage. Most have been removed, but some remain. The votive offerings relate directly to the statue of the Virgin Mary atop the church, welcoming, it is said, with outstretched arms the seafaring men who made Montréal a center for trade and commerce. The Sailor's Church was among the first places my husband took me as we courted. I remember climbing the winding staircase to the tower, imbibing the city from various lookouts as we ascended and being struck speechless by the marriage of heaven and earth. No more romantic spot in town.

DAY ONE: afternoon

When you descend the tower and leave the church, turn left and amble along **rue St-Paul,** Montréal's first street and once its main commercial thoroughfare. As you near Place Jacques-Cartier, you may hear music and lots of chatter coming from an old stone building. The sound heralds your luncheon spot.

LUNCH

Chamber music plays in the leafy courtyard at **Le Jardin Nelson** (407 Place Jacques-Cartier; 514–861–5731; inexpensive). Enjoy a stuffed crepe or a salad (and don't forget a glass of wine) under the large, flowering tree in good weather or head for a table on the *terrasse* to people-watch. In winter, the restaurant is cozy inside as well.

After lunch, walk to the top of **Place Jacques-Cartier**, former site of an outdoor public market in the early 1800s and now a lively gathering point rimmed with shops and restaurants. Head for the building with the high copper roof and large clock (275 rue Notre- Dame Est). They don't take reservations at **Hôtel de Ville**—which means City Hall *en français*—but the guards here have had many inquiries about the price of rooms over the years.

The balcony of the facade is famous in Québec as the spot where General Charles de Gaulle uttered his famous "Vive le Québec libre" during an official visit in 1967—interpreted by some as a clarion call for Québec's independence from Canada—a topic still hotly debated today. Climb the stairs and enter the building for a brief look inside. Redecorated in the Roaring Twenties after the interior was destroyed by fire, Hotel de Ville has a swanky lobby, with a marble floor laid out to resemble a Persian carpet, priceless Tiffany lanterns in each corner, and a one-ton chandelier made in Paris that can be raised and lowered for cleaning. If you can peek in the council chambers across the hall, you'll see rich teakwood from India and five stained-glass windows illustrating five factors that shaped life in Montréal: religion, agriculture, the port, industry, and finance.

Cross the street and spend about an hour in the beautifully landscaped **Château Ramezay** (280 rue Notre-Dame Est; open daily from 10:00 A.M. to 6:00 P.M. June to September; Tuesday to Sunday from 10:00 A.M. to 4:30 P.M. the rest of the year), one of the most striking residences ever built in what was then called New France. Erected in 1705 for Claude de Ramezay, then Governor of Montréal, the majestic residence lured other notable families of that era to the area. In 1775, the Château was requisitioned by Benedict Arnold and rebel American forces. Ben Franklin stayed here trying to convince Montréalers to back the independence movement—but the revolutionaries were chased away by the advancing British Army. If only the walls could talk!

"Things are always at their best in their beginning."
—Blaise Pascal

Today the Château is a museum and houses a collection of eighteenth- and nineteenth-century furniture, costumes, and household items. During summer, artisans are often on hand to demonstrate nearly forgotten arts like weaving, quilting, or lacemaking. The most gorgeous room (alone worth the $4.00 price of admission) is the Salle de Nantes with its rich Louis XV mahogany paneling, a gift from the West India Company, which bought the house from Ramezay's heirs in 1745 and used it as a storehouse for spices—a humble function for such a glorious space.

Retrace your steps to Place Jacques-Cartier and plan to spend at least an hour—and maybe the rest of the afternoon—oohing and aahing over the remarkable collection of native art in the **Galerie Le Chariot** (446 Place Jacques-Cartier; 514–875–4994; open every day in summer, restricted days and hours in winter). Showcase after showcase fill three floors in this combination gallery/shop. The stunning carvings are done by artisans from Canada's arctic or other native communities, including the Mohawk people. Among the most prized pieces? The sculpted soapstone by Inuit artists living in Cape Dorset, particularly Dancing Bear by Pauta Saila, a world-famous carver now in his eighties whose pieces are distinguished by ivory teeth and rounded feet. Saila's bear is dancing toward the moon, moving toward the spirit. Don't miss the ammolite gemstones from southern Alberta (the only precious stone found in Canada) or the caribou antler jewelry and the jewelry crafted from prehistoric ivory. I defy you to leave here without buying something—or at least vowing to come back tomorrow. Galerie Le Chariot delivers anywhere in the world. Back to the hotel now to freshen up for dinner.

DAY ONE: evening

DINNER

You're in Place Jacques-Cartier again for dinner this evening at **La Marée** (404 Place Jacques-Cartier; 514–861–8126; expensive). You'll want to dress up a bit, especially if it's Saturday night—I learned that lesson when we were turned away one summer evening because the men in the party were wearing shorts, albeit nice ones. The heritage of La Marée is as interesting as its much-lauded menu. The stone house was built in 1807 by innkeeper Pierre del Vecchio, but the land was awarded by Paul de Chomedey, sieur de Maisonneuve, to Andre Demers thirteen years after the founding of Ville Marie. Today, the restaurant's dining room, which seats seventy, is very intimate and private, with linen tablecloths, upholstered chairs, and a fireplace. In summer, request a table on the *terrasse*, which is rimmed with flower boxes. Enjoy the night breeze and the action in Place Jacques-Cartier. On weekends, cars are prohibited from the public square, and mimes, musicians, and magicians compete for attention.

Fish is the house specialty at La Marée, as you might have gathered from the restaurant's name, but veal, duck, and beef are also on the menu. The clam chowder is pure ecstasy, as is the salmon with chives, but the menu changes according to season. La Marée is noted for *guéridon*, or cart service, which means a waiter with a flair for performance will prepare your platter tableside with a flourish. The service is quietly vigilant, and you'll feel like the center of attention.

If you're still up for action after dinner, head to sultry **L'Air du Temps** (194 rue St-Paul Ouest; 514–842–2003) for live jazz. Dotted with antiques, the tiny club has become a favorite of the crowds in town for the International Jazz Festival. A rocking horse hangs from the ceiling, a gilt-framed mirror occupies much of one wall, and a velvet couch looks seductive on the second-floor landing. After the show (the cover charge varies according to the performer), you can walk or grab a cab back to the inn.

DAY TWO: morning

BREAKFAST

Breakfast in the inn's greenhouse is a delightful affair. The sun warms your body and mood even on wintry mornings, and parrots prattle from perches inside the room. Fresh-baked croissants, some filled with almond or fruit, are always on the menu, as are cereal, juice, and coffee. Trottier will also prepare to order eggs any style, with bacon and toast, or an omelette if you desire. It's easy to fill up here, so you may want to begin a walking tour right after you've savored the last bite. Be sure you're not dressed in jeans or shorts: you'll spend the day exploring the western part of Old Montréal and will go to dinner directly after your tour, so you'll want to be dressed appropriately.

Who's Looking at You, Kids?

In the dining room at La Maison Pierre du Calvet, an imposing portrait hangs above a cozy table in the corner. Gaetan Trottier's maternal grandparents, who honeymooned in New York in 1899, brought this enormous photograph of themselves back on the train, already framed. Have a cup of tea under the watchful eyes of Arthur Pierre Beaupré and his bride Seraphine Perrin. Remember that in Calvet's day the dining room where you're sitting was a courtyard where horses deposited their riders.

Your first destination is the city's best-known church: **Notre-Dame Basilica** (116 rue Notre-Dame Ouest; 514–842–2925). It was built in 1829 by a Protestant architect, James O'Donnell, who was so taken with the project that he converted to Catholicism. Notre-Dame has twin towers that leap 227 feet in the air, a ten-ton bell that can be heard miles away, a feathery, turquoise canopy ceiling emblazoned with gold stars, and one of the most powerful organs in North America, making it a favorite site for concerts and weddings—singer Céline Dion married her manager here in an extravagant ceremony in 1994. The **Montréal Symphony Orchestra** holds a Mozart Plus Festival here in July and August (tickets are needed), and organ master Pierre Grandmaison gives hour-long concerts in the cathedral five evenings every August. You're not likely to hear the organ during your morning visit, but you might catch a rehearsal by the MSO (call the Basilica for the rehearsal schedule). Guided tours are available daily (from mid-May to June 24 and Labor Day to mid-October) and include the museum at the back of the Basilica. The church is so majestic, you'll want to linger and imbibe the beauty.

DAY TWO: afternoon

Your next destination is an easy fifteen-minute walk to the western end of the district—but take your time and play explorer in this quieter, lesser-known sector of Old Montréal. Follow rue Notre-Dame west to rue St-Pierre, then take a left and walk south toward the river. As you stroll, duck into tiny side streets filled with old-world buildings that now are used for commercial purposes. You'll pass blocks that contain architectural treasures now inhabited by furniture designers, glass blowers, and other artisans. You might want to branch off and explore a couple of these peaceful *rues* as you amble down rue St-Pierre.

Continue until you reach the **Musée Marc-Aurèle Fortin** (118 rue St-Pierre; 514–845–6108; open Tuesday to Sunday from 11:00 A.M. to 5:00 P.M.; $4.00), the only museum in Québec devoted to one artist. Founder of a school of landscape painting, Fortin's trademark was using black backgrounds and gray skies to highlight his renditions of the Québec countryside. His gargantuan elm trees are a marvel. The intimate setting in the museum leaves you with a real feel for the artist, who died in 1972 and would have been stunned to see the price tags his work commands today.

SNACK

If there's a gnawing feeling in your stomach, stop at **Stash's Café Restauracja Polska** (200 rue St-Paul Ouest; 514–845–6611; inexpensive) where the pine benches and tables are offset by exposed stone walls and silk lanterns and where the motto is: "Anything tastes better with vodka. Even vodka." The scrumptious fruit squares served with sweet cream are renowned (as are the pierogi and the Polish pancakes), but you'll be eating a robust dinner, so don't fill up. Why not share something?

Now you're only a short walk from the exact site where Montréal was founded in 1642 by a band of French settlers. The triangular plot where the settlers landed is marked by **Pointe-à-Callière** (350 Place Royale; 514–872–9150), an archaeology and history museum and repository for treasures unearthed from years of excavation. Take at least two hours here to trace the city's evolution and have a conversation with Elizabeth Begon, who lived in Montréal in the 1600s and had quite a love life. Have I intrigued you? Don't leave without visiting the top floor for an excellent view of the Old Port, the St-Lawrence River, and Old Montréal. From the museum, it's a short walk to the former Youville Stables—where you'll have dinner.

A Musical Interlude

Concerts take place at the Château Ramezay on the last Sunday of every month. A harpsichordist performing baroque music one Sunday might be followed the next month by the rousing voices of a gospel choir. Three performances are held on those selected Sundays —at 1:30, 2:30, and 3:30 P.M. Tickets are $5.00, and a tour of the museum is included.

DAY TWO: evening

DINNER

Gibby's (298 Place d'Youville; 514–282–1837; moderate; reservations recommended) is located in a complex of gray stone warehouses built in 1825. In summer, explore the courtyard and have a cocktail before dinner on the patio. In winter, a fire glows inside, and generous portions of beef, veal, and fish are served at antique wooden tables. Request a table downstairs in the back, where it's quieter and more intimate, and prepare for a treat. The house salad is a model of freshness, the sautéed mushrooms are scrumptious, and the main courses are wonderful. If you have room for dessert, try the Key lime pie, the chocolate mousse, or the homemade ice cream. After that, you'll really look forward to your twenty-minute stroll back to the inn along rue de la Commune, which borders the river and is lined with street lamps. Gaze at the piers and the boats in harbor and take a long look at the St-Lawrence. You'll be saying *au revoir* after breakfast tomorrow.

FOR MORE ROMANCE

If you'd like to see a play during your stay, you're in the right place. The only English-language theater company in the city operates from Old Montréal's **Centaur Theatre** (453 rue St. François-Xavier; 514–288–3161). Major works are staged here; make sure to book tickets in advance.

Latin Blood
THE PLATEAU AND THE LATIN QUARTER

*T*HE VIBRANT PLATEAU AND THE BOHEMIAN LATIN QUARTER are the city's most effervescent areas—and still largely unexplored by tourists. The Plateau holds a hefty chunk of Montréal's heart and soul. If Old Montréal is where French adventurers lived long ago, the Plateau is where French-speaking adventurers live now. The Latin Quarter, Montréal's equivalent of the Sorbonne area in Paris, is where they study, philosophize—and play.

Both quarters absolutely must be walked around to be appreciated—during the day and at night. Strolling through the Plateau, you'll see countless versions of the area's trademark corkscrew staircases attached to long, narrow homes on streets that seem to stretch forever. Flowers gush from window boxes and spruce up even tiny plots that residents have adopted around telephone poles. You'll wander down *rues* and *ruelles* to see where people live, and you'll frolic in the one of the city's most beautiful parks. When the sun goes down, you'll step into the night to dance and romance. On this moderately priced itinerary, you'll feel as if you're in Paris in your heart—without feeling it in your wallet.

PRACTICAL NOTES: Heavy on walking, this itinerary works best from May through October—strolling season. Keep in mind, however, that Lover's Lake in Parc Lafontaine stays open only during the summer as does the park's illuminated fountain, which features fifty-four water jets and nine lighting sequences.

♦ Check into **Le Jardin d'Antoine** (2024 rue St-Denis; 514–843–4506; 800–361–4506), a renovated nineteenth-century mansion, then spend the afternoon exploring the charming rues and ruelles in the fabled neighborhood known as the Plateau. End your tour at Parc Lafontaine, where you'll navigate a row-boat along Lover's Lake.

♦ Dine in the intimacy of **Aux Baiser Volés**—the name means "stolen kisses" (371 rue Villeneuve Est; 514–289–9921), but first steal a kiss in a tiny park nearby that is a romantic gem. Spice up your life even more after dinner at **Le Cactus** (4459 rue St-Dennis), where you'll dance the salsa till the wee hours.

♦ After breakfast at your B&B, spend the day walking the city's **Latin Quarter**, where you'll visit the oldest music store in town, see a foreign film, and enter a church door—only to discover a university.

DAY ONE: morning

Step off the Latin Quarter's main drag and step into a private home that once symbolized wealth and privilege. You've entered **Le Jardin d'Antoine** (2024 rue St-Denis; 514–843–4506; 800–361–4506; Sherbrooke station; $75 to $165, including full breakfast), where owner Antoine Giardina has created a precious gem from a badly tarnished bauble, managing to salvage some of the original interior from the former mansion built in the late 1800s. All twenty-five rooms in the inn are extremely romantic and all are different—some with rose-printed wallpaper, brass beds, whirlpool tubs, separate showers, thick carpet, lace curtains, and television hidden in an armoire—but what's surprising is that even the smaller (and less expensive) rooms have a special warmth and beauty provided by an entry off the ground-floor courtyard.

If you are honeymooning or celebrating an anniversary, splurge on one of the seven suites, each with a sitting room apart from the bedroom. Suite No. 21 features wood doors from the original mansion, a huge whirlpool bath, and a sleigh bed. Suite No. 32 has a Jacuzzi bathtub right in the bedroom, and Suite No. 35, with more than 400 square feet of space, has a king-size bed and a sinfully large tub and shower. Settle in to your new digs and get ready to take the métro (Sherbrooke station) directly to the heart of the Plateau (Mont-

Royal station), where you'll be seduced by street life on your morning walk and charmed by a residential and commercial mix unequaled anywhere else in town.

Exit the metro station on **avenue Mont-Royal,** and you feel as if you've entered a scene from a play. Mont-Royal is street theater in the raw and the epicenter of commercial activity in the **Plateau,** whose boundaries are hazy even in the minds of longtime residents. The area is actually comprised of four small villages developed at the start of the 1860s, when workers from the Québec countryside flocked to what was once farmland looking for jobs in the nearby limestone quarries and tanneries. The workers built simple homes—narrow boxes that sometimes stretched as much as 100 feet from the street —and they built them side by side. By 1914 no vacant lots remained in the area. By strolling down any street in the Plateau, you can see the tight quarters people shared. This is the most densely populated neighborhood on the island of Montréal. There are more than 300 merchants on avenue Mont-Royal alone to serve the population.

Tour the Plateau a bit before lunch. Directly across from the métro exit, the impressive building with the elaborate pinnacle is a **Maison de la Culture** (465 avenue Mont-Royal Est), one of nineteen neighborhood cultural centers dotted around Montréal. Built in 1896, it originally served as a Catholic boarding school for girls. Today, it houses a library. Its three upper floors have been converted into apartments for senior citizens.

Walk east on avenue Mont-Royal a few paces. **Notre-Dame-du-Très-Saint-Sacrement** (500 avenue Mont-Royal Est) was built from quarry stone in the 1890s and is a combination monastery, church, and present-day historic landmark. The businesslike look of the church belies the fanciful interior designed by architect Jean-Zephirin Resther. Visitors can meditate or pray in the church every day of the week. Resther, for whom a street in the Plateau is named, had a crucial role in the development of the area. He served as executor of the will of J. A. Massue, who owned the land that is now avenue Mont-Royal and operated a popular racetrack on the property. After Massue's death in 1891, Resther had the land subdivided into lots to create a neighborhood around the church and the monastery he'd been commissioned to design.

As you explore the Plateau, note the absence of high-rise buildings. Even from the busiest stretch on avenue Mont-Royal, you still have a clear view of the Olympic Stadium tower and the steel cross atop Mont-Royal that is lit every night. Turn right on rue St-Hubert, where you'll see homes constructed for the wealthy French—the home at 4455 rue St-Hubert once belonged to Camilien Houde, mayor of Montréal from 1928 to 1954. The spiral staircases that have become the area's signature speak volumes about the religious influence so prevalent at the time. Urged by the Catholic church to procreate, French-Canadians often had more than a dozen children, and an outside staircase saved space inside for children. In the 1950s new construction of outdoor staircases was banned when they were declared icy danger zones in winter, but the ban was recently lifted.

As you walk a block or two, note the balconies—a means of socialization at the time—and the signs of prosperity—elaborate cornices and stained-glass windows. Return to avenue Mont-Royal and continue east a block. You'll pass a Belgian pastry and chocolate shop, **Patisserie Bruxelloise** (860 avenue Mont-Royal Est; 514–521–1122), an institution in the neighborhood. Peek in the window, but don't be tempted to enter now. We're going a few steps farther. It's time for lunch.

What's in a Name?

Street names in the Plateau reveal a great deal about power, interests, rivalries—and love. For example, Dr. Pierre Beaubien (1796–1881), a member of a wealthy land-owning family, wanted to immortalize his wife Marie-Justine Casgrain (1804–1882) and her son by a previous marriage, Hannibal Dellagenta. He created streets with their names in 1867 —and named another street after himself.

LUNCH

A motorcycle hangs from the ceiling in the streamlined space at **l'Avenue** (922 avenue Mont-Royal Est; 514–523–8780; inexpensive), a sleek eatery that shouts retro cool. Yet behind the high-tech decor, there's warmth, too. Just out the back door, you can glimpse one of the many *ruelles*, or alleyways, that have always distinguished the Plateau and provided rough-hewn playgrounds for generations of children. As befits a neighborhood populated by students, artists, and academicians—whose waking hours are wildly varied—l'Avenue's claim to fame is breakfast service until 3:00 P.M.—so if you're still in a brunch mode, try an omelette or waffles, crepes or French toast. If you're ready for lunch, try l'Avenue's half-pound hamburger topped with your choice of Brie or goat cheese.

DAY ONE: afternoon

Continue walking on avenue Mont-Royal after lunch (but backtrack first to the pastry shop to pick up a little something for later) and eye-ball the assortment of businesses, many of them longtime enterprises. **St-Viateur Bagel** (1127 avenue Mont-Royal Est; 514–528–6361), in Montréal since 1957, claims to make the best bagel in the city. That's a hotly debated claim, especially among out-of-towners. But Montréalers love their special brand of bagels, which look like pretzels and taste, to me (a native New Yorker), somewhat like pastry. Buy a few and judge for yourselves. Keep walking east to one of the oldest businesses in the area. The jewelry store **Bijouterie J. Omer Roy & Fils** (1658 avenue Mont-Royal Est, corner rue Marquette; 514–527–2951), has been in the same location since 1919 and now sells diamond rings to the grandchildren of original patrons. Maybe you might find something you like as a souvenir of your trip?

Backtrack one block and make a left on rue Fabre. Here you'll see fine examples of typical Montréal housing as you amble down the street. Sons and daughters of residents who fled the Plateau in the 1940s and 1950s are now returning to gentrify these homes built shortly after the turn of the century.

At rue Marie-Anne, turn right and walk west. At rue Brebeuf, you'll see a rustic two-story home attached to its three-story neighbor; a local bakery is across the street. Fifty years ago, you could find either a restaurant or a general store on almost any corner in the Plateau. The stores, called *depanneurs,* used to offer everything from bread and milk to mending services. The proprietor would also watch your pet bird if you went on vacation. Depanneurs are still everywhere today (five exist within a mile of my home), but the personalized services have pretty well disappeared. You will, however, find some depanneurs that carry ethnic foods, fine chocolate, or flowers, and some that even have a table or two for a sit-down snack.

Today, though, most depanneurs specialize in the staples and also dispense lottery tickets. Why not pop into one on avenue Mont-Royal and take a chance on winning a bundle while you're here?

At the corner of rue Brebeuf and rue Rachel, you may notice commuters coming home from work on bicycles. You're on a main cycling artery in Montréal, a city crisscrossed by some 240 kilometers of designated bike path. The path on rue Rachel leads right up the mountain. Cross the street and enter **Parc Lafontaine**. You'll spend the rest of the afternoon here, strolling through 180 shady acres of former farmland used in the mid-1800s by the British War Ministry for military maneuvers. After you've done a turn around the park and seen the impressive monument to composer, poet, novelist, actor, and ambassador of French-Canadian culture Felix Leclerc (1914–1988), rent a pedal boat or a rowboat and venture onto Lover's Lake. On the water, surrounded by greenery and in the shadow of the mountain, dive into your luscious cache of Belgian pastry and feel decadent.

When you're ready to return to the inn, take rue Cherrier, which branches off from rue Sherbrooke Est across from the monument to Sir Louis-Hippolyte Lafontaine, for whom the park is named. Continue to rue St-Denis and to the hotel.

DAY ONE: evening

Change into clothes appropriate for a lovely dinner destination, but wear comfortable shoes. You'll be walking tonight. Leave yourself at least an hour of daylight before dinner to view a precious park that is a romantic gem. Take the métro once again to Mont-Royal station. This time, turn left and walk west on avenue Mont-Royal to rue Drolet. Turn right and walk into the park on your left. More than 650 parks are in Montréal—you saw one of the largest this afternoon. Nearly half the parks are tiny, neighborhood affairs, but few are as private as this tiny oasis of calm that is called, simply, **Parc Drolet**. Take a moment to savor the seclusion offered here. No better place for a kiss will present itself tonight.

In the middle of this sylvan setting, turn right and walk up the path. Turn right on rue Gilford, once named chemin de la Carrière (Quarry Road), then left on rue de Grandpré, a sugar-coated picture postcard of color and Victorian style. You'll see the oldest house in the Plateau (No. 4660 rue de Grandpré, built by Irishman Cornelius Lorge). Observe the elaborate balconies on Nos. 4663 through 4698, and imagine the working folk coming home from the job and chatting with the neighbors before dinner. Your own dinner, by the way, is just steps away.

DINNER

At the corner of rue de Grandpré and rue Villeneuve is **Aux Baisers Volés** (371 rue Villeneuve Est; 514–289–9921; moderate). The name means stolen kisses, and if your stolen moment in the park fanned your ardor, you can steal many more in this diminutive restaurant that accommodates only thirty. Aux Baiser Volés is the ideal site for a cozy tête-à-tête. A table d'hôte features fine French cuisine. Have a glass or two of wine before dinner. The night has just begun.

Exit the restaurant and walk one block west onto rue St-Denis. Walk south to **Le Cactus** (4459 rue St-Denis; 514–849–0349; open Wednesday to Saturday; $3.00 admission), where sensual salsa dancing will spice up your life. Le Cactus, which attracts an over-thirty crowd, is an intimate club with brick walls, wood floors, and piñatas hanging over the bar. Couples proficient at salsa exhibit their skills, but don't be shy. Everyone is welcome. The music is a magnet. Before long your feet will be flying and your bodies will be moving seductively. The action doesn't start until 10:00 P.M. and doesn't stop until 3:00 A.M. When it ends, grab a cab back to the inn.

DAY TWO: morning

BREAKFAST

Sleep late. The Jardin d'Antoine serves a full breakfast until 10:00 A.M. in a cozy dining nook on the ground level facing a gray stone wall from the original mansion. Wrought-iron tables covered with white linen cloths are set in front of a buffet table laden with bread, croissants, fresh fruit, scrambled eggs, cheese, muffins, and cereals. Eat outside on a private terrasse reserved for guests if you'd like. After breakfast, you'll walk a bit on the trendiest street in the city.

Walk north on rue St-Denis just past rue Sherbrooke. On your left is Montréal's most beautiful public square. **Carré St. Louis** is bound by turn-of-the-century Victorian homes marked by fanciful touches—colorful roofs and elaborate cornices. Avenue Laval, which extends north from the square, was the home of romantic poet Émile Nelligan (1879–1941), who lived at No. 3688, and the late actor, writer, and filmmaker Claude Jutra, who resided at No. 3492 and died in 1986. Film critic Pauline Kael of the *New Yorker* called Jutra's movie *Mon Oncle Antoine* an "international masterpiece" and called him "a mixture of Truffaut and Tati." At Avenue des Pins turn right, walking to rue St-Denis in the direction of the hotel.

On the stretch of rue St-Denis between rue Sherbrooke and rue Ste-Catherine and spreading east to rue Berri, you'll find young-at-heart shopping and discover the Latin Quarter's intellectual bent. **Mona Lisait** (2054 rue St-Denis; 514–849–0987), up a flight of stairs from the street, is a good browse for French books and a smaller selection in English. Across the street are three sports outfitters that cover camping, hiking, skiing, and just upscale casual dressing: **Azimut** (1781 rue St-Denis; 514–844–1717), **Altitude** (1701 rue St-Denis; 514–845–9145), and **L'Aventurier** (1647 rue St-Denis; 514–849–4100) all cater to the adventurous.

Keep the adventurous streak alive as you head for some instant escapism at the screening room of the **Office National du Film du Canada** (National Film Board of Canada; 1564 rue St-Denis at the corner of boulevard de Maisonneuve), which has the world's only cinérobothèque ($5.50 for two hours; open Tuesday to Sunday, noon to 9:00 P.M.; 514–496–6887). At the NFB, the two of you can sit in comfortable chairs in a common viewing room where you'll share a small private viewing screen. Although others around you may be watching different films, the chairs at the NFB are specially constructed to envelop you in the sound of your own selection. You'll be catered to by a robot when you make your choice from more than 4,000 films. Why not choose Claude Jutra's *Mon Oncle Antoine*? It was voted the best Canadian film of all time in 1984. It's available with English subtitles or in a dubbed version. Point your finger at the title, and your servant will deliver the goods. Enjoy the movie in your space-age seats.

TEA or SNACK

Since there was no popcorn at the NFB, you might want a snack. You're right across the street from the **Second Cup** (1551 rue St-Denis; 514–285–4468; inexpensive), which serves an extensive array of beverages, hot and cold sandwiches, and desserts. Have a light bite on the outdoor terrace, a great people-watching perch. Afterward, you'll continue exploring the Quarter.

Walk one block east and one block south to **Archambault Musique** (500 rue Ste-Catherine Est; 514–849–6201), in business more than one hundred years in the same spot. In 1896 Edmond Archambault, a young piano teacher, began giving lessons in the establishment of J. A. Hurteau, who sold pianos. Archambault bought the Hurteau building in 1919, and his descendants have continued a century-long tradition of selling musical instruments and providing music lessons. On the first floor, you'll find a great collection of tapes and CDs from French-speaking artists worldwide. Why not buy a tape of a Québec artist as a memento of your romantic weekend? Don't fail to see the musical instruments on the second and third floors, where music lessons have been given for generations.

Exiting the store, you'll be automatically drawn to the church with a statue of the Virgin Mary on top. A halo around her head glows at night. She stands guard over **La Chapelle Notre-Dame-de-Lourdes** (430 rue Ste-Catherine Est; 514–845–8278), built in 1873 and one of the few heritage buildings that remains intact in the Quarter after extensive renovations to accommodate the **Université du Québec à Montréal** in the 1970s. The Chapelle was designed by Napoléon Bourassa as an homage to the Virgin Mary, and the elegance of the curving interior that leads to the cupola gives the church a feminine grace. Visitors are welcome day and night.

From here, continue to rue St-Denis and turn right. On your right is another church—but, alas, it is only a facade. Enter the doors, and you're really at the Université du Québec à Montréal, built in 1974; it kept the facade of an old church as its entryway. Farther north across the street you'll find the **Bibliothèque Nationale du Québec** (1700 rue St-Denis), where the stained-glass windows in the front of the building are a treat to view from the street. (The library, unfortunately, is closed on Sunday, so if you want to visit, squeeze it in before 5:00 P.M. on Saturday.)

Now you're ready to return to the hotel and prepare for dinner.

DAY TWO: evening

DINNER

Down a few doors from your hotel is **La Sila** (2040 rue St-Denis; 514–844–5083; moderate; table d'hôte, $20 to $33), one of the city's most romantic restaurants. Dimly lit and cozy with exposed brick on the walls, La Sila specializes in Italian food and offers a table d'hôte with three courses built around pasta, veal, and fish. It also offers one of the city's finest wine lists. Have a quiet, intimate dinner in this cavern-like restaurant and savor the moments that remain in your getaway.

FOR MORE ROMANCE

If last night's dancing only gave you a taste for more, when darkness falls head to **Tango Libre** (rue Marie-Anne Est; 514–527–5197), a dance studio that becomes a bar on weekends. On Friday, Saturday, and Sunday nights at Tango Libre, lights are dimmed and the studio becomes a sultry spot where the dance that originated in Buenos Aires in the late 1800s is showcased. For a $6.00 cover, you can join the action and see whether it truly takes two to tango. Tango Libre artistic director Gerardo Sanchez offers private instruction to couples ($45 per session), should you want to perfect your technique.

Meet the Elite
GOLDEN SQUARE MILE

I N THE 1800s, MOST OF CANADA'S WEALTH lay in a slice of Montréal nestled at the foot of Mont-Royal. The first residents of the posh Golden Square Mile, as the area is now called, were mostly Scottish immigrants who arrived after the British conquest of New France in 1763 and eagerly seized opportunities denied them at home. They came to dominate business in Montréal for more than a century and a half, and left a lavish legacy in the mansions, churches, and museums along rue Sherbrooke. Follow their footsteps and plunge into old-world splendor, and in so doing, come to understand the two solitudes that comprise Québec—English and French —and how they've attempted to touch each other through the years.

PRACTICAL NOTES: You'll be walking over almost every square inch of the Square Mile, so wear comfortable shoes—or boots, depending on the time of year. The architectural heritage is so rich— and the shopping opportunities so appealing—you'll want to cover this territory on foot.

DAY ONE: morning/early afternoon

Identified by its trademark black metal porte-cochère designed long ago to shelter guests alighting from carriages and fancy sleighs, the **Ritz-Carlton Kempinski** (1228 rue Sherbrooke Ouest; 514–842– 4212; station Peel; $200 plus; ask for promotional rates) is not only Montréal's oldest hotel—built in 1912—but the epitome of Edwardian elegance and the exemplar of Scottish money and influence. King Edward VIII called it "the grande dame of Sherbrooke Street," a name that has endured.

*R*om*a*nce
AT A GLANCE

◆ Step inside the very first **Ritz-Carlton Hotel** in the world (1228 rue Sherbrooke Ouest; 514–842–4212), where Swiss hotelier César Ritz established his exacting standards; deposit your bags, then take a grand tour of the neighborhood that was the wealthiest in all Canada during the 1800s.

◆ Stroll arm in arm along **rue Sherbrooke,** Montréal's Fifth Avenue, where you'll admire some of the finest furs, jewelry, and antiques in the world, situated in shops that are surrounded by heritage homes and museums.

◆ Get cozy on a carriage ride up **Mont-Royal** at sundown. Since one Montréal tradition deserves another, alight from the carriage and have dinner in Montréal's most traditional restaurant, the **Beaver Club** (900 boulevard René-Levesque; 514–861–3511), which was founded by fur traders in 1785 and is one of two restaurants in Canada to receive five stars in the Mobil Guide.

It is also the first hotel to bear the chain's hyphenated name, a story documented in the book *No Ordinary Hotel* by Adrian Waller, published on the seventy-fifth birthday of the Ritz. The hotel was the dream of four Scottish businessmen: railway engineer Herbert Holt (later president of the Royal Bank); Charles Gordon, president of Dominion Textile and a director of Molson's Bank; shipping tycoon Hugh Montagu Allan; and Charles Hosmer, a self-made man who built Canadian Pacific Telegrams to international fame. The four wanted a place to lodge their wealthy friends. Impressed by the Carlton Hotel in London, they used it as a model. They courted Swiss hotelier César Ritz—then the talk of Europe—and convinced him to endorse the effort. He agreed, but only if the hotel were run according to his precise standards.

Over the course of almost a century, those standards have attracted everyone from heads of state to rock stars. Queen Elizabeth and Prince Philip once checked in on short notice but couldn't get the seventeen-room Royal Suite because it was already occupied by Liberace. Liz Taylor and Richard Burton were married here on the spur of the moment in 1964. Mick Jagger was asked to wear a tie when the Rolling Stones dined in the Ritz. He complied.

You'll feel the history in this limestone building with 230 rooms, forty-five suites, an exquisite ballroom, and a sweeping staircase that is truly glamorous. Major renovations completed in the spring of 1999 mean the rooms at the *grande dame* have a fresh new elegance while retaining touches like original woodwork. Select a room with an old-world flavor, or you may prefer to request rooms No. 533 or 633, the only rooms in the hotel, aside from the suites, that have fireplaces. In any case, settle in to the room and take a few moments to freshen up. Now, you're ready for lunch.

LUNCH

If you're visiting in summer, you'll head straight for the **Ritz Garden**, rain or shine. Patrons sit under awnings set around a landscaped Japanese garden that includes a waterfall and a pond dotted with baby ducklings. On rainy days, the ducklings make a game of trying to catch droplets in their mouths. Order wine by the glass and begin to unwind. Then move to the table d'hôte menu consisting of a soup and main course ($26 to $35). In winter, lunch moves inside to the **Café de Paris**, where the same selection awaits you.

DAY ONE: afternoon

The Square Mile is bounded by avenue Université to the east, Côte des Neiges to the west, avenue des Pins to the north, and boulevard René-Levesque to the south. You'll start your journey at the eastern edge. Expect to spend at least four hours this afternoon reveling in the history of a golden era.

Walk to the **McCord Museum of Canadian History** (690 rue Sherbrooke Ouest; 514–398–7100, closed Monday; admission $8.00), which houses a wonderful collection of Canadiana and aboriginal artifacts donated originally to McGill University by David Ross McCord. An impressive collection of furniture and costumes from the past are also here. The museum's biggest claim to fame, however, is the Notman Photographic Archives—an unparalleled record of Montréal history photographed by William Notman, who came to Montréal from Paisley, Scotland, in 1856 and was soon in demand by high society. Notman's portraits of the well-to-do residents of the Golden Square Mile—and their mansions—provide, in some cases, the only picture of what demolition crews destroyed before heritage preservation groups halted the eradication of architectural history in Montréal.

Across the street from the museum, you can't miss the curved Roddick Gates leading to **McGill University** (801–865 rue Sherbrooke Ouest), a school with international renown. Scottish founder James McGill came to Montréal in 1766 after attending the University of Glasgow, which made him perhaps the only Square Miler with a university education. He married into an established French-Canadian family, made a fortune in fur trading, and, upon his death in 1813, willed his forty-six-acre Burnside estate for a college that would bear his name. Classes began in 1829. The gates in front are a 1924 memorial to Sir Thomas George Roddick, a surgeon and former dean of medicine, who was said to be obsessed with punctuality. Notice the clock atop one of the columns. McGill's tomb sits outside the Arts Building that crowns the main drive on campus. His remains were transferred there when the city's old Protestant cemetery was dug up in 1875 to make room for Dorchester Square.

Love consists in this,

that two solitudes protect,

and touch, and greet each other.

—Rainer Maria Rilke

Don't leave the campus without visiting an enchanting treasure trove. The **Redpath Museum** (on the west side of the campus; 514–398–4086; free admission), built in 1882 with money donated by sugar tycoon Peter Redpath, holds Canada's second-largest collection of Egyptian antiquities, including a mummy that lies in a viewing case near the entry. Well-preserved dinosaur bones, other examples of extinct species, and a stuffed lion on the landing between the second and third floors (pet his nose—everyone does) are delightful highlights of Canada's first building designed expressly as a museum.

Begin your tour of Square Mile homes at **Baumgarten House** (3450 rue McTavish; 514–398–6391), built in stages from 1887 to 1902 and now the McGill Faculty Club. Owned by Alfred Baumgarten, president of the St. Lawrence Sugar Refinery and whose father was the personal physician to German monarch Frederick Augustus III, the house is distinguished for its indoor swimming pool (which no longer exists), a ballroom built on springs, and a layout that includes three stories. It's worth knocking on the door and asking if you can take a look around, since almost all the other homes in the area are privately owned or are used as offices and don't allow visitors. The consulates of Russia, Poland, Switzerland, Mexico, and Italy are today housed in former Square Mile homes.

Another home that has taken on a new vocation is **Ravenscrag** (1025 avenue des Pins Ouest), a Tuscan-style villa you can see clearly from the top of the hill on McTavish. Sir Hugh Allan, one of the four Scots who brought the Ritz to Montréal and the richest man in Canada in his time, built this castle on the hill in 1863 and named it after the Marquis of Lorne's residence in Scotland. From the central tower of his sixty-room house, the shipping magnate could keep an eye on the action in port—when he wasn't entertaining dignitaries and statesmen. In 1943, when the building was deeded by the Allan family to the Royal Victoria Hospital and converted to a psychiatric institute (Allan Memorial), the interior was virtually destroyed. Remaining original touches on the exterior include the cast-iron gate.

Returning to rue Sherbrooke, walk a few blocks west to see three houses that evoke the glory of Sherbrooke in a bygone era. First comes the **Mont Royal Club** (1175 rue Sherbrooke Ouest; 514–842–5454), built by New York architect Stanford White at the behest of Square Milers on a site that used to be the home of Canada's third prime minister, John Abbott. White designed what looks like an Italian Renaissance palace. Membership at the club is by invitation only, so you can only gaze upon it from outside the door. What a pity.

Don't despair. Admission to a grand Square Mile residence can be gained at the former home of Louis J. Forget, head of the most power- ful brokerage in Canada in the 1800s, the wealthiest French-Canadian businessman of his time, and the first French-Canadian member of the Canadian parliament. The **Forget House** (1195 rue Sherbrooke Ouest) had a private chapel, which is now used as a restaurant for veterans. You can't eat here, but you can enter and take a peek at the chapel sky- light, the fine mahogany woodwork, and a stained-glass window made by Tiffany.

The third notable home is **Maison Corby** (1201 rue Sherbrooke Ouest; 514–288–4181), owned since 1951 by Corby Distilleries. The house was built in the 1880s for Thomas Craig, then redesigned for new owner James Reid Wilson, a banker.

Before ducking back into the Ritz-Carlton, take a quiet moment to view the **Erskine and American United Church** (1339 rue Sherbrooke

Ouest; open only for services), which celebrated its centennial in 1994. Scottish millionaires worshipped here, and its collection of eighteen stained-glass windows represents the largest grouping of work by Louis Comfort Tiffany outside the United States.

You are steps from the hotel. Make your way back to your room, slip off your walking shoes, put your feet up, and relax. When you're recharged, change clothes for dinner. Square Mile tycoons, as you noticed on your walk, were not all Scottish. French-Canadians had some influence on the Mile initially, and today restaurants serving both French and Québecois cuisine are plentiful in the Mile. We'll try one tonight. As you the leave the hotel at dusk, don't miss the pink and yellow sky as the sun sets with Mont-Royal in the background.

DAY ONE: evening

DINNER

Victorian decor melds with classic French cuisine at **Le Lutétia** (1430 rue de la Montagne; 514–288–5656; closed Sunday; moderate to expensive; four-course table d'hôte between $19.75 and $32), which is located in the **Hotel de la Montagne**, around the corner from the Ritz-Carlton. You might want to arrive at Hotel de la Montagne for happy hour (between 5:00 and 7:00 P.M.), when the sumptuous lobby, marked by crystal chandeliers, a fountain, mirrored walls, and a polished baby grand piano, sometimes fills to overflowing. My husband took me here when we were courting, and I was so taken with the place, I considered getting married here. (We ended up exchanging vows in the U.S.)

When you've had a drink and admired the surroundings, move to the restaurant on the mezzanine level, where the rococo decor is even more intense. Salmon-pink linen cloths and fresh seasonal flowers decorate tables placed under a hand-painted sky-blue dome. Specialties of the house include rack of lamb, breast of duck, and the finest beef from Alberta.

You'll want to linger here, especially on Thursday, Friday, and Saturday nights, when a jazz combo entertains in the lobby in full view of restaurant patrons. The decibel level is soft during dinner, but

Prenuptial Agreement

On December 2, 1776, when James McGill wed Charlotte Guillimin, a young widow with two sons, the couple agreed on an unusual marriage contract for the time. According to McGill's biographer, Stanley Brice Frost, they signed papers declaring each of them to be separate as to property. Frost suggests that they were undoubtedly thinking that if McGill failed in the fur trade business, Charlotte would not lose her own property to his debts. No such disaster occurred, of course, and James and Charlotte grew old together.

at 10:00 P.M. the music becomes more animated. Then it's time to move from the table to the lobby for an after-dinner drink. Get close. Snuggle on a leather settee, enjoy the music, and admire the opulence. Around midnight, stroll back to the hotel, where you'll get even closer.

DAY TWO: morning

BREAKFAST

Why not order room service? The waiters are the model of discretion and are fully accustomed to serving sleepy couples in nighttime attire at bedside. Expect flowers on the table, even at breakfast, along with the finest linen and china. Honeymooners often request a mimosa cocktail and caviar. Another favorite with romantics is a bottle of champagne and a bowl of strawberries (to be dipped in the champagne), followed by eggs Benedict or buckwheat pancakes, served, of course, with thick maple syrup from Québec. Pop a strawberry into her mouth; pop one into his. Shameless behavior, but so delightful.

When you can pry yourselves away from the bedroom, you'll walk around the corner to shop where Square Milers did years ago—and still do. **Ogilvy** (1307 rue Ste-Catherine Ouest; 514–842–7711) is a huge department store founded in 1866 by James Angus Ogilvy. Tradition still oozes inside these doors. For instance, at noon a kilted bagpiper marches through the main floor playing Scottish tunes to signal the hour, and until recently the ancient elevators were hand-operated.

The store has been thoroughly modernized. Its wide aisles spread over five fabulous floors and include a marvelous bookstore (Nicholas Hoare), designer clothing (Canadian trend-setters Jean-Claude Poitras and Alfred Sung are showcased), and antiques and furniture. Indulge—and take home a memento of Scottish distinction. Why not buy a plaid scarf for each of you?

DAY TWO: afternoon

LUNCH

Shopping certainly builds the appetite. When the bagpipe sounds, head downstairs to the lower level at Ogilvy for a bite at **Café Romy** (inexpensive). Delicious sandwiches, quiche, or salads are served at cozy tables for two. You can also choose *le plat du jour*, or daily special, which might be poulet (chicken) de Bistro as the main course and include soup and dessert ($9.00).

From here, it's just a short walk to the **Musée des Beaux-Arts** (1380 rue Sherbrooke; 514–285–1600; closed Mondays; admission $10), the oldest art museum in Canada (founded in 1860), and so large, it is spread over two sides of the street. You'll head for the **Benaiah Gibb Pavilion** on the north side of the street, opened in 1912, and named after a prosperous tailor who loved art. It was fashioned from white Vermont marble by architects Edward and William Maxwell, favorites of the Scottish elite. These days, it houses Canadian art—much of it from the homes of early Square Milers—so you can see what hung on the walls of those luxurious mansions you eyeballed yesterday.

Before daylight has faded, return to the Ritz and requisition a horse and carriage for a sunset ride up Mont-Royal. You've pre-arranged with the concierge for a pickup at the hotel. As the *calèche* pulls up, imagine the first visitors to the Ritz using the same mode of transport nearly a century ago. Imagine when Sherbrooke was a tree-lined road and when the only way to visit the mountain, other than on foot, was by horse and carriage. Hold hands as you ascend the mountain for a view of the city and the river. You've reached a peak height-wise, but you're still climbing when it comes to adventure. Dinner awaits.

DAY TWO: evening

DINNER

Montréal's coat-of-arms includes a beaver, an industrious animal that was a prime source of revenue in Montréal's fur trade heyday. The fur trade is venerated at the **Beaver Club** (900 boulevard René-Levesque; 514–861–3511; expensive; reservations required), formed in 1785 with membership restricted to those who'd spent at least one season exploring the northern fur trade routes. James McGill was a charter member. Benjamin Franklin, John Jacob Astor, and Washington Irving were invited to club meetings, at which officers were responsible for organizing dinner and libation. Today the club has some 900 members in more than forty countries. Some fly across continents to attend a traditional annual banquet the last Friday in January, when everyone dresses in fur trade garb for a five-course dinner.

You can experience the same sentiments every night at the Beaver Club, one of two restaurants in Canada to receive five stars in the 1996 Mobil Guide. British chef John Cordeaux prepares venison and beef with a French flair. A wine cellar caters to the discerning connoisseur —with selections quite a bit more diverse than when the original club members got together. Be sure to see the 60-foot-wide stained-glass window depicting Montréal in the mid-nineteenth century.

You'll head back to the Ritz after dinner, thinking about the warmth and utter luxury of fur. Perhaps a visit to a fur salon is in order? (See "For More Romance.")

FOR MORE ROMANCE

If your budget allows the extravagance, shop for furs in **Holt-Renfrew** (rue Sherbrooke at the corner of rue de la Montagne; 514–842–5111), another Scottish institution. The department store was founded nearly 160 years ago as a fur shop in Québec City and formerly supplied furs to British royalty.

Arts and Flowers

Private Passions
ART, ARCHITECTURE, AND DANCE

IF YOUR ARDOR RISES WHEN SURROUNDED BY BEAUTY, FORM, and movement, expect to become passionate in Montréal. Architectural treasures, some of them dating back centuries, are everywhere in Montréal, engaging the eye and comforting the soul. Art, as well, is everywhere in Montréal, even in the metro stations, where stained-glass panels and brightly colored murals soothe the weary commuter—and delight the adventurous traveler. As for dance, a potent argument could be made for calling Montréal the North American capital of contemporary dance. It is a hotbed of experimentation.

So be experimental when you explore your private passions in Montréal. Here, beauty and form are part of the landscape. Your beautiful forms will fit right in.

PRACTICAL NOTES: This itinerary works year-round, except on Mondays, when the museums are closed. Art lovers who can extend their stay should consider purchasing the Montréal Museum Pass at the Infotouriste Centres or at the museums. A three-day pass (and the days don't have to be consecutive) costs $28 and admits you to nineteen city museums. In addition, arrange your weekend to coincide with a dance performance by Les Grands Ballets Canadiens (call 514–849–0269 for a schedule), with a visiting company at Place des Arts (514–842–2112)—or with the festival of modern dance held every other year in late September. Reserve seats in advance for one of these performances. The Musée d'art contemporain also showcases modern dance (514–847–6212), so inquire there as well.

Romance AT A GLANCE

◆ Enter a beautiful B&B, where your hostess is a sculptor, and use her Victorian mansion as a departure point for your exploration of the city's finest art.

◆ Admire a famous pair of pouting lips at the **Musée d'art contemporain** (185 rue Ste-Catherine Ouest; 514–847–6212), along with more than 5,000 works of contemporary artists. Spend the afternoon taking in the collection, pausing for lunch at the museum's elegant **La Rotonde** restaurant, which provides a breathtaking view of **Place des Arts**—Montréal's version of Lincoln Center.

◆ Make it a double-whammy by visiting the world's only museum devoted to architecture in the morning, **Centre Canadien d'Architecture** (1920 rue Baile; 514–939–7026), and then venturing to Montréal's famous **Musée des Beaux-Arts** (1380 rue Sherbrooke; 514–285–1600) in the afternoon. Cap off your art-filled day by dining at **Le Passe-Partout** (3857 boulevard Décarie; 514–487–7750), a marvelous French restaurant with an art gallery on the premises.

DAY ONE: morning/afternoon

Rub your eyes as you approach your lodgings. It's not a dream. It's architectural splendor. **Aux Portes de la nuit** (3496 avenue Laval; 514–848–0833; métro Sherbrooke; $75), a century-old Victorian mansion, is located on what many consider the most beautiful street in the city. Rejoice a second time when you walk through the door. Your hostess is a sculptor who works from a studio at home. Her husband, a physicist who is fully bilingual, loves to play the baby grand piano in the living room. They both love talking arts and ideas. So do you. What a match.

Aux Portes de la nuit was formally recognized for its hospitality by the province in 1994–1995, when it won a regional prize for excellence. It's even better now, having undergone renovations early in 1997. Each of the three guest rooms in the B&B has its original woodwork and parquet floor.

After you check in, start your exploration of structure and form right in the B&B, where your hostess displays two or three pieces of her own work on a revolving basis. Step out the door, and you're directly facing **Carré St-Louis**, a public square surrounded by fanciful Victorian homes. Tear yourself away from this beautiful setting, and take the nearby métro to the **Musée d'art contemporain** (185 rue Ste-Catherine Ouest; 514–847–6212; station Place des Arts; closed Monday; admission $6.00). You'll have lunch at the restaurant here before you begin exploring.

LUNCH

Designed like an outdoor terrasse, **La Rotonde** (514–847–6901; inexpensive; table d'hôte $10 to $15) provides a breathtaking view of the esplanade of the Place des Arts—Montréal's version of Lincoln Center and the place where the symphony, opera, dance, and theater find a home. The French restaurant offers a three-course daily special: soup or salad, a main dish of fish, veal, or pasta, and dessert.

After lunch, stroll outside to the esplanade, a vantage point from which Montréal's modern art museum is not easily missed—especially by lovers. A perfectly shaped pair of big red lips graces the roof and sets the mood for—well, use your imagination. Artist Geneviève Cadieux's 1992 piece, an illuminated billboard titled *La Voie lactée*, actually lights up at night.

Inside, the avant-garde museum houses 5,000 works dating back to 1939, more than half by Québec artists, including Jean-Paul Riopelle, perhaps the most acclaimed Canadian painter of this century. Romantics must seek out Jim Dine's acrylic on canvas called *At Smithfield*, a dramatic rendering of a heart. Albert Dumouchel's passionate portrait of a couple entitled *L'Étreinte* is also a must-see for lovebirds.

The most romantic gallery here is the intimate Salon Senateur Louis P. Gélinas, which houses part of the permanent collection. You feel a sense of calm and peace as soon as you enter the light-filled salon. It's a perfect place to pause for a moment just to relax and enjoy each other's company.

Don't leave without visiting the Boutique in the main hall of Place des Arts, where crafts made by Québec designers are for sale. When you've finished browsing, return to your room to dress for dinner. You'll want to wear something chic. There's no dress code at the restaurant where you're heading, but the fashionable and trendy crowd dines here, so you'll want to fit right in. Take a cab or walk, if you're in the mood for a ten-minute stroll, to a place where the food is so beautifully presented it looks almost too good to eat.

DAY ONE: evening

DINNER

Chef Normand Laprise has been hailed as a culinary genius for his cutting-edge creations at **Toqué!** (3842 rue St-Denis; 514–499–2084; reservations required; expensive), where the designs on the plate are a work of art—and taste incredible, besides. *Toqué!* is French for nuts—as in crazy—but Laprise exhibits a divine form of madness with regional products. The restaurant decor mirrors the food: streamlined, no-frills, and totally refined. Ask for a table in the nook by the window, where it's quieter. Service is first-rate here, and the wine list is excellent.

After dinner, stroll down rue St-Denis and peek in the windows of the stores on the city's funkiest shopping street. The stores stay open until 9:00 on Thursday and Friday nights, so if you've finished eating early, you'll surely want to peruse the galleries and boutiques that line the street. No matter what hour you finish dining, end your evening with a nightcap at **Café Cherrier** (3635 rue St-Denis; 514–843–4308), a hangout for French-speaking artists, actors, and writers. This is a place to see-and-be-seen, and patrons are continually keeping an eye out for the famous—or infamous. Take a seat on the terrasse (if the weather permits), and let others speculate about your claim to fame.

When you're ready to leave center stage, return to your charming B&B literally steps away. Sleep soundly in your elegant manor house, surrounded by opulence enjoyed by occupants a century ago.

DAY TWO: morning

BREAKFAST

Wake up to another work of art—a frothy, fresh fruit drink made by your hostess. Her breakfast menu changes every day so that guests staying more than a single night don't grow tired of repeated dishes.

A typical breakfast offers a selection of breads from one of the top bakeries in the city, French toast or pancakes, and a selection of cheese and fresh fruit. All is artfully presented and served, of course, in the mansion's dining room.

After breakfast, take the métro to station Champs-de-Mars to visit another architectural treasure—the oldest part of the city. Browse through the galleries in Old Montréal (see the list of possibilities in "For More Romance"). Whether you're looking for paintings by Canadian artists, native soapstone carvings, copper sculpture, or finely crafted jewelry, these galleries will satisfy your desires. Take your time looking at pieces that, in some cases, can't be found elsewhere in Canada. Then take the métro to the only museum in the world devoted to the study and history of architecture.

The **Centre Canadien d'Architecture** (1920 rue Baile; 514–939–7026; station Guy-Concordia; closed Monday and Tuesday; admission $6.00) was founded by architect Phyllis Lambert, one of the richest women in the world, heir to the Seagram liquor fortune, and a bona fide heroine when it comes to saving Montréal's past. Renowned for her work preserving heritage homes and buildings in the city, Lambert was named an officer of the Ordre des Arts et Lettres by the French government in 1992 for her efforts to preserve Montréal's architectural splendor.

The CCA, which opened in 1989, has multiple functions. It is, at once, an architectural archive, a library devoted to architecture, and an exhibition center that presents thematic shows on important buildings and architects worldwide. A recent CCA exhibition, presented in galleries with vaulted ceilings that soar to a height of 20 feet, used photographs to document the work of landscape architect Frederick Law Olmsted, who designed Central Park in New York City as well as Parc Mont-Royal in Montréal.

In addition to the functions mentioned, the CCA building is, in itself, a wonderful example of architectural ingenuity. Lambert literally rescued the centerpiece of the building—the **Shaughnessy House** —from the wrecker's ball after it was pinpointed for demolition to make way for a highway. Years later, she and architect Peter Rose incorporated this 1874 structure, now classified as an historic monument, into the design of the Centre. The actual building is so striking,

In the Eye of the Beholder

Be sure to linger a while at eight of the most romantic paintings in the permanent collection at the Musée des Beaux Arts. Suggested by museum staffer Marie-Claude Saia, they are sure to inspire affection.

✳ *October* by James Jacques Joseph Tissot (1877)

✳ *Ludmille Komar, Princess of Beauvau-Craon* by Hippolyte (Paul) Delaroche (1849)

✳ *Wooded Landscape with Peasant Courting a Milkmaid* by Thomas Gainsborough (1755)

✳ *Under the Shadow of the Tent* by Helen Galloway McNicoll (1914)

✳ *Sappho* by Jules-Joseph Lefebvre (1884)

✳ *With the Current* by William Raphael (1892)

✳ *Venice, Looking Out Over the Lagoon* by James Wilson Morrice (1904)

✳ *Crown of Flowers* by William Bouguereau (1884)

it's worth the trip simply to look at the exterior and to then walk across boulevard René-Levesque and stroll through an urban sculpture garden created by artist/architect Melvin Charney. Built upon a 12-foot-high escarpment that cleverly screens out the sight and sounds of the nearby autoroute, it is an oasis of serenity. The pieces in the garden relate to the history of architecture and to the industrial city that lies below the hill.

If there's not currently an exhibition that catches your fancy at the CCA, you still might want to tour the building and the Shaughnessy House. (The building is open Wednesday through Sunday from 11:00 A.M.; call ahead for the tour schedule.) The Centre also has an impressive bookstore that explores subjects related to architecture. Peruse its shelves for volumes on city planning, the history of gardening, photography, and design. When you have finished admiring the structure, inside and out, lunch awaits.

DAY TWO: afternoon

LUNCH

You're a five-minute walk from **Le Faubourg Ste-Catherine** (1616 rue Ste-Catherine Ouest; 514–939–3663; inexpensive), a bustling international food court that offers authentic cuisine from more than twenty nations. You'll be charmed as you stroll past specialty grocery stores on the first floor and work your way up to an array of small restaurants on the third level. According to your mood and preference, choose from such ethnic treats as sushi, curry, and souvlaki. If you'd like a draft beer to go with your meal, drop by **Petite Europa**, which offers imported and local brands. Then settle at a wrought-iron table in the festive atrium, where 18-foot kites hang from the ceiling. Now's the perfect moment to discuss that wonderful soapstone carving you saw this morning—and whether you'll return to buy it.

From here, it's just a short walk north to the **Musée des Beaux-Arts** (1380 rue Sherbrooke; 514-285-1600; closed Mondays; admission $10). Founded in 1860, it is the oldest art museum in Canada, and it spreads across both sides of the street. The Benaiah Gibb Pavilion on the north side of Sherbrooke is devoted primarily to Canadian art, but you are going to explore the architecturally striking **Desmarais Pavilion** on the south side of Sherbrooke. Opened in 1991, it more than doubled the museum's space and houses contemporary international art and decorative arts from the Middle Ages to the present.

Architect Moshe Safdie wanted the new Pavilion to reflect the city —and it does, from all seven floors. At each level, you catch a slice of the mountain or the rooftops in the city. If you want to see the most romantic paintings in the collection, look for those mentioned in the "In the Eye of the Beholder" sidebar in this chapter, but be advised that the works rotate; not all the paintings will be on display.

When you have finished admiring the works, visit the museum boutique. The perfect memento of your afternoon here might be one of the mirrors from Peru, a piece of Mexican ceramic or Chinese porcelain, or a piece of jewelry made by a Québec artisan.

After shopping here, return to the B&B and change for dinner into clothing suitable for a fine restaurant. You're going to a hidden gem located in an unlikely spot near a major highway.

DAY TWO: evening

DINNER

Take a cab to **Le Passe-Partout** (3857 boulevard Décarie; 514-487-7750; open for dinner Thursday, Friday, and Saturday; expensive), where chef

James MacGuire shares space with an art-gallery owner who happens to be his wife. With seating for only thirty, reservations are an absolute must here. MacGuire, a French-trained chef who grew up in New York, oversees a classic French kitchen on the main floor, while Suzanne Baron-Lafrenière, his French-Canadian wife, runs an art gallery in the lower level. Baron-Lafrenière exhibits her collection of contemporary prints on paper in the restaurant. In the small bake shop on the premises, she also shows a collection of exquisite plates made by earthenware artisan Mareck Aillerie, who uses clay from Limoges and methods dating back three centuries. MacGuire too displays special talents: He smokes his own salmon, is renowned for his sourdough bread, and has been lauded by critics for producing flawless haute cuisine.

After dinner, take a cab to the Place des Arts, where you have reserved seats for the 8:00 P.M. curtain. Perhaps you have tickets to the Les Grands Ballets Canadiens, which has performed both classic and modern ballet for more than thirty-five years. More likely you're seeing a visiting troupe—perhaps from Spain or South America. Or perhaps you secured tickets to see a thoroughly modern local dance company—either La La La Human Steps or Marie-Chouinard. Let yourselves be transported by a highly charged performance you'll recall long after you leave Montréal. Afterward, you may want to put on your own highly charged performance back at the B&B.

FOR MORE ROMANCE

Collectors suggest these galleries as unusual. *Always* call ahead for hours, as they are not conventional.

Galerie d'art Yves Laroche (4 rue St-Paul Est; 514–393–1999; station Place d'Armes): Housed in a century-old building, the gallery showcases Canadian talent in painting, carving, and copper and metal sculpture.

Galerie Le Chariot (446 Place Jacques-Cartier; 514–875–4994; station Place d'Armes): Canada's largest gallery dedicated to Inuit art, this establishment highlights soapstone carvings from Cape Dorset and carries precious jewelry from Alberta.

Galerie Kastel (1368 avenue Greene; Westmount; 514–933–8735; station Atwater): In business for forty years, the gallery carries the best Canadian art. On its three floors, you'll find works by Antoine Bittar, Serge Brunoni, Liliane Fournier, Frank Nemeth, and Pierre Patry.

Galerie Shayne (547 avenue Royalmount; 514–739–1701; station de la Savane): Paintings and sculpture (including engaging musicians made entirely of wire) are combined here with jewelry, ceramics, and glass pieces that make wonderful gifts.

Galerie Red Cedar (6127 avenue Monkland; 514–489–8644; station Villa Maria and Bus No. 162): The largest collection of Northwest Indian art in eastern Canada is here. Pieces are culled directly from tribes in British Columbia and Washington State. The masks and medicine boxes are stunning.

A Big Bouquet
THE BOTANICAL GARDENS AND THE FLORAL PARK

OVE BLOSSOMS IN MONTRÉAL, where the city's natural beauty is a turn-on for residents and visitors alike. Mont-Royal and the St-Lawrence River are top natural landmarks in Montréal, but lovers are especially seduced by a fragrant dream on the eastern edge of the city. The Botanical Garden is the second-largest botanical garden in the world and the perfect place to promote a budding love, revive a wilted love, or nurture a love already in glorious full bloom.

The Garden's former director was elected mayor of Montréal in 1994 (and again in 1998), campaigning on a promise to turn the entire city into a garden if he won. Has Pierre Bourque succeeded? You two can judge for yourselves when you stop and smell the roses in Montréal.

PRACTICAL NOTES: This itinerary works best when the flowers are in bloom from June through September, but if there's a particular flower you're interested in seeing, call the Botanical Garden (514–872–1400) for a pamphlet entitled *The Wonders of the Seasons*, which describes precisely what you can expect to see in any particular month. In addition, bring sporty clothes suitable for your bike ride on Day Two.

DAY ONE: morning

Champagne—and flowers—await in your room if you make arrangements in advance with your hostess at a lovely B&B across from Parc Lafontaine called **B&B on the Park** (1308 rue Sherbrooke Est; 514–528–1308; station Sherbrooke; $110 to $145). Your weekend

Romance AT A GLANCE

♦ Enter a B&B that was once a Jesuit retreat, drop your bags, and then go for a stroll through verdant Parc Lafontaine to get a feel for the natural beauty that awaits.

♦ See the entire city of Montréal from a perch atop the world's tallest inclinded tower. Descend and then explore four habitats under one roof at the **Biodome** (4777 avenue Pierre-de-Coubertin; 514– 863–3000). Venture into the great outdoors at **Botanical Garden** (4101 rue Sherbrooke Est; 514–872–1400), where you'll walk through a river of roses, sniff the fruit of a cocoa tree in a tropical jungle, and see orchids that could star in an XXX-rated flick.

♦ Rent bicycles, then hop on the ferry for a short ride to the **Jardin des Floralies** on Ile Notre-Dame, where you'll ride through magical floral gardens designed by artisans from France, Italy, and England. Have lunch in the midst of splendor at an open-air café on the edge of the floral park.

love nest is a beautiful peach-colored room on the first floor of this seventy-seven-year-old house formerly owned by Jesuit priests. Your spacious chamber has a private bath with a Jacuzzi and a peaceful aura that your hostess believes comes from the spiritual occupants of the space in days gone by. Your bilingual hostess loves to spoil her guests. Given advance notice, she'll shop for that floral surprise so it can be in the room when you arrive. She'll be happy, as well, to design a private cocktail hour for you. She'll select a bottle of champagne, a wedge of soft cheese, and a creamy pâté—and serve you the feast in your room.

Settle into your room now, change into casual clothing, and you'll be ready to lose yourselves in a fragrant dream. I'm not referring only to the flowers you'll sniff this afternoon. I'm referring to the mouth-watering aroma wafting from a restaurant that serves the best French fries you've ever eaten.

DAY ONE: afternoon

LUNCH

Stroll hand in hand on the wide pathway through Parc Lafontaine, where you'll spy lovers stretched out on the grass or pedaling bicycles. It's a twenty-minute walk—when you're in love it takes longer —to **Frite Alors** (433 rue Rachel; 514–843–2490; inexpensive), a Belgian bistro located in a building that looks like a garage. Behind the hardware chic lurks the best fries in town—no contest—served with a choice of nine sauces. Québecers routinely dip their fries, but even the most discerning Québecer comes away impressed by the array of dips here, which range from Aioli (heavenly) to Dijon Mayonnaise (even more heavenly). The Hamburger Frite Alors is a juicy marvel laden with onions, mushrooms, and cheese, but salads and fabulous sandwiches are also on the menu for those who prefer, shall we say, lighter fare. The best seat in the house is near the garage door, which is always raised in summer and overlooks the passing parade of folks traversing the hip Plateau.

When the last *frite* has vanished and the dip is depleted, walk two blocks north to the Mont-Royal métro station. Take the métro to **Stade Olympic** (4549 avenue Pierre-de-Coubertin; 514–253–3434; station Viau), designed for the 1976 Summer Games held in the city —the Games where pigtailed gymnast Nadia Comaneci scored her perfect 10s—and follow signs to the Tourist Hall.

The Olympic Stadium—jokingly dubbed the Big Owe for the mountain of debt it left behind after the Games—is home to major league baseball's Montréal Expos. The Stadium's Inclined Tower (514–252–4141; open daily; admission $9.00) has permanently altered the Montréal skyline and provides one of the best vistas in the city. A funicular cable car travels up the spine of the tower every ten minutes (except in February, when the car is closed for its annual checkup). From 575 feet above ground, you'll view the distant surroundings and the Garden you'll visit later.

When you descend, explore other parts of the Olympic complex. You'll venture into the Arctic and a tropical forest—under one roof. The **Biodome** (4777 avenue Pierre-de-Coubertin; 514–868–3000; open daily; a $15.00 joint admission with the Botanical Garden saves $3.50), located where the Olympic cycling competition was held, was created by city botanists, biologists, and zoologists to showcase four ecosystems and thousands of plants and animals in their natural habitats. Two of the ecosystems can be found locally near the St-Lawrence River—one a marine habitat (where a mother duck feeds her babies) and the other a forest, where you'll catch sight of beavers, river otters, and a Canadian lynx roaming among pines and maples.

After you've seen birds in the tropical jungle and penguins in the frozen tundra, grab a free shuttle from Olympic Park to the **Botanical Garden** (4101 rue Sherbrooke Est; 514–872–1400). Picnickers eat at tables near the entry, and concessions offer snacks. Have a soft drink while I tell you about the place. Opened in 1931 (the art deco administration building attests to the era), the Botanical Garden was the brainchild of Brother Marie-Victorin, who loved the idea of theme gardens and exhibition greenhouses right in the city. Today, the Botanical Garden is second in size only to Kew Gardens in Surrey, England. If you're here from August through October, a wall of dahlias along the stone wall near the snack area will delight your eyes—as will a parade of brides and grooms.

The Botanical Garden is the most popular spot for wedding photos in Montréal. On any given Saturday in July, some fifty couples head to the park with their photographers. You'll see dueling wedding parties jockeying for space near the fountains at the entrance, determined brides who refuse to remove their gloves in the sultry heat, and groomsmen in velvet tuxedos who look like they're about to liquefy under a broiling sun. Enjoy the spectacle. Raise a glass to their happiness.

Consult the map you received upon entering the garden. There's a lot of ground to cover—so to speak—but you'll pause at only the most sensual spots. Begin at the economic tropical plants in the Exhibition Greenhouses (No. 23 on your map), which focuses on plants that turn a dollar for the local economy. Here you'll find a cocoa tree, which produces the heavenly bean that chocolate lovers worship, and a vanilla tree as well. The fruit of both trees, if not actually blooming when you visit, can be observed up close in a display case.

An adjoining greenhouse focuses on orchids, a flower laden with sexual connotations. The shape of an orchid, the way the lips frill, the column right in middle of the lips—botanists here joke that orchids could star in an XXX flick.

After you've toured the greenhouses, walk to the Roseraie (No. 20), where beds of roses are meant to simulate a long and sinuous river winding through a forest. Sweep along a riverbed of roses until you reach a spectacular display of climbing roses on the pergola, a favorite spot for wedding photos. At the end of the garden, you'll find a collection of antique roses acclaimed for their color and perfume. Get ready to swoon.

Now jump on a free red tram to the Jardin Leslie-Hancock (No. 4), where rhododendrons in several shades form a shimmering bauble of color in late May—but stay sparkly only a few weeks. All summer, however, the grass here is so exceptionally soft that you'll have to take off your shoes and walk through it barefoot.

Take the tram or walk to Jardin du sous-bois— the shade garden (No. 10). Here, pale blue forget-me-nots bloom in early spring. Now walk to Les Étangs—the ponds (No. 7)— where huge willow trees almost 3 feet in diameter surround two creeks. Sit down to rest your feet and watch the ducks paddling along.

Your last stop is Jardin de Chine (No. 18), the largest Chinese garden in the world outside Asia. It was designed in Shanghai and assembled here by Chinese artisans. Seven pavilions were built around the garden's lake. One houses penjings—miniature trees that are generations old. This stunning garden is the perfect spot to end your visit as the sun sets and the stillness of evening descends.

Montréal en Fleurs

The city's coat of arms is a bouquet of sorts. It features four floral designs meant to represent the city's population in 1832, when Montréal was formally incorporated: a fleur de lys for the French settlers; the Lancastrian rose for the English; the thistle for the Scottish population; and the shamrock for those of Irish descent.

DAY ONE: evening

Take the métro back to your B&B (station Sherbrooke) and rest your weary feet. Why not use the Jacuzzi before dinner, after pouring yourself a glass of bubbly from the bottle you asked your hostess to secure? While you're in the bath, sip the sparkling wine and admire the roses she picked up earlier for you at the flower market. When you finish your bath (and the wine), don a summer outfit (but no jeans or shorts). Then walk to the métro, watching the sun set over Mont-Royal.

DINNER

In keeping with the floral theme, you'll dine tonight at the lush-looking **L'Orchidées de Chine** (2017 rue Peel; station Peel; 514–287–1878; closed Sunday; moderate), which combines elegant decor with gourmet Chinese fare. Though located on a bustling city street, the restaurant's second-floor perch, well-spaced tables, and ample booths immediately convey a feeling of tranquility. The food here is a balanced blend of spicy and sweet flavors. Owner George Lau visits with patrons and is adept at matching your desires with his menu choices. As well, Lau has worked hard to match his menu with a commendable wine list and will be happy to suggest a red or white to complement your choices. Spend a languid evening remembering the racy orchids you beheld earlier, then take a cab back to the B&B —and behold each other.

DAY TWO: morning/afternoon

BREAKFAST

You'll have a hearty vegetarian breakfast this morning in the modern kitchen of the B&B. Your hostess, a vegetarian, offers five kinds of bread (including croissants) and a variety of spreads; she also offers a bounty of fresh fruit, granola and other cereals, and juice, coffee, and tea. Try the bread with raisins and nuts. No need to count calories. You'll be getting plenty of exercise today.

After breakfast, exit the B&B dressed for a bike ride. You'll again walk to rue Rachel, where you'll rent a bike at **Cycle Pop** (978 and 1000 rue Rachel; 514–526–2525). Staff here will guide you to rue Berri and the designated bike path that takes you to the Old Port and the St-Lawrence River, a distance of about 3 miles. It's an exciting ride through a large slice of the city, past the downtown corridor, and then into the oldest part of Montréal. You'll whiz by modern skyscrapers and suddenly be confronted with old-world buildings. The contrast is a pleasant surprise.

When you catch sight of a body of water that seems to extend forever, you've reached your destination. Ride over to the **Navette**

Fluviale (on Quai Jacques-Cartier; opens at 10:30 every morning; fare, $3.00 per person) and board the ferry with your bike. Get ready for a brief, but romantic ride across the St-Lawrence. The sea breeze plays with your hair as you travel to Parc Drapeau, formerly Parc-des-Îles, which was renamed in September 1999 after the death of legendary Montréal mayor Jean Drapeau. It is composed of Île Ste-Hélène and Île Notre-Dame and was the site of the World's Fair (or Expo) held in 1967.

When Montréal began planning for Expo '67, city officials soon realized that Île Ste-Hélène would not be adequate to accommodate dozens of pavilions and nearly fifty million visitors. So the city literally built another island from scratch, fashioning Île Notre-Dame in ten months from tons of dirt left from digging the métro tunnel.

Debark at the landing on Île Ste-Hélène and follow signs to the Kiosque d'Accueil. Ask for a map of the park. From here it's just a short bike ride to Île Notre-Dame.

Here, surrounded by water and crisscrossed by canals, is the **Jardin des Floralies**, a stunning floral park that is the legacy of an international competition held in 1980. Thousands of roses, flowers, shrubs, and trees are arranged in a series of picturesque gardens representing more than fifteen nations. Cycle around astoundingly beautiful acreage designed by landscapers and horticulturists from France, Italy, and the United States—and note that Britain's rose garden was created in tribute to the Queen Mother on her eightieth birthday. When hunger pangs call, leave the lilacs and begonias for a while and have lunch.

LUNCH

At the edge of the floral park, in a bowl-shaped patio, you'll find **Café Terrasse Fleur de l'Île** (inexpensive). Dotted with picnic tables topped by parasols, the café is a combination restaurant/snack bar. Order a sandwich and a glass of wine or beer, and enjoy the simple but tasty fare in the open air, surrounded by the finest plants and flowers the world has to offer. Take a well-deserved break, and when you're ready, hop back on the bike.

Continuing exploring the Floral Park (have you seen the ornamental shrubs?), but remember, you still have to pedal back to the Plateau. Leave yourself ample time to catch the ferry back to the Old Port and retrace your path. Once you've returned your bike, it will be late afternoon. Walk back through Parc Lafontaine to your B&B, where a happy hour (Québecers call it *cinq-à-sept*) is about to commence—in your room. Your hostess has taken care of the details. Race each other to the Jacuzzi (or settle snugly into the tub together), and afterwards, put your feet up, uncork the champagne, and whisper the words: *Je t'aime*.

DAY TWO: evening

Dress up tonight for dinner. Ask your hostess to call you a cab (you've done your share of exercise today) and zip off to a favorite hideaway for lovers.

DINNER

Pale blue cloths grace the tables at the very intimate **La Gaudriole** (825 rue Laurier Est; 514–276–1580; open every night; moderate), where chef and proprietor Marc Vezina prepares what he calls fine cuisine "métissée"—a mix of foods with northern heritage, Mediterranean roots, and Québec simplicity. A cuisine, he says, that is "full of contradictions reconciled." The menu is in constant evolution, but a sample table d'hôte (appetizer, main course, and dessert) might include smoked salmon blinis, rabbit stuffed with apricots (or shrimp in saffron butter, for those less adventurous), and, to close the evening, strudel filled with figs, apricots, and nuts. Or you might want to close the meal by playing Le Grand Jeu, the big game, and ordering an assortment of homemade desserts to share. This way, you'll have many sweet memories to take home with you.

FOR MORE ROMANCE

If you can, squeeze in a visit to **Ogilvy** (1307 rue Ste-Catherine Ouest; 514–842–7711), a boutique-style department store with a fabulous garden shop in the basement level. **Dig This** carries seeds from

England, fancy garden tools, flowered gloves, floral gift cards, fountains, sculptures, sundials, and a wonderful collection of bowls, pots, and pitchers with floral designs. Break out the credit card and indulge.

Get Physical

In Tandem
BIKER'S PARADISE IN THE OLD PORT

MONTRÉAL IS A FREEWHEELING CITY GEARED TO COUPLES who enjoy sightseeing from a higher plane—and maybe in tandem. Be assured that Montréal can fulfill any biker's needs and desires. The city sponsors Le Tour de l'Île every June, attracting 45,000 participants to what the Guinness Book of Records calls the largest gathering of cyclists on earth. And in 1999, Montréal was named the best cycling city in North America by *Bicycling* magazine.

A whopping 150 miles of designated bike path crisscross the island of Montréal. Much of the marked bike path radiates from the Old Port, which is the city's most popular tourist attraction, your headquarters for a spirited weekend, and a cyclist's paradise.

The Old Port bike path offers you two a scenic ride along the water, a panoramic view of the city skyline, easy transport to top attractions, and a smooth ride to fun and romance. Why hesitate? Strap on your helmets and get ready to roll.

PRACTICAL NOTES: Your lodging has storage facilities for bicycles should you choose to bring them, and the métro allows bikes in the tail cars. Cycling paths are open from April through October, and you can obtain maps before your trip from **Maison des Cyclistes** (1251 rue Rachel Est; 514–521–8356). Have an Italian coffee at Café Bicicletta, right on the premises. Feel free to bike farther than the itinerary indicates. With a map as a guide, you can tailor the mileage to your own capabilities—and desires.

Rom**a**n**c**e AT A GLANCE

♦ Gaze at the waterfront from your bedroom window at **Auberge du Vieux Port** (97 rue de la Commune Est; 14–876–0081), a former leather factory transformed into a perch on the St-Lawrence, then break away from the view to explore Montréal's harbor by bike.

♦ Spend the day biking along the **Lachine Canal,** a paved stretch that runs 11 miles, stopping for lunch at an outdoor market. Pedal through one of the largest outdoor sculpture gardens in North America, where works of art are displayed around the waterfront.

♦ Leave your bikes behind when night falls, but stay at the water's edge as you visit the **Casino de Montréal,** a European-style gaming house overlooking the St-Lawrence, where you'll have dinner and then tempt Lady Luck.

DAY ONE: morning/afternoon

Views of the St-Lawrence River, the Jacques-Cartier Bridge, and even the Casino de Montréal are spectacular from **Auberge du Vieux Port** (97 rue de la Commune Est; 514–876–0081; $175 to $225, breakfast included; station Champs de Mars). A former leather factory erected in 1882 has been transformed into an inn, with an original wood beam or exposed stone wall retained in each of twenty-seven rooms spread over five floors. Wood floors and brass beds mix with modern touches like a Jacuzzi bath, a marble shower, and two wineglasses on a side table—and an elevator for patrons who love the intimate ambience of an inn but don't like to take the stairs. During the **International Fireworks Festival** in July and August (for more information, see the "Big Grin" itinerary), patrons have a ringside seat on the pyrotechnic display from the inn's roof.

Check-in time at the inn is 3:00 P.M., and you've reserved room No. 302 (with a Port view), but you can set your bags down much earlier and start pedaling. If you haven't brought a bike, rent a ten-speed nearby at **Montréal En-Ligne** (47 rue de la Commune Ouest; 514–849–5211; $25 a day for each bike).

To scope out the 11-mile (one way) route that you will travel on today, bike to the ivory-colored clock tower on the eastern end of the pier. **La Tour de l'Horloge** (on Quai de l'Horloge), known as the Sailor's Memorial Clock Tower, was constructed in 1922 to commemorate sailors lost in World War I. It houses four clocks legendary for their accuracy. Climb the 192 steps to the top, where you'll see the clockworks from the inside out, hear the sound of the pendulum swinging, and view the harbor from three observation points.

You'll see the dramatic outline of the Jacques-Cartier Bridge, the foliage on the Expo Islands (you'll be there tomorrow), and the magisterial dome of the Marché Bonsecours, the farmer's market that served as city hall in the 1800s.

Descend from the tower and bike west to **Parc des Écluses** (Locks Park, corner rue McGill and rue de la Commune), where you'll link up with the **Lachine Canal**, built in the early 1820s by hundreds of Irish laborers who finally managed to tame the wild rapids that had formed a barrier to shipping and trade for some three hundred years. Get the whole story at **Maison des Éclusiers** (514–283–6054; free admission), an interpretation center that explains the canal's history from conception to construction to closure in 1970.

Now you're ready to travel on the bike path that runs alongside the canal. Lunch is about 2 miles down the path.

LUNCH

Look for the clock tower denoting **Atwater Market** (138 avenue Atwater at rue Notre-Dame; 514–935–5716), established in 1932 and notable in summer for its cut flowers, plants, herbs, and fabulous produce—indoors and out. Park your bikes in the stands and head upstairs to the second floor. **Première Moisson** offers more than twenty kinds of bread, including a fabulous loaf with an onion built into the middle. The bakery also sells an array of *terrines*—nicely spiced meat loaves made with lamb or deer or bison. Pick up a bread and some terrine, or you can have a sandwich made to order. *Et voila!* Exit the market and head for the picnic tables near the canal. From this protected, quiet spot, you can watch the parade of cyclists, strollers, joggers, and rollerbladers whizzing past.

By now, you can see the bounty Montréal offers to cyclists. This is just a start. Le Tour de l'Île, the largest cycling event in the world, attracts tens of thousands of participants each June for a 65-kilometer (39-

mile) ride through city streets. If you'd like to participate in next year's Le Tour de l'Île, register now with the Maison des Cyclistes.

After lunch, resume your ride. On the extreme western end of the canal you'll find the **Fur Trade National Historic Site** (1255 boulevard St-Joseph, Lachine; 514–637–7433; $2.50 admission; open every day in summer), roughly forty-five minutes by bike from the Old Port. Built in 1803, the building is the only remaining warehouse left from that era. In this tiny museum you'll wander among bundles of precious fur, touch pelts of deer and raccoon, and laugh at each other as you each try on a beaver top hat and gaze in the mirror at your distinguished image. In the Fur Trade museum you can easily envision the roles of the Indians who trapped the fur, the French-Canadian *voyageurs* who hauled goods by canoe for barter, and the Scottish merchants who brokered the deals.

From the museum, veer off boulevard St-Joseph and onto a stretch of land that juts to the left. You've discovered **Parc René-Levesque** and **Le Musée Plein Air de Lachine**— one of the largest collections of outdoor sculptures in North America. Thirty-two sculptures, some crafted by artists of international repute, are placed around the Lachine waterfront—half of them on this strip you're traversing. You'll be enchanted by this artistic oasis. Park your bikes and sit on a bench to study and admire works of stone, granite, and metal. Linger as long as you'd like in this museum under the sky, admiring the art from various angles. Admire each other, as well, at this quiet rest point, which is so little traveled it's

Long-Distance Romance

Île Ste-Hélène was discovered in 1611 by French explorer Samuel de Champlain, who named the island after his young wife. They were betrothed when Hélène was twelve and Samuel forty—and they married two years later. Hélène stayed in France while her husband traveled between the Old World and the New—giving a whole different spin to the term, "commuter marriage." When Hélène finally ventured to Québec, she found the bitter winters too hard to take and returned to France.

almost a private world. You've reached the end of the road for today. Return to the Old Port using the same route by which you came.

By the time you return to the inn, it should be early evening, although during summers in Montréal, the sun doesn't set until after 9:00 P.M. Why not take a relaxing soak in the Jacuzzi and then watch the sun go down from the rooftop?

As darkness descends, amble hand in hand on the cobblestone street to a new restaurant that has captivated longtime admirers of Old Montréal.

DAY ONE: evening

DINNER

A sense of history is evident the moment you enter **Pavarotti** (408 rue St-François-Xavier; 514–844–9656, closed Sunday and Monday night; moderate), where antiques cover the fireplace mantel, a chandelier made of wood dominates the small room, and pictures of Old Montréal adorn the walls. Classical music adds to the old-world flavor as you select from a menu designed to provide just the right fuel for another day on the bike. Homemade soups and fresh pasta are the specialty here. Try the chunky minestrone filled with vegetables, and perhaps seafood pasta for your main course. You won't be able to resist the olive bread in the basket, ready to dip in olive oil. After you've loaded up on carbs, stroll back to the inn and sink into your brass bed.

DAY TWO: morning/afternoon

You covered a fair bit of territory yesterday, so take it slow this morning. Start with an old-fashioned breakfast to fuel your muscles for today's ride.

BREAKFAST

Breakfast is served at the bottom of a narrow, wrought-iron spiral staircase in the inn's basement level. The staircase is more than one hundred years old and dates back to the building's saddle-making days. By the way, you don't really have to take the spiral staircase downstairs—the breakfast area is accessible also by elevator. No matter which route you take to reach it, you can't beat the ample meal offered by the innkeepers. Fresh fruit, muffins, cereals, and your choice of eggs or waffles provides the energy to pedal a distance.

After breakfast, you'll visit a different bike rental shop and secure a deluxe tandem bike at **Vélo Aventure** (Quai King Édouard; 514–847–0666; $45 a day). Your destination is **Parc Drapeau**, site of the World's Fair (or Expo) held here in 1967. The two islands that compose Parc Drapeau are often referred to as the Expo Islands, and they're accessible from the bike path on the Lachine Canal. The path runs through an industrial area, then through a residential complex called **Cité du Havre** before reaching the Pont de la Concorde, where you'll cross the river to the islands, called Île Ste-Hélène and Île Notre-Dame. The ride should take about an hour.

As you bike along Cité du Havre, admire **Habitat '67**, one of the most famous works of architect Moshe Safdie, who was only twenty-six when he created it. Habitat is a high-density apartment complex composed of three-dimensional prefabricated modules. It was inspired by the hillside villages in Israel, where Safdie grew up. Habitat created a tremendous sensation at the Expo. After the World's Fair, the units were sold to private individuals and are still considered choice property.

Keep cycling until you cross over Pont de la Concorde and catch sight of an enormous silver globe that seems to twirl on an axis. The **Biosphere** (160 rue Tour de l'Îsle; 514–283–5000; $6.50 admission) is housed in a 200-foot-high geodesic dome that was designed by architect R. Buckminster Fuller as the American Pavilion for Expo '67.

Québec, amazingly, produces 10 percent of the world's fresh water supply. The relationship between water and the province—and between water and humankind—is explored at the Biosphere through interactive exhibits on conservation, pollution, and marine life. Make certain to see award-winning filmmaker Frédéric Back's animated history of the St-Lawrence River before you visit the other exhibits. It's been described as a Chagall painting brought to life. Revel in the vibrant images that give the river meaning.

Explore the museum until hunger pangs hit. Then take a break at the Biosphere restaurant.

LUNCH

L'eau Vive (inexpensive) offers daily specials of chicken, pasta, and beef as well as sandwiches and quiche. The restaurant has a terrasse where you can dine alfresco, but if the weather won't cooperate, windows all around the restaurant provide a fine view of Parc Drapeau. Enjoy the greenery. The islands are filled with trees and flowers.

The view from the restaurant is certainly lovely, but when it comes to vistas, you'll want to head for the fourth floor of the Biosphere—a perch that would carry a much higher floor number in a more conventional structure. The lookout offers a superb view of the city, the river, the South Shore, and the Jacques-Cartier Bridge. Compare the view here to the one you saw yesterday from the Clock Tower. Which do you prefer?

When you leave the Biosphere, turn left and bike through one of the most beautiful parks in Montréal. **Parc Hélène-de-Champlain** has pathways lined with shrubs and flowers. Stop at the observation deck that tops a building dating back more than a century and a half. When you've admired the scenery, return to the Old Port the way you came—or transport your bike in the tail car of the métro. Back at the inn, soak your tired feet in the Jacuzzi tub in your room. You'll be chasing Lady Luck tonight.

DAY TWO: evening

Action awaits at the **Casino de Montréal** on Île Notre-Dame, located in the architecturally stunning French Pavilion built for Expo '67, Montréal's World's Fair. Arrive before sunset so you can catch the light streaming in from wraparound windows that overlook the city and the St-Lawrence River; the casino presents a happy contrast to the artificially lit settings in which most other gambling palaces are housed. It is open twenty-four hours a day, has 113 gaming tables, nearly 3,000 slot machines, and an off-track betting lounge. Juice, soft drinks, and coffee are served free of charge on the gaming floor, and cocktail lounges are scattered over different levels. When it opened in 1993, the casino was expected to draw 5,000 visitors a day, but administrators badly underestimated. As many as 18,000 visitors a day streamed in, and before long, it became apparent that the French Pavilion was not sufficient to handle the crowds. In 1996, the French Pavilion was linked by tunnel with another Expo '67 relic. Enter the tunnel and head to the former Québec Pavilion, where you'll be having dinner.

DINNER

With its old-world atmosphere and red-and-white checked table-cloths, **Via Fortuna** (1 avenue du Casino; 800–665–2274; inexpensive) offers a delightful three-course table d'hôte at bargain Las Vegas-style prices. Try the salade focaccia, rigatoni with mushroom sauce, and tiramisu for dessert. *Bon appétit*—and *bonne chance* when you leave the dining table for the gaming table.

FOR MORE ROMANCE

Avid bikers will want to discover the **P'tit Train du Nord**, a cross-country trail described in "The Alps" itinerary, which turns into a first-rate bike trail in summer. Drive roughly forty minutes from Montréal to the foothills of the Laurentian Mountains in St-Jérôme, where the path begins, and cycle through quaint villages as far as 200 kilometers north.

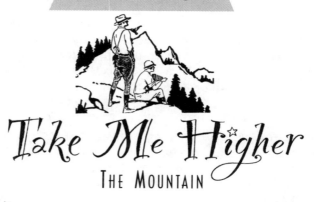

Take Me Higher

THE MOUNTAIN

LOVERS WILL ALWAYS REACH A HIGH POINT on Mont-Royal. City fathers have decreed that nothing rises higher than the mountain. By law, no building in the city may be taller than its 763 feet (232½ meters). The city's highest building at 1000 rue de la Gauchetière is 761 feet (232 meters), ensuring that romantics will always get the highest high on the mountain.

In this town, you can't get much closer to nature—or heaven, for that matter—than Mont-Royal. Ask Montréalers what turns them on about the city, and "the mountain" is way up there on the list of features. Living with a mountain in their midst is almost like living with a cherished monument—the Acropolis in Athens or Notre-Dame Cathedral in Paris. Like residents of those cities, Montréalers both revere the city's distinguishing feature—and take it for granted.

On this budget-minded itinerary, you'll traverse acres of mountain. When you're not exploring the peak, you'll discover its unique surroundings. If you two love the outdoors unadorned, you're on the right path.

PRACTICAL NOTES: The itinerary works best from May to October, when climbing, hiking, and picnicking are practicable. Wear solid shoes. Your feet will thank you.

DAY ONE: morning/afternoon

You're seeking charm, not sterility, so avoid the modern tower recently added to your lodging and be sure to reserve a room in the original section of the **Château Versailles** (1659 rue Sherbrooke Ouest;

◆ Check into the **Château Versailles** (1659 rue Sherbrooke Ouest; 514– 933–3611), a series of Victorian town homes now combined into a hotel, and get ready to find paradise on earth at a most unlikely site: Mount Royal Cemetery. Designed as a Garden of Eden, it's where the city's elite lie buried in natural splendor.

◆ Visit a mountainside basilica where the faithful flock for miracle cures— some of them climbing 283 steps to the main portico on their knees. After you've debated the notion of miracles, arrive at the **Champs Élysées** for dinner. No, you haven't been miraculously transported to Paris. The Champs Élysées restaurant is across the street from your hotel (1800 rue Sherbrooke Ouest; 514–939–1212).

◆ Hike to the top of **Mont-Royal,** where you'll spread a gourmet picnic on the mountaintop, splash each other while boating on Lac aux Castors and view the legendary cross on the mountain, placed there originally in 1643.

514–933–3611 or 800–361–7199; $95 to $135, but ask for the weekend package). Four Victorian town homes, dating back to 1911 and all designed by Scottish architect James Seath-Smith, who lived in one of the houses, comprise the original portion. Since you've requested a deluxe room with a view of rue Sherbrooke, you should be setting your bags down in No.108 on the main floor or Nos. 201, 204, or 320, all of which have king-size beds.

When Seath-Smith built the stately mansions, rue Sherbrooke was not yet paved west of rue Guy. Each of the homes had a series of owners and renters through the years, some of them well known—like Narcisse Perodeau, notary, politician, and eventual lieutenant-governor of Québec. Seath-Smith and his wife Gwendoline lived in No. 1657 until they sold it in 1935 to a widow who turned it into an exclusive boardinghouse for well-to-do bachelors and widowers in the Square Mile district. A subsequent owner made it a French pension catering to genteel European families arriving in Montréal without a place to stay after World War II. André and Marie-Louise Villeneuve were just twenty-four years old when they purchased No. 1669 in 1958, remodeled it, and turned it into the Versailles Lodge. Over a period of eighteen years, they acquired three other adjacent homes. Today Château Versailles has seventy rooms—and treasures galore—

like the art deco lamp made of Italian alabaster in the foyer and the Delft tiles in the fireplace of the former breakfast room, originally part of the Seath-Smith house.

The Villeneuves didn't learn until after they christened Versailles Lodge that nearly three centuries ago a French religious order had constructed a château on the same grounds, patterned after the Versailles of Louis XIV and complete with gardens and a fountain. No sign of the old château exists, but it's not hard to imagine the respect that the site once commanded when you study its position overlooking the old quarter of the city. Take a few minutes to settle into your room, and then have a quick lunch. You want to have lots of time to explore the neighborhood.

LUNCH

Van Houtte (1538 rue Sherbrooke; 514–934–4836; inexpensive) is a time-saver for busy Montréalers, who flock here at lunch for nourishing soups and salads and tasty sandwiches and desserts served cafeteria-style. Take your trays over to a café table-for-two and sit down for a few intimate moments. When you've refueled, you'll travel to a most unlikely romantic spot—a cemetery.

You'll climb the mountain on foot tomorrow. Today you'll get to the top more quickly. Grab a cab outside the restaurant, and be whisked off to a quick high. You're moments from the main entrance to **Mount Royal Cemetery** (chemin de la Forêt), conceived as a sort of Garden of Eden in 1847. Even today it seems to exist in some heavenly realm light-years away from the city.

As birds warble (birders have counted more than 145 species, some found nowhere else in the province) and tiny chipmunks dart through the grass (you might also spot a pheasant or a fox), follow the green line on the asphalt to the cemetery office. Here you'll pick up a map containing a historical walking tour of the grounds as well as information on bird-watching and the cemetery's collection of trees and flowering shrubs.

The cemetery covers 165 acres on the north slope of Mont Royal, formerly the site of old farms. Its sinuous pathways were created a generation before Frederick Law Olmsted built Parc Mont-Royal across the road. Its design is generally attributed to J. C. Sidney, who was commissioned by the Protestant community to create a Garden of Eden—a paradise for the living to visit their dear departed. Although he could not foresee what would come to pass, Sidney's vision of paradise was helped along tremendously by careful management from three generations of gardeners in the Roy family, who cared for the grounds from 1890 to 1990.

According to Sidney's plan, the pathways in the cemetery wind and curve and roll, taking advantage of the land, which is shaped like a basin. Wherever you wander in the valley, the view changes, and so does the shadow and the light. The markers here are discreet, but many are works by celebrated artists. The foliage ranges from crab apple trees and Japanese lilacs in May and June to blazing maples in autumn. Conifers add color year-round. An oak and a white ash have entwined trunks to form one tree; a screech owl has hollowed out a home in a white birch; trilliums, peonies, ferns, ivy, thyme, phlox, lupines, and hundreds of roses dot the grounds.

The famous are buried here: Sir John Abbott, first native-born prime minister of Canada; hockey legend Howie Morenz, the greatest player of his era and the Canadiens' scoring leader for seven seasons; famed photographer William Notman; and members of the Molson family on a plot distinguished by a round obelisk, a symbol of wealth. But the most-visited grave might be that of Anna Leonowens—governess to the King of Siam's sixty-four children and inspiration for the play *The King and I.*

When you've ambled through the engaging garden-like setting, follow the green line to adjoining **Cimetière Notre-Dame-des-Neiges**, a Catholic cemetery where more than a million people are buried. In complete contrast to the cemetery you just left, the graves here are organized almost like city blocks. The icons are much more elaborate and religious in nature, including archangels on the crucifix positioned at the main entrance.

Among the Québec elite buried here is Sir Georges-Etienne Cartier, a father of the Canadian confederation who died in 1873. His tombstone reads *Franc et Sans Dol*—honest and without deceit—and overlooks Lac des Deux Montagnes and Lac St-Louis, two of the five waterways that encircle Montréal.

Through the trees in the Catholic cemetery, you can catch a glimpse of the copper dome at **Oratoire St-Joseph** (3800 chemin Queen Mary), where you're heading now. Draw a deep breath. The massive structure is awe-inspiring. The dome is second in size to St. Peter's in Rome. From the street, there are 283 stairs leading to the Corinthian-style columns that soar 60 feet at the main portico. Each year the stairs are climbed by more than two million people, a mix of tourists and devout pilgrims who believe that miracles can happen here; some climb to the door on their knees.

The church is both an homage to St-Joseph, patron saint of Canada, and to Brother André, an orphan by age twelve who left Québec to work in the textile mills of New England. He returned, joined a religious order, and, by age thirty, working as a doorman at the Collège Notre-Dame across the street from the present oratory, started drawing public attention for miraculous healings. In 1904, the Miracle Man of Montréal built a humble wooden chapel on the site of

I Can See for Miles and Miles

From these lookout points you can see forever:

* Observatoire de l'Est du Mont-Royal (on voie Camilien-Houde Parkway).

* Observatoire du chalet (in Parc Mont-Royal).

* Chemin du Belvédère (on chemin Belvédère in Westmount).

* Tour du Stade Olympique (at 4141 avenue Pierre-de-Coubertin; 514–252–8687).

* Observatoire de l'Oratoire St-Joseph (at 3800 rue Queen Mary; 514–733–8211).

* Observatoire de la Chapelle Notre-Dame-de-Bonsecours (400 rue St-Paul Est).

* La Tour de l'Horloge (on Quai de l'Horloge, off rue de la Commune, in the Old Port).

what later became Oratoire St-Joseph. Today you can see canes, crutches, and wheelchairs left by the grateful in the shrine. In the crypt-like church, you can see stained-glass windows representing the life of St-Joseph. Outside, fifty-six bells weighing 24,000 pounds and originally intended for the Eiffel Tower in Paris are on view. Also outside you can walk along the chemin de Croix (Way of the Cross), featuring sculptures of polished stone. The observatory at the Oratory provides a splendid view of the city (see sidebar).

Descending the steps of the Oratoire, pause near street level to gape again at the building's grandeur—and at the mountain in the background. The spiritual and the earthly mesh on this site. Do miracles really happen here? As you debate the notion, continue with your miraculous romantic encounter. Return to the hotel by cab and change for dinner—and entertainment.

DAY ONE: evening

DINNER

My French teacher, Madame Charlotte, once told me to meet her at the **Champs-Elysées** for lunch. I had to call her back to make sure I'd heard correctly. Yes, the Champs-Elysées is a restaurant—and it's not in Paris. Right across the street from your hotel, it's located at 1800 rue Sherbrooke Ouest (514–939–1212; moderate). Fine French cuisine is served here daily, and on Saturday night, there's music at dinner—ranging from a jazz trio to a singer/guitarist.

After dinner, stroll along rue Sherbrooke and window-shop. The street is Montréal's version of New York's Fifth Avenue. Link arms and imagine how it looked in Seath-Smith's day, when it was simply a wide avenue lined on both sides with trees.

DAY TWO: morning

BREAKFAST

Don't jump out of bed right away. Rev up for you hike slowly. Why not indulge and order room service? Make the call and minutes later, fresh-squeezed orange juice will be brought to your room along with an assortment of croissants and jams and coffee and tea. After you've had a leisurely wake-up, you're ready for the trek ahead. Leave your bags in the lobby for a pickup late in the afternoon. Don't forget to bring along your backpacks. They will hold your picnic.

Before you begin climbing, take a short cab ride to the **Westmount Greenhouse** (at the corner of rue Sherbrooke Ouest and Landsdowne;

open 10:00 A.M. to 5:00 P.M. on Saturday and Sunday), on the same complex as the recently renovated **Westmount Library,** Québec's first public library, founded in 1899. The greenhouse was started in 1926 expressly to supply plants for parks in Westmount, a wealthy residential city enclosed within Montréal's borders. The gardeners in the conservatory stopped taking inventory of the collection years ago, but here you'll find one large room and four smaller ones exhibiting everything from a bird-of-paradise to a banana tree. It's an oasis in the urban landscape—much like the mountain you're about to ascend.

Now, walk west a few blocks on rue Sherbrooke to **Patisserie de Gascogne** (4825 rue Sherbrooke; 514–932–3511), where you'll put together a first-class picnic from the city's best pastry shop. Actually so much more than a patisserie, Gascogne is also a catering shop and is expert at designing fancy lunches. Order a gourmet sandwich on a baguette—maybe smoked Norwegian salmon with cream cheese, onions, capers, olive oil, and romaine lettuce. Or maybe the house roast beef with Dijon mustard, romaine lettuce, tomatoes, onions, pickles, and shallots. Or maybe prosciutto with Parmesan, olive oil, romaine lettuce, and tomatoes. Hmmm. So difficult to choose. Side dishes include potato salad, tabouli, and celery rémoulade. Desserts are a wrenching decision. You'll find juices here and Perrier, but why not walk a few paces to **Société des Alcools du Québec** (4855 rue Sherbrooke Ouest) and buy a bottle of wine? (Remember to ask for cups before you leave the patisserie.) Now you're ready to trek.

You'll take a long and leisurely walk to Parc Mont-Royal, past the fine neo-Tudor homes, art deco mansions, and landscaped gardens in Westmount. It's uphill, so be prepared. Walk east on rue Sherbrooke to avenue Clarke and turn left. At the Boulevard—one of the most exclusive addresses in Montréal—turn right and keep walking until you cross chemin de-la-Côte-des-Neiges. Once across the busy street, continue walking uphill until you reach Hill Park Circle. Take a right and climb a flight of stairs. At the top, keep to your left. Now you're entering the park, laid out in 1874 by Frederick Law Olmsted, who urged city fathers to allow a design that preserved the natural setting. Olmsted accomplished that goal by carving walking paths through dense woodland.

Head for Lac aux Castors, an artificial lake surrounded by picnic tables. (An adjacent pavilion contains washrooms.) The slope on one side of the lake converts in winter to a downhill practice run for beginning skiers. In summer, however, it's covered with sun wor-shippers. Before lunch, settle yourselves in a peaceful, secluded spot —maybe near a large rock and some bushes. Get comfortable. Kiss. It's easy to find a slice of tranquility in this pristine setting.

LUNCH

Should the kiss stir up hungers of the ordinary sort, spread your royal picnic on a table near the lake. Make a toast to nature as you watch the pedal boats on the water. Devour your gourmet meal as you admire the oaks and maples. After lunch, take a pedal boat ride your-self—or dip your toes in the water and splash.

More than a century after its original design, the park looks much as Olmsted envisioned. Spruce-crested paths wind through maple and oak and offer the spiritual respite from the city that Olmsted intended.

DAY TWO: afternoon

When lunch and water play are finished, walk east toward the **Chalet du Mont-Royal** (Parc du Mont-Royal; 514–844–4928), a country cottage designed in the 1930s for community use. Inside are works depicting Montréal's early history. Some of Québec's most noted painters were commissioned for this project. Marc-Aurèle Fortin and Paul-Émile Borduas are among the artists. But the interior is eclipsed by the view from the terrace. Stop here to enjoy the sight of Montréal's downtown, the St-Lawrence River, and, on clear days, the U.S. border roughly 60 miles south.

From the chalet, walk to the steel cross on the mountain, the spiritual heart of the park and a legendary symbol. According to leg-end, on Christmas Day in 1642 the waters of the St-Lawrence River began to swell and threatened to inundate the tiny outpost of Ville-Marie, as the newfound colony was called. Paul de Chomedey, sieur de Maisonneuve, founder of the colony, vowed to plant a cross on the mountain if the waters subsided. They did, and in January of 1643, Maisonneuve himself carried a rough-hewn oak cross on his shoulders and, accompanied by all the colonists, climbed to the top of Mount Royal, where Mass was celebrated. The wooden cross Maisonneuve carried no longer remains. In the 1920s, long after the original had decayed, schoolchildren took up a collection to replace it. On Christmas Eve in 1924, the 83-foot steel cross was erected. In a thoroughly modern touch, it is now illuminated at night.

Now you can say that you've been to the mountain.

When you're ready to leave, exit in a novel manner that'll put you very close to your hotel. Begin your descent down the mountain via a winding asphalt path just steps from the cross. It will return you to the chalet. As you approach the chalet, look to your left. You'll find a very long staircase that goes down the entire side of the mountain. It's not steep and there is ample room to stop and grab a breath if needed. At the bottom, you'll be on avenue des Pins. Walk south in the direction of Centreville, just a few steps from your hotel.

FOR MORE ROMANCE

The story of Paul de Chomedey, sieur de Maisonneuve, and his trek up the mountain with the cross on his back is illustrated in one of fourteen dramatic stained-glass windows in Notre-Dame Basilica (110 rue Notre-Dame Ouest; 514–842–2925). If you have a chance to visit, you'll love the majesty of this grand church. Luckily, too, after your mountaintop odyssey, you'll understand the symbolism of the window.

Scoring Big
HOCKEY HOLIDAY

I T'S OFTEN SAID THAT HOCKEY IS A RELIGION in Canada. The sport was invented in Montréal, and has become, through the years, a secular bond that ties a geographically vast nation together. A hockey weekend will tie you together, too, as you worship at hockey's cathedral—the home of the winningest team in North American professional sports.

But you'll also venture far from the Canadiens modern rink, opened in 1996. This moderately priced itinerary elevates hockey to romantic heights with an intimate pre-game dinner, a post-game stroll down trendy Crescent Street, and a twilight walk along the Stanley Cup parade route, which just happens to be a major shopping venue. Whether you share a passion for hockey—or simply have a passion for a hockey fan—you'll find Montréal is not only the best place for the game but the best place for the game of romance.

PRACTICAL NOTES: The Canadiens play at home on select Saturday nights from October to April, though play-off games can stretch into June. I suggest a Friday arrival so you can build up slowly to the big game. The **Marriott Château Champlain** has fifty season tickets reserved for guests, which could make planning this romantic holiday a snap. You must call in advance, however, to have the tickets set aside. Be sure to check, at the same time, that the visiting team is actually staying at the hotel. All but three of the visiting squads stay at the Marriott Château Champlain, but make sure you don't choose a game where the out-of-towners are elsewhere. After all, stargazing is part of the fun.

Romance AT A GLANCE

◆ Rub shoulders with National Hockey League stars when you check into the **Marriott Château Champlain** (1 Place du Canada; 514–878–9000 or 800–200–5909), game-day hotel for visiting teams. Then take a nostalgic tour of the Montréal Canadiens' new home, the **Molson Centre** (1250 rue de la Gauchetière; 514–932–CLUB), where you'll discover relics of the team's storied past.

◆ Trace the Stanley Cup parade route along **rue Ste-Catherine,** where you can also shop till you drop. When your feet won't go another step, head for a movie theater toting a bag of genuine Canadian sweets.

◆ Take to the ice yourself. Rent skates and take a few turns on the indoor rink located in the atrium lobby of the city's tallest office building. Afterward have a pre-game dinner at **Da Vinci's** (1180 rue Bishop; 514–874–2001), a favorite haunt of hockey players and other sports figures. The staff will make certain you're out in time to watch the Canadiens play.

If you're driving to Montréal and own ice skates, you may want to bring them along. Otherwise they can be rented for the excursion on Day Two. One further tip: It doesn't hurt to pack warm clothes and boots, even in fall. This is Montréal, after all, where the weather is as capricious as love.

DAY ONE: morning

Drop your bags at the **Marriott Château Champlain** (1 Place du Canada; 514–878–9000; 800–200–5909; station Bonaventure; rooms from $109, including breakfast), distinguishable by the huge half-moon windows all around the hotel that provide a terrific view of the St-Lawrence River or Mont-Royal, depending on where you stand. Best bet? Request a room above the tenth floor, facing the city. The view of **Mont-Royal** is striking. In addition, the Marriott Château Champlain offers romantic options that are bargains on weekends. Consider the Concierge Level, with private lounge for a complimentary continental breakfast (or full breakfast, depending on the package), evening cocktail hour, free local phone calls, bathrobes in the room, and other amenities.

Chances are good you'll see a player you recognize in the lobby or on the elevator—the visiting squad not only stays in the hotel but also eats here in a private dining room. Keep an eye out for Serge Savard. The former Canadiens player and ex-general manager has a financial stake in the hotel and eats lunch here every day.

The **Centre Molson** (1250 rue de la Gauchetière; 514–925–5656) is literally steps from your hotel. You can walk outside or stay cozy and walk there through the underground city. Plunge into hockey nostalgia by first taking a guided tour of the new arena, which is owned by Molson Brewery. You'll learn that the Canadiens chose red, white, and blue as the team's official colors in 1910; that the team produced forty Hall of Famers (you'll see each one immortalized in a bronze plaque); that the state-of-the-art scoreboard weighs more than sixteen tons, and that renowned goalie Georges Vezina had twenty-two children. You'll see the Oldtimers Lounge (with dark wood tables emblazoned with the familiar CH logo) and the press box, with places for 300 journalists, on a catwalk 90 feet above the ice. If the team is not practicing that day, you'll even see the famous locker room. These words from John McCrea's poem *In Flanders Field* are inscribed here and have been challenging players for more than half a century: *"To you, with full hands we throw the torch. Be yours to hold it high."*

Tours of the Centre cost $7.00 and are given every day (in English) at 11:00 A.M. and 2:00 P.M. Tickets can be obtained at the box office, and saved stubs get you a 15 percent discount at **La Boutique des Canadiens** (1220 de la Gauchetière; 514–989–2836), which sells hockey sticks, keychains, official team jerseys, and a CD-ROM detailing the storied history of the team. Or you can use the stubs for the same percentage discount at the restaurant where you'll have lunch.

DAY ONE: afternoon

LUNCH

Ovation Resto-bar (enter on rue de la Gauchetière) is where you'll lunch after the tour. Here you'll find more memorabilia, including the Canadiens bench from the old Forum. Choose the more intimate first floor of the restaurant, where windows face the street. Crowds pile into this bustling, inexpensive eatery at noon for the daily specials, the club sandwiches, and the burgers. No need to get caught up in the whirl, however. You're here to unwind. Order a beer, and anticipate a romantic afternoon strolling and shopping.

After lunch, leave Molson Centre and walk north on de la Montagne, then left on rue Ste-Catherine and over to rue Atwater for a long, last look at **The Forum** (2313 rue Ste-Catherine Ouest), hockey's temple, abandoned by the Canadiens in March of 1996 when they moved to new quarters. City fathers have decided to turn the landmark building into a multiplex theater. From here, you'll venture along rue Ste-Catherine tracing the traditional Stanley Cup parade. On Friday nights, stores lining both sides of the street stay open late. The street is hot hot hot until the wee hours even if the temperature is cold cold cold.

You're heading for **Le Centre Eaton** (705 rue Ste-Catherine), the largest shopping complex in the downtown core, where you'll find more than 200 shops and boutiques in an atrium setting under a skylight. Before you get there, though, dash into a candy store named for a genuine Canadian heroine (see sidebar). **Laura Secord** (1045 rue Ste-Catherine Ouest) sells luscious light and dark chocolates with hard and soft centers that almost reach out from the show-case and grab you. Buy your treats here and tuck them away. You'll bring them out again when you enter the movie theater on the top floor of Le Centre Eaton for an early show. Shop till you're ready to drop, then head for the theater with your bag of sweets—and your sweetie.

The Courage
of Laura Secord

The Americans had Paul Revere, but during the War of 1812 Canadians had patriot Laura Secord of Queenston, Ontario. According to legend, Laura overheard some American soldiers planning a surprise attack on a British outpost not far from Niagara Falls. She walked many miles through the wilderness to warn British soldiers of impending danger. Thanks to her, Canada won the Battle of Queenston Heights —and Laura won a place in history.

DAY ONE: evening

DINNER

After the movie, you're in the mood for more serious sustenance. Backtrack on rue Ste-Catherine and duck into **Le Paris** bistro (1812 rue Ste-Catherine Ouest; 514–937–4898; moderate) for good French food in a delightful atmosphere. Tables are this close, waiters zip around deftly, and the menu is refined by forty years of unbroken family ownership. Try the salmon buerre blanc, cooked in wine, butter, and shallots, or another trademark, calf's liver. *Alors*, back to the hotel by cab—or on foot. Maybe you've saved some of those Laura Secord chocolates for a bedtime snack. Put on your terry-cloth robes and indulge.

DAY TWO: morning/afternoon

BREAKFAST

It's game day, but the excitement will build slowly. Why not sleep late and have breakfast in bed? The Marriott almost expects couples staying here on the weekend special to cocoon in the hotel room and pass a lazy morning. Peek out your half-moon windows. If it's snowing, don't fret. Your activities this morning don't require you to step outside for a single moment—even though you'll see plenty of action. After you've indulged in juice, croissants, toast, eggs, bacon, and coffee, dress for the day and grab your skates, if you brought your own.

You're fortified now to hit **l'Amphithéâtre Bell** indoor ice rink at 1000 rue de la Gauchetière, located in the lobby of the tallest office building in town and situated just one building east of your hotel (through the underground city). Bathed in natural sunlight and open every day of the year, the rink charges skaters $5.00 for admission and $4.00 more to rent skates. Hold hands and glide around the glistening 10,000-square-foot rink. On weekdays, it's not unusual to see men and women skating in business attire, using their lunch break for some exercise. On Saturdays, though, you're likely to see couples and families. When you're ready for a break, pause for hot chocolate—and a light bite—at the restaurant concessions that surround the rink.

LUNCH *or* SNACK

You're having an early dinner before the game, so don't fill up here. You can choose from about a half-dozen restaurant concessions offering everything from Chinese fast food to chef's salad. Of course, you'll each want to order a hot chocolate. But why not share a main dish item—and perhaps a piece of chocolate cake? Enjoy your food at a rinkside picnic table, where you can watch other couples glide across the ice—and maybe be inspired to take a few more turns.

When you've removed your skates for good, why not pamper those sore muscles by returning to the Marriott and relaxing in the hotel's whirlpool and steam room? If you're so inclined, yield to temptation and treat yourselves to a massage—the hotel offers four kinds—but you must book your appointment in advance. After your massage or steam bath, change into clothes for dinner—nice slacks and a sweater are perfect. You've reserved a cozy table for your pre-game dinner at 5:30 P.M.

DAY TWO: evening

DINNER

Da Vinci's (1180 rue Bishop; 514–874–2001; reservations requested; moderate to expensive) is a favorite haunt for Canadiens players and other sports figures. Request a table by the fireplace, near the wine cellar, or in the corner looking into the garden. This family-owned restaurant has catered to the famous for thirty years but has only one dish named after a celeb—linguine Lasorda—for the ex-Dodgers coach who never fails to stop by when in town. Pasta, fish, lamb, chicken, and veal are primo here, and the staff is skilled enough to serve you graciously yet make certain you arrive at the Molson Centre, a five-minute walk, with time to spare before the game begins.

Now, for the reason you came. Head for the rink and find your seats. As you go, eyeball the crowd, which is often much glitzier here than in other arenas in the NHL. You'll see plenty of fur coats and chunky jewelry on a Saturday night in winter, particularly in the rows behind the Canadiens bench, where team bigwigs and their guests sit. In Montréal, hockey is an occasion—like the theater or the symphony. As the lights dim, you'll see twenty-four Stanley Cup banners hanging from the rafters and the retired jerseys of seven Hall of Famers. A singer dressed in a tuxedo takes center ice to render "O! Canada" in French. During the national anthem, thousands of tiny lights form a Canadian flag on the scoreboard and its trademark maple leaf waves gently above the rink.

There are no other gimmicks before a Canadiens game—no laser lights, no booming music. Here, the purity of hockey prevails. Seal the moment with a kiss and let the game begin. Between periods, sweeten the evening by dashing to the concession stand for a couple of sinful chocolate chip cookies made by **Monsieur Felix et Mr. Norton**—Québec's equivalent of Mrs. Field. *Ménage à trois* is a wonderful choice; this cookie has three kinds of chocolate chips and is deliciously gooey.

If you hear the crowd yelling, "Boo-boo-boo," just when the Canadiens players seem to be charging hard down the ice, don't think Montréalers have lost their minds. "But" (pronounced *boo*) is the French word for goal. At the Molson Centre, the two of you can boo all night.

When the action on the ice is over, part of the human wave moves to the strip of bars, clubs, and restaurants on rue Crescent, one block west of de la Montagne. Stroll along the street and try **Hurley's Irish Pub** (1225 rue Crescent; 514–861–4111), biggest supplier of Guinness Irish stout in North America and home to Celtic music every night. Pubs are traditional places of courtship in Ireland, and Hurley's has four small, separate rooms where romance can bloom. One of these is the Snug, where couples can be seen deep in conversation on comfortable chairs. Return to the hotel whenever you're ready. Hurley's doesn't close until the wee hours—and you've arranged a late checkout on Sunday.

FOR MORE ROMANCE

A true hockey fan knows there's one player who commands more love and respect in Québec than any other. If time permits, pay a visit to the **Univers Maurice "Rocket" Richard** (2800 rue Viau; 514–251–9930; closed Mondays), a museum devoted to Canada's answer to Babe Ruth and Québec's answer to God. The Rocket, who played for the Canadiens from 1942 until he retired in 1960, is an icon. The museum, located in a long-standing hockey arena named after Richard, documents the life of the first player in the National Hockey League to score fifty goals in fifty games. The man who wowed millions with his determination, talent, and pure grit grew up so poor he'd make goalposts from scraps of wood found in a field. At the museum, you can trace Richard's humble beginnings and his rise, and learn the reason he chose number 9 for his jersey and how he earned the nickname Rocket.

Land's End
THE UNDISCOVERED ISLE

RE YOU PASSIONATE TRAVELERS WHO TAKE PRIDE in discovering the undiscovered? I'll tell you a secret. A beautiful segment of Montréal remains a mystery to many who live in the city and to almost all visitors. Such a shame. While we lavish attention on the St-Lawrence River and its surroundings, we all but ignore the ribbon of blue and its historic shoreline on the north side of the island.

If you two like to take the road less traveled, start walking and biking along a little-known riverside and through miles and miles of exquisite swampland. As the undiscovered island is revealed, you and your love will revel in a private world.

PRACTICAL NOTES: Bike paths are operative from April 15 to November 1, but the area is drop-dead gorgeous in late summer and early fall, when the trees and flowers are luxuriant and the weather is still warm enough to enjoy strolling and biking. No matter when you come, start the itinerary on Friday, when the shops are open late. So pack up your bicycles—or your walking shoes—and dare to be different.

DAY ONE: morning/early afternoon

Land's End is so unspoiled in parts—and so residential in others—that no lodging actually exists in the area. Along boulevard Gouin, in fact, where you'll spend most of your time, public lodging is actually outlawed.

> ## Romance AT A GLANCE
>
> ◆ Take a walking tour in **Sault-au-Recollet**, visited by explorers Jacques Cartier and Samuel de Champlain centuries ago. Admire heritage homes dating back to the 1700s, and visit **Eglise de la Visitation** (1847 boulevard Gouin Est), Montréal's oldest church, which contains some of the most beautiful wood sculptures and ecclesiastic art in the city.
>
> ◆ Spend the afternoon and early evening shopping along a strip of upscale stores in the area on **Promenade Fleury** (on rue Fleury), and if time permits, book a facial or a body wrap.
>
> ◆ Devote the next day to nature as you bike or hike along pathways surrounded by shoulder-high flowers and plants. Work your way to a stone lighthouse, **Pavilon des Marais** (12300 boulevard Gouin Est), which provides a panoramic view of the swampland that makes up a good percentage of Montréal island. Break out a picnic in the middle of marsh.

I'm booking you, therefore, in the newly renovated **Hotel President Laval** (2225 Autoroute des Laurentides, Laval; 450–682–2225; $110 for a deluxe room with a continental breakfast), where it's just a ten-minute drive across the Papineau Bridge to Montréal—and Land's End. Your comfortable room at the attractive hotel has a king-size bed, a sofa, a hair dryer, and a coffee machine. You'll find free parking here as well.

Once you've checked in, put on casual clothes for a day of strolling and shopping. Take a right out of the hotel parking lot onto the service road of Autoroute 15. Look immediately for signs indicating Route 440 Est. Travel on 440 Est until you see signs for boulevard Dagenais (Autoroute 19 South). As you cross the Papineau Bridge, you'll see church spires to your right. You are now in Sault-au-Récollet, which owes its name to Récollet priest Nicolas Viel, who disappeared in the rapids (*sault*) when returning from a journey to Huronia with an Indian guide called Ahuntsic.

Continue along avenue Papineau until rue Fleury. Take a right and park in a lot on Fleury or on a side street near avenue Christophe Colomb. You'll have lunch here, then walk north on Christophe Colomb to the historic district, returning late in the afternoon to Fleury for shopping.

LUNCH

Fortify yourself for the walk ahead at **Café Le Petit Flore** (1145 rue Fleury Est; 514–387–2640; open every day from 10:00 A.M.; inexpensive), an adorable bistro across from a St-Paul-de-la-Croix church. It offers French cuisine and the music of Jacques Brel in the background. Owner Jacques Ouellette sought to recreate the feeling of being in Paris in the 1960s, with poster art on dark walls and cozy tables for two. He wanted patrons to feel comfortable reading the paper and lingering over coffee. They do. The house blend is delicious, and Ouellette offers more than thirty other coffees as well. At lunch, an omelette is a staple on the menu, as are a chicken dish and a meat dish like boeuf bourguignon. Imported beer and wine by the glass are sold at very moderate prices. Have a glass. Then make a toast to your audacity. You two are about to discover the undiscovered isle.

Leave the restaurant primed for adventure. Walk north on Christophe Colomb. It's hard to believe now that this area was farmland up until the 1950s. Today, it is a commercial and residential quarter, and the heritage homes on boulevard Gouin, where you're heading, are surrounded by huge waterfront mansions east and west of the historic district.

You'll be walking along a bike path that starts near **Parc Louis Hébert** (corner boulevard Gouin and avenue Christophe Colomb), named for one of the first colonists in New France. Hébert was an apothecary and a justice of the peace. As you walk east, you'll see a number of lookouts and benches along the **Rivière-des-Prairies**. Pause to gaze across the water. You're looking at Laval, an island like Montréal and the site of your lodging. A conglomeration of mostly rural villages now united under one governing body, Laval is still composed largely of farmland and is dotted with local producers of fruits and vegetables.

Walk farther and you'll see **Collège Sophie-Barat** (1105 and 1239 boulevard Gouin Est), started by a French order of nuns recruited by Montréal's second bishop in the mid-1800s. Les Dames du Sacré-Coeur settled on the banks of the Rivière-des-Prairies and built a convent school for girls. All that remains of the original complex is the building at No. 1105.

You'll now start to see ancestral homes like the one at No. 1737. You'll have to look hard for it. The fieldstone home with a blue roof is tucked behind trees and a fence. **Maison David-Dumouchel**, built in 1839, belonged to a carpenter. A few paces farther and a church with twin silver spires, which you glimpsed earlier, comes into view. Set majestically on the riverbank at the end of a long driveway, the church will take your breath away.

Église de la Visitation (1847 boulevard Gouin Est) is the oldest church still standing on the island of Montréal. Built between 1749 and 1752, the church has a fascinating history—and a splendid interior. Plaques on the facade note Jacques Cartier's landing here in October of 1535; Joseph Le Caron, a Récollet priest, said mass here for a group that included Samuel de Champlain in 1615. The chapel's beauty has much to do with an intense rivalry between the parish here and another farther west, which had just built a church. In the game of one-upmanship, there's little doubt the folks in Sault-au-Récollet prevailed.

Inside, you'll see some of the finest wood carving in Québec. The hand-carved wood pews, the robin's-egg blue pulpit, the gilded altar, the egg-shaped vaulted ceiling, the stained-glass windows, and the oil paintings all make the church look like the private domain of a French monarch. Indeed, the Louis XV-style interior took more than seventy years to complete. Sit in a pew and take in the glory. The beauty is staggering; you'll want to linger a while.

When you exit, keep walking east. The heart of the historic village lies east of the church and east of the Papineau Bridge leading to Laval. Here you'll find homes dating back to the 1700s, including **Maison Boudreau** (No. 1947), a charming cottage with a sloped roof and three windows sitting behind a wrought-iron fence. It was built around 1750. You'll see an old general store (No. 2010), and farther along, you'll find a tiny commercial strip where sculptor **Fernand Caron** (2080 boulevard Gouin Est; 514–383–1923; open daily 9:00 A.M. to 6:00 P.M.) has an *atelier* (workshop) that blends seamlessly into the surroundings. Caron sculpts from wood. You can buy his work—or that of other sculptors from outside Québec—in the atelier. If you arrive around the noon hour, Caron may have stepped out for a sandwich. Be patient. He will return.

Turn left on rue du Pressoir and walk to the end of the cul-de-sac. **La Maison du Pressoir** (10865 rue du Pressoir; 514–280–6783; free admission, but call ahead for a schedule) is now an information center where you can pick up a brochure denoting the homes in the area and telling their histories. It's also an exhibition center focusing on the pressing of apples into cider. Around 1810, Didier Joubert built a cider press on this property, and his home, remarkably well preserved, is used for demonstrations of cider pressing—and for other happenings (see "For More Romance").

From here, you'll continue east along boulevard Gouin a bit before you backtrack to explore Île-de-la-Visitation regional park. You'll find **La Maison du docteur** (No. 1995), built in 1866 for Dr. Jules Chopin. When he died in 1901, it was bought by another doctor, Hector Pelletier. At No. 2084, you'll find **La Maison de l'entrepreneur**, built in 1810 for Pascal Persillier dit Lachapelle, who owned the mills you're about to see on Île-de-la-Visitation. Lachapelle constructed several bridges into Laval—one of them bears his name. Before turning back, check out No. 2273. Built in 1835, it was the home of Antoine Brousseau, former mayor of Sault-au-Récollet.

Return to La Maison du Pressoir and follow the wooded path to **Maison du Meunier** (10897 rue du Pont; 514–280–6709; open to the public; call for hours), an art gallery now, but once a miller's house. Between 1726 and 1960, the mills here—which are just badly deteriorated stone remnants now—formed one of the oldest industrial sites in Québec. If you wish, cross over to **Île-de-la-Visitation**, a natural preserve with walking and cycling trails, picnic tables, and two fishing holes.

Wrap Me Up!

"Les soin du corps" treatment at the Institute de beauté St-Cloud Lté has you lying in the buff on a plastic sheet covering a padded table that is delightfully heated from below. Algae specifically chosen for your needs are applied from your neck down. Next, the plastic sheet is wrapped snugly around your body. While the algae perform their magic, you drift off to sleep, lulled by peaceful music coming from the headphones placed on your (unwrapped) ears.

DAY ONE: late afternoon

Roughly three hours have passed since you left the restaurant—given that you probably browsed for a bit in Caron's atelier. Now return to the commercial venue where you had lunch; walk west on boulevard Gouin to rue Taché. Take a left and walk south to Fleury. Take a right. You're now on **La Promenade Fleury**, where you'll spend the rest of the afternoon exploring the stores—and maybe pampering yourselves.

In a four-block area, you'll find jewelry stores, a furrier, a bookstore, a Swiss-trained shoemaker who makes the old look new (**Cordonnerie Biagio**, 1125 rue Fleury Est; 514–387–7926), a couple of men's clothing shops (including **O Singulier**, 1374 rue Fleury Est; 514–387–4342), several women's clothing stores (including **Camille Brets**, 1316 rue Fleury Est; 514–382–6334), gift shops (including **Casa Luca**, 1354 rue Fleury Est; 514–389–6066), and an antiques store (**Claude L'Heureux**, 1374 rue Fleury Est; 514–387–3595).

If you enjoy the luxury of a special beauty treatment in a discreet setting, call in advance and book an appointment at the **Institut de beauté St-Cloud Lté** (1302 rue Fleury Est; 514–381–1720; 9:30 A.M. to 7:00 P.M. on Tuesday through Friday). Here you can enjoy an expert facial, waxing, pedicure, manicure, or perhaps *les soins du corps*, a European treatment that relies on essential oils and algae to rejuvenate tired muscles, reduce stress, or refresh the skin all over. Proprietress Hugette Schafer has been on rue Fleury for nineteen years. Her sister, Lyse Huet, joined her three years ago. Together, in a cozy second-story walkup, they lavish personal attention on the male and female clientele.

Before you leave La Promenade Fleury, visit **Patisserie l'Opéra** (1185 rue Fleury Est; 514–383–8558), where Claude and Martine Ruchat and their two sons make and sell *terrines*, pâté, mini-quiches, croissants, and luscious pastries. Here you'll stock up on items for your picnic tomorrow. The hotel will refrigerate the perishables for you.

DAY ONE: evening

DINNER

The dining room in the Hotel President Laval is not the chain-style eatery you'd expect from a hotel restaurant just off a highway.

La Grigliata (moderate to expensive, table d'hôte $32) is an intimate dining spot with linen cloths and flowers on the table. Fish, lamb, and beef are prepared to tasty perfection while you watch; the chef does his magic in a glass-enclosed grill in the dining room. A basket of scrumptious baguettes begins the service, to be dipped into a blend of pure olive oil, balsamic vinegar, and freshly grated cheese. The menu is weighted toward Italian fare with a marked emphasis on the delectable grilled selections. What makes the meal more special is the musical accompaniment. A combo and a singer render tunes popularized by artists ranging from Frank Sinatra to Roberta Flack on Friday and Saturday nights (a pianist performs Tuesday through Thursday). It's lovely to slow-dance on the tiny wood dance floor near the bar.

DAY TWO: morning

BREAKFAST

The hotel has a continental breakfast consisting of fresh fruit and juice, muffins, croissants, tea, and coffee. If you wish, have it served in the room. Pack your bags after breakfast, retrieve your picnic from the fridge, and check out.

As you did yesterday, you'll end up on boulevard Gouin this morning on the banks of the Rivière-des-Prairies, but this time the location is far less tame. Follow the same directions out of the hotel, but bypass the exit you took yesterday and continue along Autoroute 440 until you see signs for boulevard Pie IX (Autoroute 25 South). Take the Pie IX bridge to exit Henri Bourassa Est. Follow Henri Bourassa Est to Léger and along Léger, take a left to Gouin. You'll continue on Gouin for about twenty minutes, until you see signs for **Pointe-aux-Prairies regional park,** where you'll find a parking lot ($3.00 a day) at the **Chalet Rivière-des-Prairies,** the park's visitors center (12980 boulevard Gouin Est; 514-280-6767).

Thirteen kilometers of cycling and walking paths in the park take you through the nearby marshland. Once on the path, follow the ample signage. Navigate past shoulder-high cattails, purple loosestrife, and flowering rush. You'll hear birds warbling. Depending on the time of year, you may see blazing maples, oaks, and sumacs. You may also see a snake, a rabbit, or a beaver.

But before you take to the trails, leave the park just briefly. Start your exploration today a few hundred feet from the entrance of the park—on property now owned by the city. **La Maison Bleau** (13200 boulevard Gouin Est; 514–280–6698) is a heritage home built originally in 1721 and occupied continuously until 1961 by seven generations of the Bleau family. The current structure, which dates from 1890, hosts artists-in-residence and is open to the public on Saturdays from mid-June to mid-September. Ride or walk a bit farther west on boulevard Gouin, and you'll see a marvelously preserved home that dates back to 1737. The Armand home is privately owned but is a treat to observe from the road.

Now reenter the park and continue west. Carefully observe the terrain and the flora. By the time you find your way to **Pavillon des Marais**, a round, stone building that resembles a lighthouse and serves as an interpretation center in Pointe-aux-Prairies (12300 boulevard Gouin Est; 514–280–6688; open daily from 11:00 A.M., April to mid-October), you may have guessed what you'll find. Climb the spiral staircase to the purple parapet that surrounds the building, and while a squirrel scoots along the rail, lean forward to see the long stretch of pale green swamp that cuts a mysterious swath through the park. On the permanent display boards downstairs, you'll learn that a chunk of the delicate habitat here is swamp and that—not surprisingly when you think about it—marshland accounts for 10 to 15 percent of the total land mass on the island of Montréal.

Leave the Pavillon des Marais via a wood-plank footbridge nestled in the park. The bridge traverses a sector of marshland where, in fall, industrious muskrats build tent-like houses out of cattails as protection from the impending deep freeze and from predators that include the red fox. On your way out of the area, watch out for the furry black caterpillars with an orange stripe across their middles. They take their sweet time crossing the pathways.

Big Stripe, More Snow

The first time I spotted the caterpillar mentioned to the left was right before Halloween, so his black-and-orange outfit made perfect sense. But the getup has added significance, according to a sweet bit of folklore. The wider the stripe around the waistline, the harsher the upcoming winter.

You can confine your exploration to the park, or if you're adventurous, bike along boulevard Gouin to Île-de-la-Visitation (where you were yesterday) and picnic there. It's a 38-kilometer round trip.

DAY TWO: afternoon

Whether you go the entire distance or simply stay within the beautiful confines of the park, you'll find picnic tables and benches in several spots along the route. You'll pass a monastery where **Les Récluses Missionnaires** (12050 boulevard Gouin Est; 514–648–6801), a group of reclusive nuns with voices like angels, carry out their mission: continuous prayer twenty-four hours a day. They accomplish their goal by taking turns in the chapel around the clock. If you call ahead to let them know you'd like to come, you can hear them sing at mass, which is held twice daily; be sure to make prior arrangements.

As you continue your journey, you'll see fieldstone homes in the old village of Rivière-des-Prairies and the village church, **Église St-Joseph**, built by Montréal architect Victor Bourgeau between 1875 and 1879. You'll also see enormous modern homes that look like estates along the riverfront.

LUNCH

Break out your picnic in the park or somewhere along the bank of the Rivière-des-Prairies and admire the bucolic scene. After you've eaten your cheese, pâté, and croissants, return the way you came, making sure to stop for crème glacée at one of several places in the village of Rivière-des-Prairies. Believe me, soft ice cream has never tasted so good.

Return to where you started, confident that you're among the few who have explored this side of the island.

FOR MORE ROMANCE

Around the time of the full moon, **La Maison du Pressoir** holds intimate concerts in the attic of the heritage home. A baritone might perform, for instance, accompanied by a flutist. Admission is free, but tickets must be obtained in advance.

In-Town
Indulgence

Table-for-Two
GASTRONOMES UNITE!

AD MEALS SIMPLY DON'T EXIST IN MONTRÉAL. It's as if City Council has banned them. Even an ordinary weekday lunch in a Montréal restaurant is culinary art. Color, shape, texture, and form—not to mention taste—are all part of the mealtime equation.

If Québecers elevate lunch to such a high plane, just imagine how they treat dinner and breakfast. You'll find out on this itinerary, where the process from farm stall to table will reveal itself eloquently —three times a day (and maybe in-between).

PRACTICAL NOTES: Table-for-Two works best in August, when produce is at its peak and the markets are bursting with flawless fruit and vegetables. Try to schedule your visit concurrent with Les Fêtes Gourmandes Internationales de Montréal (514–861–8241), which runs for ten days in August and showcases foods and culture from five continents.

DAY ONE: morning/afternoon

Step back centuries when you enter the discreetly marked **Auberge Les Passants du Sans Soucy** (171 rue St-Paul Ouest; 514–842–2634; station Place d'Armes; $100 to $125 double occupancy, including breakfast for two). Nestled on a cobblestone street in Old Montréal, the foundations of the auberge were laid in the 1600s. Owners Michael Banks and Daniel Soucy spent years and tons of money renovating the former fur factory so that remnants of the original gray stone walls remain within each of the nine guest rooms. Every room is *très romantique*, pairing antiquity

Romance AT A GLANCE

♦ Stay in the heart of Old Montréal at **Auberge Les Passants du Sans Soucy** *(171 rue St-Paul Ouest; 514–842–2634), where the rooms are romantic simplicity and breakfast is a homemade feast. From the inn, stroll to the **Atwater Market** (138 avenue Atwater), where vendors sell farm-fresh produce outside and offer everything from micro-brewery beer to ostrich meat within. Munch on bacon bread and exotic cheeses as you make the rounds.*

♦ *Take the métro to **Parc des Îles**, where you'll spend the day visiting the **Stewart Museum** (514–861–6701), which examines life centuries ago in New France, then plunge into present-day sights and smells at **Les Fêtes Gourmandes Internationales de Montréal**. Here you'll sample food and drink from five continents, including wild game, buffalo, and seal meat from Québec.*

♦ *Splurge when you dine by candlelight at **Les Caprices de Nicolas** (20272 rue Drummond; 514–282–9790), an elegant Victorian home built in the mid-1800s, where you can sit on a velveteen banquette and pretend you're living in the last century.*

with modernity by mixing Persian rugs, brass beds, and delicate antique tables with voice mail, TV, and Jacuzzi tubs (in some rooms). Rooms on the street side have shuttered windows that open onto rue St-Paul, so you can hear the clip-clopping of the horse-drawn *calèche* and stick your head out to observe the street life.

Settle yourselves in your room, then head back downstairs to the common areas of the auberge. If you can tear yourselves away from the display of local artists and artisans in the reception area, or from the antiques-filled lounge leading to the breakfast nook where Daniel works magic in the morning, or from the fireplace mantel lined with artifacts, including a butter crock that the owners dug up during the renovation, you'll soon be out the door and on your way.

Your fun-loving hosts will direct you to the waterfront, where you'll take a leisurely forty-five-minute walk toward **Atwater Market** (138 avenue Atwater at rue Notre-Dame; station Lionel-Groulx), the oldest continuously operating market in town. Opened in 1932 and easily identified by its soaring tower, the market's outdoor stalls are operated by local farmers who sell directly to the public. Vendors let you taste plump strawberries and tender raspberries. At **Légumes Gourmet et**

Exotique, a husband-and-wife team of growers from outside Montréal offer the sweetest cherry tomatoes imaginable, more than ninety kinds of hot and sweet peppers, and contoured eggplant colored white, green, and mauve. Slim green and purple beans, small buttery potatoes, and miniature yellow crookneck squash are so precious, they're almost irresistible. So don't resist. Buy some raspberries to share later in the day.

When you've seen the outdoor vendors, head for the interior mall, spread over two floors, where some twenty-five stores offer delicacies all year-round. Don't forget to stock up on Québec maple syrup for your home table. Québec produces 75 percent of the world's supply. As you scout for syrup, look for other goodies and put together a delectable lunch in the process. To begin, climb the stairs to the second floor.

LUNCH

Shops lining both sides of the market here offer an array of breads, pâtés, and desserts. Buy what your fancy dictates. You won't want to miss **L'Épicerie du Marché Atwater**, operated by former politician Fernand Jourdenais, who stocks forty types of beer from microbreweries in Québec and also carries an array of condiments and relishes made by local producers. After engaging in discussion with the amiable merchant, pick up a few cold beers and proceed downstairs to **La Fromagerie du Marché Atwater**, where Fernand's son, Gilles, offers nearly 500 cheeses from around the world—many of them from Québec—including an outstanding goat's-milk cheddar aged more than two years. Ask Gilles for a recommendation that will suit your pâté and bread. Thus armed, return upstairs and find a cozy table in the market to enjoy your feast.

After lunch, walk back to the inn, stopping often to admire Montréal's architectural heritage from your vantage point along the waterfront. Now it's time to rest your tired feet. Once you've settled into your room, slip into the Jacuzzi and take turns feeding each other the succulent raspberries you bought earlier at the market. A little treat won't spoil your appetite. Good thing. You'll be dining tonight in what many consider the best restaurant in the city—and maybe the most romantic. Dress up.

DAY ONE: evening

DINNER

Take the metro to **Les Caprices de Nicolas** (2072 rue Drummond; 514–282–9790; station Peel; closed Sunday; expensive), a sensual experience from the moment you descend the stairs, enter the dimly lit restaurant, and saunter past the long, oak bar. Les Caprices is located in a magnificent Victorian building that is more than 150 years old. Choose to sit either in an indoor courtyard near a fountain or the more formal dining room with its red velvet banquette in the corner.

A *caprice* is a whim. The chef here has plenty of them, much to his patrons' benefit. The food is inspired, the service impeccable. Begin with a salmon and caviar potato crepe or cold asparagus salad with white truffle vinaigrette and a crisp Parmesan wafer. For the main course, savor a roasted veal chop with home-style gnocchi or roasted duck breast with fresh figs. Dessert might be crème brulée topped with lavender flowers and with a pecan crust underneath. Every morsel is ambrosial.

Linger over dessert and coffee, then take the metro or a cab back to the inn. The only sensual experience better than what you've just experienced is the one you're about to invent in the privacy of your room.

DAY TWO: morning

BREAKFAST

Breakfast at the Auberge is utter indulgence, served around an old-fashioned dining table in a cozy nook. Owner Daniel Soucy rises at dawn to bake strawberry cake and chocolate croissants, served with fresh fruit or fresh-squeezed juice, and your choice of French toast or an omelette made with cheese and herbs. Café au lait tops off the meal. *Magnifique!* Mornings don't get any better than this.

After (or before) breakfast, spend some time in the sitting room in the Auberge, where the day's newspapers and other reading material are spread on the table. The atmosphere is so pleasant and unhurried, you may want to hold hands and linger a bit before heading for the métro.

When you're ready to head out, make sure you're wearing comfortable clothes and shoes for a day of strolling. Take the métro to Île Ste-Hélène, where you'll explore a museum that puts life long ago in New France into perspective. After that, if you're here in August, you'll island-hop—by foot—to a food festival nearby, carrying along a pen and paper just in case you want to jot down a recipe.

When you exit the métro at Île Ste-Hélène, don't miss the Alexander Calder sculpture called *Man* as you emerge into daylight. Admire the piece, then obtain a map of the island and neighboring Île Notre-Dame from a nearby information kiosk. Following the map, stroll to the **Stewart Museum** (514–861–6701; open daily, 10:00 A.M. to 5:00 P.M.; admission $5.00). Located in an old fort built by the British in the 1820s to stave off an anticipated attack from the United States, the museum's stone walls are almost 10 feet thick in some places.

During the summer, military life centuries ago is reenacted here by troops dressed like the French soldiers who defended New World outposts in the 1600s. Bagpipers from the Olde 78th Fraser Highlanders also perform authentic eighteenth-century military maneuvers. Inside, the museum is a treasury of old maps, firearms, and navigational equipment, presenting a picture of life here more than 300 years ago.

DAY TWO: afternoon

From the museum, take another lovely stroll to the bridge connecting Île Ste-Hélène with Île Notre-Dame. Pause on the crossway to admire the view behind, then cross the bridge and head for the big tent that houses an annual gastronomic fantasy—**Les Fêtes Gourmandes Internationales de Montréal.**

LUNCH

Circle around the premises to fully appreciate the sights and smells, many of them exotic. You can sample food from five continents and taste more than twenty types of cuisine—including wild game, buffalo, seal, and caribou meat from Québec. Musicians from the city's cultural communities entertain visitors daily. A cooking demonstration takes place every day under the big tent, and, as an added treat, wine-makers from Québec's Eastern Townships offer samples of their wines at a booth on the grounds. Take a variety of dishes to a nearby picnic table or just keep nibbling as you make the rounds. Speak to the chefs, if you wish. They love talking about their creations, and they willingly impart tips—and even recipes.

Globe-trotting Crowd

You may have eyes only for each other, but keep an eye peeled at Milos for celebrities, too. Mick Jagger brought a large entourage there when the Rolling Stones were in town for two concerts in 1998. Afterward, Jagger went dancing in the neighborhood.

When you have appeased your appetites, rent a pedal boat and navigate the artificial lagoon that rims the culinary display. Have fun in the sun as you relax on the boat. Dock when you're ready for another cooking demonstration—or for dessert. As the afternoon heat wanes, stroll back to Île Ste-Hélène and return by métro to the inn. If you purchased a bottle of the Québec wine you tasted earlier, have a glass now while reveling in your private time before dinner.

DAY TWO: evening

DINNER

The best restaurant in Montréal? Many people swear that it's **Milos** (5357 avenue du Parc; 514–272–3522; expensive), and those rousing endorsements have continued to follow owner Costas Spiliadas to Manhattan, where he recently opened a second Milos. Years before he hit the Big Apple, Spiliadas created an elegant taverna in the heart of Montréal's Greektown that transcended any ethnic boundary. Spiliadas is known for his fanatical preparation of fresh fish and delectable seafood, from octopus to red snapper to sea urchin. He used to drive twice a week to the Fulton Fish Market in New York (a fourteen-hour round trip) to make sure Milos had the best the seas could offer. Montréalers loved his legendary "drive for perfection." They also loved his homemade feta spread, deep-fried veggies, and goat cheese topped with honey. You will love it all.

Marvel over the decor and the food, and don't forget to visit the bathrooms at some point. They're built with marble from Crete, another detail that puts Spiliadas above the rest. After the meal you'll feel so inspired you just may feel like dancing. Mick Jagger did. So head for rue Crescent, where the late-night crowd gathers. You're bound for **Thursday's** (1449 rue Crescent; 514–288–5656), a bar and dance club with a twenty-year track record. Here's where the business and professional crowds go to disco. You've got the energy, so head for the dance floor. Stay up late. Thursday's doesn't close until the wee hours, and you want to enjoy every last second before (what else?) breakfast.

For More Romance

If time permits, explore another vibrant market—this one in Little Italy. Take the métro to **Jean-Talon Market** (7075 avenue Casgrain; 514–277–1588; station Jean-Talon), where some 130 merchants and farmers display fabulous garden produce and flowers grown locally and elsewhere. The market building is the permanent home of specialized food boutiques with an Italian flavor and also houses a horticultural center. Neighboring streets are lined with excellent restaurants.

Two days and two nights

Clinking Glasses
WINE LOVERS WEEKEND

I F YOUR IDEA OF ROMANCE IS CLINKING GLASSES over an intimate dinner with your lover—after you've already tasted the
wine, swirled it around, and sniffed its bouquet—then this itinerary will have you dreaming in red, white, and rosé.

While wine cognoscenti certainly know that French wine is
revered in Québec, few realize that Québec produces homegrown
varieties south and east of Montréal, where geography creates cli-
matic conditions favorable to the cultivation of grapes. On this
luxury-laden itinerary, you'll discover vineyards and their wineries—
and the verdant Québec countryside surrounding them. When you
return to Montréal, the city and its charming *quartiers* will delight
you as you wine and dine.

Before heading home, tuck a few bottles of Québec wine in your
luggage. Here's to you!

PRACTICAL NOTES: Since Clinking Glasses explores the vineyards,
this itinerary works best in summer and early fall, before the grapes are
harvested in late October. Additionally, many restaurants carrying fine
wine selections are closed on Sundays, so begin this itinerary on Friday.

You'll need a car to navigate the wine region on Day Two. The
Montérégie Tourism Association can send you a map of the Québec
wine route before you leave home (450–674–5555). As well, the
Hotel Vogue, where you'll be staying, holds wine tastings periodically.
See if you can coordinate your visit with a tasting.

Romance AT A GLANCE

◆ Stay in the intimate **Hotel Vogue** (1425 rue de la Montagne; 514–285–5555), where wine tastings are held regularly. The Vogue is close by the city's finest shops, including a store that carries a tremendous variety of wine and spirits and a noted selection of port.

◆ Pack a picnic and spend a full day exploring Québec's wine route. Watch vineyard owners toil in their fields (and taste the fruit of their labors) at several places along the route, including **Vignoble Dietrich-Jooss** (407 Grande-Ligne, Iberville, Québec; 405–347–6857), where a husband-wife team produces a dessert drink known as ice wine.

◆ If your pocketbook allows, book the wine cellar at **Le Latini** for a very special dinner (1130 rue Jeanne-Mance; 514–861–3166). Eat by candlelight in the enchanted cantina of this fine Iatlian restaurant, where you'll be surrounded by more than 1,200 labes from wineries worldwide.

DAY ONE: morning/afternoon

Drop your bags in the lobby of the very hip **Hotel Vogue** (1425 rue de la Montagne; 514–285–5555; Peel station; $199 to $425 for double rooms; ask for promotional rates), a small hotel with a big reputation. With 142 rooms spread over nine floors, four designed by Stanley J. Friedman of New York, the Vogue is a boutique hotel—personal and discreet—and for that reason has quite a following with celebrities, who appreciate its mix of intimacy and creature comforts that other hotels don't offer. All rooms in the Vogue have duvet bedding with white eyelet covers, whirlpool baths, separate glassed-in showers, color TV in the bathrooms, VCRs (out of the bathrooms), personal fax machines, mahogany hangers, and a Vogue umbrella by the door. Most rooms have king-size beds; other have queen-size beds with canopies that are *très romantique*.

The Vogue also has location working in its favor. In the heart of the Golden Square Mile, the hotel is sandwiched between two of the best shopping routes in town—rue Sherbrooke and rue Ste-Catherine. You're directly across the street from **Ogilvy** department store (1307 rue Ste-Catherine Ouest; 514–842–7711), and you might want to stroll over for a peek inside before lunch.

LUNCH

You'll dine under a red sunburst chandelier at the **Société Café** (moderate) in the Vogue, surrounded by Canadian and Québec art provided by the Simon Blais gallery. The cuisine here is based on French fundamentals but has a fusion flair, blending other current cuisines with the basics. The house wine is a Chardonnay from France, which goes well with the olive bread on the table. Try the leek and potato soup with mushrooms to start and then the roasted red snapper with ratatouille. After lunch, you'll begin your exploration of wine in earnest.

In Québec, alcohol sales are governed by a state-run agency called the *Société des Alcools du Québec (SAQ)*. Grocery stores are licensed to sell beer and some wine, but the choice is extremely limited. Take a left from your hotel to rue Ste-Catherine, where you'll head east and dart in and out of the shops lining this bustling corridor, which hops day and night. Stroll for about a half-mile until you reach City Councillors, then turn left and walk to boulevard de Maisonneuve.

Selection de Maisonneuve (440 boulevard de Maisonneuve Ouest; 514-873-2274; closed Sundays) has a wider selection than most SAQ's. Located in the Sommer Building, a former fur factory, this SAQ is noted for its fine selection of port. Scan the shelves, maybe buy a bottle or two, and then retrace your steps to rue Ste-Catherine and head for an impressive sandstone building dating back to the 1880s, which was once Morgan's department store. It is now **La Baie** (585 rue Ste-Catherine Ouest; 514-281-4422), part of the oldest department store chain in Canada, which takes its name from the Hudson Bay fur trading company. The store's métro level houses La Baie's Charcuterie, where you'll pick up goodies for a picnic on the wine route tomorrow.

Shelves and glass-enclosed counters in the ample Charcuterie are laden with bread, crackers, pâté, soft Brie cheese, and an assortment of mouth-watering cakes and pies. Order a container of chicken with broccoli or a cold pasta salad. Mosey over to the Belgian chocolate and sweeten the pot. The selection is huge in the Charcuterie, so take your time planning tomorrow's feast. When you've examined every specialty product—and perhaps picked up a couple of jars of preserves for your friends back home—grab a cab back to the hotel, where you've made arrangements to store your perishables in the hotel fridge. Then relax in your ultra-chic room (and maybe open a bottle of wine?) before you dress for dinner.

DAY ONE: evening

DINNER

Owner Moreno De Marchi used to park his car on the very spot where **Le Latini** (1130 rue Jeanne-Mance; 514–861–3166; station Place des Arts; expensive) stands now when he worked in a restaurant in nearby Complexe Desjardins. An immigrant to Canada from Italy, De Marchi dreamed of having his own restaurant. Inspiration struck one day when he was getting out of his car. He purchased the former parking lot and performed a minor miracle in 1979, opening what many consider the finest Italian restaurant in the city—and assembling, over time, what may be the largest collection of Italian wine in the world.

With advance notice, De Marchi will organize a romantic dinner for two in his beautiful *cantina*, a picture-perfect wine cellar that houses thousands of bottles under more than 1,200 labels. Here you

You Heard It
Through the Grapevine

Montréal oenophile and wine educator Nick Hamilton selects his top romantic restaurants in Montréal—with top wine lists, of course.

* *Le Latini (1130 rue Jeanne-Mance; 514–861–3166).*
* *La Sila (2040 rue St-Denis; 514–844–5083). See "Latin Blood."*
* *La Rapière (1155 rue Metcalfe; 514–871–8920).*
* *Le Muscadin (100 rue St-Paul; 514–842–0588).*
* *Carpaccio (2075 Université; 514-284–1115).*
* *Casa Napoli (6728 boulevard St-Laurent; 514–274–4351). See "European Adventure."*

can dine by candlelight in utmost privacy and be served by your own waiter. If your pocketbook won't stretch for such an extravagant private venture, dining in the restaurant carries its own excitement—and enchantment. From the olive oil on the table to the noodles graced with sliced white truffle to the homemade *tartufo* for dessert, every item at Le Latini is authentic and exceptional. De Marchi is always on hand to help make the wine selection easier—and to tell you a story about the vineyard from which your bottle originates. He has visited most of them.

You can have both a nightcap and a night view of Montréal from **737** (1 Place Ville Marie; 514–397–0737), a restaurant atop the city's most famous shopping venue/office tower, Place Ville Marie. You can come here for a drink only and feel like you're flying high in the clouds as you gaze out the large windows. Mile upon mile of cityscape and onward spread before you. You'll be exploring some of those miles, on land, tomorrow.

DAY TWO: morning

Plan to rise and shine early in the day so you can catch a view of the workers in the vineyards when you arrive in the wine-making region. Dress casually and comfortably. You'll be walking outdoors, picnicking at lunchtime, and returning to the hotel to change for dinner.

BREAKFAST

Have an early breakfast at the **Société Café**, which opens at 7:00 A.M. and serves an American-style breakfast featuring egg dishes and bagels, then get on the road. You'll head south into the Montérégie region and wine country, about a thirty-five-minute trip from Montréal. Cross the St-Lawrence River via the Champlain Bridge. Follow signs for Highway 10 Est, in the direction of Sherbrooke. Turn right on Highway 35 South, in the direction of St-Jean-sur-Richelieu, cross the Richelieu River, and follow Highway 35 South to the end, where it becomes Route 133 South. You'll start to see the blue tourist signs for the wineries. Turn left on Montée Bernard and right on Rang Grand Sabrevois.

Begin your tour at **Vignoble des Pins** (136 Grand Sabrevois, Sabrevois, Québec; 450–347–1073), where it's not unusual to see a father/son team laboring under beams of morning sunlight, a pristine clapboard farmhouse with a sharply slanted roof in the background. Winery owner Gilles Benoit will put down his tools and take you to his wine-tasting room, where he'll offer two whites, two reds, and Mousse des Pin, a champagne. You can savor the product in crystal glasses on a screened-in porch and then tour the on-site winemaking operation.

Buy a bottle to bring to friends back home, then retrace your steps to Route 133 and travel north. Turn right on chemin de la Grande-Ligne, where you'll find **Vignoble Dietrich Jooss** (407 Grande-Ligne, Iberville, Québec; 450–347–6857). Here you'll meet a husband/wife team from the Alsace region in France. They make an ice wine—a white dessert wine—named after their daughter. It's called Cuvée Stéphanie. Pick up another gift bottle—and tuck one away for yourselves.

Driving out of the Montérégie region and into Estrie, or the Eastern Townships, take Route 133 South, then Route 202 East. You're now on territory settled by colonists from America who wanted to remain loyal to King George during the War of Independence in 1776. Some 40,000 so-called Loyalists migrated north to Canada in protest of the Declaration of Independence. Many ended up carving out a life in this region, where you'll notice that the names of the towns are English. Take Dunham, for example, where you'll find a group of grape vineyards and wineries. Among them are **Vignoble de l'Orpailleur** (1086 Route 202, Dunham, Québec; 450–295–2763), one of the oldest and biggest wineries in Québec and makers of a prizewinning dry white wine. Three other wineries are a short distance from there: **Vignoble Les Blancs Couteaux** (1046 Route 202, Dunham, Québec; 450–295–3503); **Domaine des Côtes d'Ardoise** (879 Route 202, Dunham; 450–295–2020) and **Vignoble Les Trois Clochers** (341 Route 202, Dunham; 450–295–2034).

All the wineries give guided tours on request. No set hours are scheduled for these tours, and you can request one when you are on the site. You don't have to schedule a tour in advance of your visit, although a call ahead doesn't hurt. All the wineries also hold wine tastings (at no cost) for visitors, and sell wine on the premises. All of them also have picnic tables.

DAY TWO: afternoon

LUNCH

Whenever you get hungry along the wine route, break out your picnic—along with a bottle of newly purchased wine. Clink glasses as you eat lunch surrounded by the vineyard that made this itinerary possible. After lunch, relax and enjoy a tour of the wine-making operation at the winery of your choice. The operation at L'Orpailleur is particularly extensive. You'll head back to Montréal at the end of the afternoon—no doubt laden with gifts for yourselves and others.

It's about an hour's drive to Montréal if you use a shortcut. Follow Route 202 East, in the direction of Cowansville. Take Route 139 North, in the direction of Granby, until Highway 10 West. Follow Highway 10 West until the Champlain Bridge, which takes you into Montréal. When you arrive at the hotel, take some time in your beautiful room to freshen up for dinner.

DINNER

The wine cellar at **La Rapière** (1155 rue Metcalfe; 514–871–8920; closed Sundays; moderate to expensive) is visible from the entrance of this intimate restaurant, located on the main floor of the fanciful Sun Life Insurance building, which was once the largest building in the British Empire. Ask for a cozy corner table when you make a reservation. La Rapière was the only Montréal restaurant to specialize in the food of the Pyrenees when it opened twenty-three years ago, and today it still highlights the best cuisine from southwestern France. Owners Lise and Louis Naud offer French foie gras, duck and goose conserves, and outstanding cassoulet, a blend of white kidney beans, sausage from Toulouse, and leg of duck confit. Accompany your cassoulet with Château Grezels, a red wine from the Pyrenees. Lamb, veal, and pork are also on the menu, and the restaurant offers a wide selection of Bordeaux and Burgundy to complement your selections.

You're within easy walking distance of the hotel, so stroll back and enjoy the evening. As you return to the Vogue, stand outside a moment on rue de la Montagne and gaze at the peak for which the street is named. Kiss in the moonlight. In just hours, you'll be leaving the city, luggage bursting with the fruit of the vine.

FOR MORE ROMANCE

If you begin this itinerary on Friday and extend your weekend through Sunday, hold on to your wineglasses. Have lunch Sunday afternoon in the Laurentian Mountains at **Bistro à Champlain** (75 chemin Masson, Sainte-Marguerite-du-Lac Masson; 450–228–4988), a general store dating back to 1864 that has been transformed into a renowned restaurant with one of the best wine cellars in the world. Situated across from Lac Masson, about a seventy-five-minute drive from Montréal, Bistro à Champlain carries some 1,200 labels—and French wine is sold here by the glass. On permanent exhibit are a veritable gallery of paintings by a handful of artists, including Jean-Paul Riopelle, perhaps Canada's most famous contemporary artist. The Bistro also contains an exclusive cigar sampling salon. If money is no object, why not arrive here by seaplane? Trips can be arranged with **Delco Aviation** (450–663–4311).

Undercover

THE UNDERGROUND CITY

STORMY WEATHER IS NO PROBLEM IN MONTRÉAL. Bring on the snow, the wind, the freezing rain. Let the thermometer slide. You won't step a foot out the door on this romantic weekend.

Stay warm and cozy in Montréal's underground city, an 18-mile network of subterranean passageways all linked by métro. You don't have to freeze your tootsies as you travel from restaurant to cinema to shopping mall to concert hall—without ever walking out the hotel front door.

If your idea of a winter wonderland means never donning boots or a coat, paradise awaits in one of the coldest cities on earth.

PRACTICAL NOTES: Because this itinerary is a winter holiday, it gives your pocketbook a break. At this time of year hotel rates are lower than in warmer seasons. Begin the weekend on a Friday, since many stores and restaurants are closed on Sunday. Book your weekend to coincide with a rock or pop concert at Le Centre Molson (514–932–CLUB) or a play at Place des Arts (514–842–2112 or 514–790–1245). Both venues can be accessed via the underground network.

DAY ONE: morning/afternoon

In terms of size, no hotel in the city measures up to **Le Reine Elizabeth** (900 boulevard René-Levesque Ouest; 514–861–3511 or 800–441–1414; station Bonaventure; $300 for two nights with breakfast on weekends

◆ Leave your bags (and coat and hat and gloves) at **Le Reine Elizabeth;** (900 boulevard René-Levesque Ouest; 514–861–3511 or 800–441–1414), where John and Yoko held a love-in thirty years ago. It's your departure point for exploring 18 miles of underground passages that'll take you through the downtown core without ever stepping outside.

◆ Have lunch on an ocean liner, in a dining room patterned on the luxury ship Île de France. Spend the rest of the afternoon shopping at a mall built underneath **Christ Church Cathedral** (1440 avenue Union; 514–288–6421), which still welcomes worshippers every day.

◆ Take the underground passages to one of the best observatories in the city, which also happens to be a stunning bar and restaurant. After dining at **737** (forty-sixth floor, Place Ville Marie; 514–397–0737) and imbibing the breathtaking view, end the evening dancing at **727** one floor below.

—ask for promotional rates). With 1,020 rooms, it is Montréal's biggest lodging facility. To bring its mammoth proportions down to a friendlier scale, management introduced the Entrée Gold program, setting aside eighty rooms on floors eighteen and nineteen for clients who crave a bit more privacy and pampering. The rooms are accessed by private elevator, and once you alight, your very own concierge is there to meet your needs. On the nineteenth floor, deluxe continental breakfast is served in a private, glass-enclosed lounge with a fireplace. Local phone calls are complimentary, and a newspaper is left outside your door each morning.

Le Reine Elizabeth, also commonly known as The Queen Elizabeth, has a glorious past. From the moment it opened in 1958, it attracted an international crowd and became *the* place for dignitaries—fifty of the sixty heads of state in town for Expo '67 booked a suite here. In 1969, the hotel's reputation was sealed when John Lennon and Yoko Ono held a love-in in Suite 1742 and recorded *Give Peace a Chance.* Visitors to the hotel still ask to see the room.

Today, the hotel has adapted to changing times, adding a state-of-the-art health club and a fabulous indoor pool, and putting a premium on travelers who require the personal touch. You've requested a room with a mountain view on the nineteenth floor. When you arrive, drop your bags with the concierge on nineteen and prepare to explore the Underground City. You can leave your coat and scarf and gloves with your luggage. You won't need them anymore. Take the elevator down to the lower level, and follow signs to a tunnel that leads to the underground trains. Pay your fare and hop aboard. It's that easy. You've just linked up with the underground network that will take you everywhere you want to go—including the unusual spot where you're about to have lunch. At the McGill station, exit the métro and follow the signs to a restaurant now considered a heritage site.

LUNCH

If you think **Le 9e** (Le neuvième; 514–284–8421; inexpensive; table d'hôte, $9.50) looks like an ocean liner, you're not lost at sea. This prized restaurant on the ninth floor of what once was **Eaton's,** Montréal's largest department store, (677 rue Ste-Catherine Ouest; station McGill) was designed by art deco master Jacques Carlu, who patterned it after the dining room on the passenger liner *Île de France.* With seating for 600 diners at a time, the elongated room literally stretches a full ship's length. It's surrounded by marble columns adorned with frosted glass lanterns, and by two murals, *Dans un parc* and *Amazones.* Imagine you're on a cruise (the Love Boat, perhaps?) while you delight in the steak and kidney pie or the club sandwich made the old-fashioned way —with real chicken.

You'll spend the afternoon exploring the "city below." It covers 29 kilometers (18 miles) and links up with two bus terminals, several métro stations, seven major hotels, Olympic Park, the Université du Québec, a Montréal campus, two leading department stores, 1,700 boutiques, more than two hundred restaurants, dozens of banks and movie theaters—and a church that sits atop a shopping arcade called **Les Promenades de la Cathédrale** (625 rue Ste-Catherine Ouest). Les Promenades is linked to Eaton, so you'll proceed there directly from lunch. Notwithstanding your affiliations, pause to reflect a moment in **Christ Church Cathedral** (1440 avenue Union; 514–288–6421). A Protestant church dating back to the 1850s, this quiet refuge is open to worshippers every day. Then start shopping at Les Promenades' one hundred stores. Don't miss the **Linen Chest** (514–282–9525), where you'll find enough satin sheets to fulfill any romantic fantasy.

When your shoulders droop from the weight of your packages, return to the hotel and renew yourselves at the health club. Along with Keiser weight-lifting equipment, a treadmill, a Stairmaster, and a rowing machine are a three-lane, 40-foot swimming pool, a whirlpool, and a steam bath with showers. Breathe deeply and work to raise your heart rate. Soon your shopworn muscles will rejuvenate, and you'll forget that it's below zero outside.

But you won't forget that dinner reservation you made for tonight. Energy restored, head back to your room and dress up in your finest. Forget the slush and snow. You're going out on the town while staying indoors.

DAY ONE: evening

DINNER

Walk through the underground passages and take the elevators leading to the forty-sixth floor of Place Ville Marie, where the view from restaurant **737** (514–397–0737; moderate to expensive; three-course table d'hôte starts at $27) might produce vertigo. **Place Ville Marie**, the cross-shaped office complex/shopping arcade designed by architect I. M. Pei, kicked off the underground concept in 1962. The shopping mall's crowning glory is 737, a swinging place with a first-rate sushi bar and an international menu. A variety of wine is served here by the glass, giving you the opportunity to indulge in a choicer label without having to buy a bottle. Desserts are worth the calorie splurge.

You could return to your room after dinner—or you could go dancing one floor below the restaurant at **727**. Take the elevator down and shake your body to the pulsating beat of a disco set. If body movement of another sort interests you more, head back to the hotel. If it's snowing, watch the flakes fall against the lights on McGill College Avenue from your bedroom window. Look up toward the Roddick Gates on the McGill University campus, now dusted with snow. Raise your gaze higher to the cross on Mont-Royal. Give thanks you're inside—and dive under the covers.

DAY TWO: morning

BREAKFAST

When you're ready to emerge from your king-size bed, hit the health club, and then have breakfast (served until 11:00 A.M. on weekends) in a classy lounge with a fireplace just down the hall. The deluxe continental buffet includes fresh fruit salad, yogurt, cereal, croissants, raisin bread, date nut loaf and cream cheese, juice, and coffee. From a table-for-two in the corner of the glass-enclosed lounge, you have a daytime view of Dorchester Square, a bustling business corridor during the week. Look down at the statues of the saints gracing **Cathédrale Marie-Reine-du-Monde**, a small-scale replica of St. Peter's Basilica in Rome. You may see a wedding party entering the church. And speaking of weddings: The **Sun Life Building**, like a multitiered wedding cake, looks simply delectable across the street. From a chair in the lounge, you can almost reach out and touch the twenty-six-story structure, once the largest building in the British Empire, and run your finger around the icing. Nearby, too, is Centre Molson, home to the most successful hockey franchise in history—the Montréal Canadiens, winners of twenty-four Stanley Cups since 1929. Perhaps you've picked up tickets to tonight's game or a show there.

Gifts Galore

Would you like to shop for gifts for the holidays on your romantic weekend? If you are in the city in early December, take the underground passage to the Salon des Métiers d'Art du Québec in the west hall of Place Bonaventure (station Bonaventure) and attend one of the biggest craft shows in North America. More than 300 artists from Québec and around the world sell crafts, jewelry, and paintings in the three-week period before December 25. You might want to consider buying a carved decoy for your love. It's not as strange a suggestion as it might seem. These precious ducks are highly valued as collector's items and range in price from thirty to several thousand dollars. The ducks come large and small, are carved from rich woods, and are hand-painted in brilliant greens, yellows, maroons, beiges, and browns. Some even have a plaid ribbon tied around the neck!

Have you ever gone to a museum without stepping into the elements one tiny bit? You will now. Dress nicely; you won't be returning to change before dinner and the show tonight. Take the same route you followed yesterday from the hotel elevator to the métro. Hop on a train and head for the **Musée d'art contemporain** (185 Ste-Catherine Ouest; 514–847–6212; station Place des Arts; closed Monday; admission $8.00), where you'll get to know Québec a little better even if you're not on the streets. Montréal's modern art museum houses about 5,000 works dating back to 1939, and 60 percent of the paintings, drawings, etchings, sculptures, and photographs are by Québec artists. Spend an hour or two considering the work of artists such as Jean-Paul Riopelle, Paul-Emile Bourduas, Max Ernst, Guido Molinari, and Adolph Gottlieb. Through them, you'll see Québec without actually stepping out the door. When you've had a sufficient sampling of some of the best contemporary art Québec has to offer, hop on the métro again and spend the afternoon where the aristocracy once frolicked.

Perhaps the heftiest price tags underground can be found in **Les Cours Mont-Royal** (1455 rue Peel; 514–842–7777; emerge from the Peel station and follow signs), formerly the largest hotel in the British Empire, where the wealthy would stay when visiting Montréal. Six decades after it opened in 1922, the hotel was converted into offices and condos—and the classiest mall in the subterranean city. The best place to view the splendor is from the fourth floor. You'll get a close look at the original chandelier from the Mount Royal Hotel, as extravagant now as then. It once hung from the ceiling of a casino in Monte Carlo. From this perch, you'll also overlook some thirty designer clothing boutiques (try **Juan & Juanita**) and a handful of restaurants.

When you've browsed through the pricey stores in the mall, head to the movie complex underneath. Dotted with columns that support the structure above, the lobby of **Cinéma Egyptien** (514–849–3456) looks like a pharaoh's temple. Catch an afternoon movie here; the three theaters here offer first-run selections. Yesterday you dined in an ocean liner. Today you're cuddling close in an Egyptian temple. All this and you haven't even stepped outside!

DAY TWO: evening

Don't rush madly out of the theater. You'll be able to keep your dinner reservations without a problem. You don't have far to travel—the restaurant is on the second level of Les Cours Mont-Royal. Just take the elevator to the restaurant where diva Céline Dion dines when she's in town.

DINNER

Guy & Dodo Morali (1444 rue Metcalfe; 514–842–3636; in Les Cours Mont-Royal; station Peel; closed Sunday; reservations required; expensive) is a romantic bistro where a rose always sits on every table, even in winter. The fine French cuisine is prepared by a husband-wife team who pride themselves on their beef Wellington or rack of Québec lamb served with a choice of five sauces. Don't leave the table without dessert. It's a toss-up between Île Flottante—a floating island of meringue and crème anglaise—or La Tarte Tatin, a hot apple pie dripping with caramel sauce.

From the restaurant, take the métro back to Place des Arts or to Centre Molson (station Bonaventure or Lucien-L'Allier), new home of the Montréal Canadiens and now a popular entertainment venue. When the Canadiens aren't playing at home, Centre Molson hosts singers ranging from Luciano Pavarotti to Neil Diamond. On the other hand, if you have tickets for the theater at Place des Arts, you're likely to see a Broadway play on tour. Enjoy your evening wherever you go, carefree and snug in your underground cocoon.

FOR MORE ROMANCE

Ice-skating is an inviting proposition from an indoor vantage. **L'Amphithéâtre Bell** (1000 rue de la Gauchetière; 514–395–0555; station Bonaventure; admission $5.00; skate rental fee $4.00) is a 10,000-square-foot indoor rink located in the lobby of the tallest office building in town. You'll be bathed in natural sunlight as you pirouette in comfort.

Love Among the Ruins

Antiquing in Montréal

HAT ANTIQUE COLLECTOR HASN'T FANTASIZED about finding a certified treasure? It actually happened a few years ago in Montréal's "Antiques Alley"—a stretch of nearly forty antiques shops lining one street—when five small Paleolithic sculptures were uncovered among the bric-à-brac in Napoléon Antiques. They are believed to predate Christ by thousands of years.

I can't promise you'll find treasure on this itinerary, but I can promise you'll have fun trying. Every imaginable type of antique—from church relics to a sumptuous chaise longue—may be found here. Hardware, doorknobs, chandeliers, furniture, clocks, jewelry, vases, paintings, toys, stained glass—and reproductions of these same items—are among the bounty awaiting you. Your happy hunting will take you through several *quartiers* of Montréal—and all on a budget-conscious plan. By watching your pennies, you can splurge on your very own treasure without even a pang of guilt.

PRACTICAL NOTES: The itinerary works at any time of year, but it can be particularly romantic in winter, since you'll be spending so much time indoors, anyway, and will welcome the cozy ambience of the shops. Rates at the B&B are also lower at that time of year, an attractive feature when you'd rather put your money toward a treasure. A couple of other provisos: I suggest you start your weekend on Thursday or Friday. Antiques stores have quirky hours, and many close on Sunday. At any of the stores listed below, you can buy a handy guide to antiquing in Montréal. Called *Antiquités, Friperies and Gourmandises* ($3.00), it will help you nav-

Romance AT A GLANCE

◆ *Stay in a guest house once owned by well-known Montréal artist Marcel Barbeau located in the midst of the city's retro antiques district. After leaving your bags at* ***Roy D'Carreau Guest House*** *(1637 rue Amherst; 514–524–2493), spend the day exploring a district that few Montréalers know exists, but which attracts filmmakers seeking deco treasure for movie sets.*

◆ *Take another day to discover Antiques Alley, a stretch of some forty stores harboring choice finds from Québec and all parts of Europe. Pause to ponder a possible purchase (and grab a scrumptious lunch) at* ***Ambiance Tea Room*** *(1874 rue Notre-Dame Ouest; 514–939–2609), where even the chair you're sitting on is for sale.*

◆ *When the treasure hunt is over, mellow out after dark at* ***L'Air du Temps*** *(194 rue St-Paul Ouest; 514–842–2003), an antiques-filled jazz club featuring live music.*

igate the terrain and also plan your day. When it comes to antiquing, you see, I've found that the early bird doesn't always get the worm—but rather finds a sign that reads "OPEN AT 11."

DAY ONE: morning

Plunge into the world of art and antiques when you arrive at **Roy d'Carreau Guest House** (1637 rue Amherst; 514–524–2493; station Berri-UQAM; $95, including private bath and continental breakfast for two), a turn-of-the-century brick row house once owned by famed Montréal artist Marcel Barbeau. Your gracious hosts, veteran innkeepers, took Barbeau's fabulous house (which includes a courtyard and a basement workshop covered by a skylight) and in 1997 created a four-bedroom guest house filled with art, antiques, and charm. Periodically your hosts open the guest house to local artists for an unveiling of their new work. Naturally, you're invited to join the fun on opening night.

The house is smack dab in the middle of a small antiques district that not even many Montréalers realize exists. Located on the fringe of the downtown core, the district attracts a mix of young and old, monied and poor, gay and straight—a blend as varied as the items you're about to see this afternoon in the shops. By the way, if you fall in love with a pricey item here, don't hesitate to mention it to your hosts. They know most of the merchants in the district, and might persuade them to be gentle on your pocketbook. But before you begin to bargain, pause for lunch.

DAY ONE: afternoon

LUNCH

At **Chez Caroline** (1844 rue Amherst; 514–522–5880; inexpensive), the international aspect of antiquing comes through loud and clear in the tiny dining room.

There's a couch instead of a banquette in the corner; a wall is colored burnt orange; and there's an assemblage of lighting fixtures in this Vietnamese restaurant, one of several Asian restaurants in the district. All come recommended, but I'm fond of Chez Caroline. You absolutely must try the Soupe Tonkinoise—or noodle soup—but be forewarned. What sits steaming before you is no mere bowl of soup. Soupe Tonkinoise is a veritable meal. Brimming with chunks of beef and vegetables—and loaded with noodles—the perfectly spiced soup may be the most delicious starter you've ever had. Order a stir-fry or a chicken brochette with rice and, duly fortified, you'll be ready to face every antiques dealer in sight.

After lunch you can stop by **Phil'z** (rue Amherst; 514–523–2435) and admire his mostly retro antiques dating from the 1920s to the 1970s. His shop is filled with sensuously shaped love seats and chairs from the 1920s—the kind that make black-and-white movies of the time look so glamorous. You might find a seductive lamp here to bring home to the friend who introduced you two.

Then slowly work your way down the street to rue Ste-Catherine, where the district ends. Be sure to look carefully on both sides of the street—some stores don't have signs.

The district specializes in deco and retro-style antiques, although other eras are represented—and you don't have to worry about crossing the border with an antique. At customs, antiques bought in Canada are treated the same way as any furniture. When it comes to industrial objects of more recent vintage, **Le Retro Stop** (1851 rue Amherst) offers a profusion of blenders, fans, toasters, hair dryers, bird cages, and radios that recall how we lived in the not-too-distant past. A pair of vintage boxing gloves might hang on the wall as you enter **Antiquités Curiosités** (1769 rue Amherst; 514–525–8772). Artfully displayed inside could be a dentist's chair and a psychiatrist's couch as well. **Cité Déco** (1761 rue Amherst; 514–528–0659), a deco lover's dream, looks like a movie set and, indeed, is called upon, like many shops on this street, to supply period pieces to film production companies. **L'Antiquaire Joyal** (1475 rue Amherst; 514–524–0057), with its turquoise walls and teacups placed just so on finely restored Canadian-made furniture, looks like a museum. The store is very romantic; French crooners perform (on tape) as you shop. Don't miss the rooms downstairs. The furniture here is beautiful and extremely well priced.

> *And ruin'd love, when it is built anew,*
> *Grows fairer than at first, more strong, far greater.*
> — Shakespeare, Sonnet 119

Cross the street to **Librairie Québeçoise** (1454 rue Amherst; 514–848–9888), and you won't be disappointed. Though the exterior of this bookstore looks drab, inside are thousands of used French and English books in good condition and used magazines from around the world. The French sign out front translates as follows: "HERE WE GET RICHER WITHOUT GETTING POORER." Now cross the street once more to **Antiquités Pednault** (1447 rue Amherst; 514–521–4447), site of what used to be the oldest jewelry store in Montréal. Fernand Pednault, who bought the jewelry store more than a decade back, kept the spiral staircase inside and stocked the place with a mix of deco, trunks, tables, lamps, knickknacks, and religious icons, which are important reminders of Québec's patrimony.

For a change of pace—but in keeping with the theme—visit a former public bath building that has been given new life as the home of the **L'eco-musée du Fier Monde** (2050 rue Amherst; 514–528–8444; open Wednesday through Sunday; $5.00)—a museum that traces the history of industry and work in Montréal, particularly in the sector of city in which you now stand. Constructed in the Roaring Twenties by architect Joseph-Omer Marchand, the former Bain Généreux (public bath) was named after a city councillor. Preservationists are buoyed by the recent restoration of the building and fervently hope the move bodes well for other Montréal public baths that are no longer operative—but fondly remembered.

After the museum visit, why not take a break and talk about that wonderful marble statue you saw earlier? With its coffee roaster made of copper on the premises and lots of luscious-looking French and Italian pastries in the display case, **La Boîte à Café** (1112 boulevard de Maisonneuve Est, at the corner of rue Amherst; 514–525–5823; inexpensive) is a cozy spot where you can get close and talk over everything you've seen—and plot a return, if need be. When you've finally decided (to buy, of course), head for the guest house with packages under both arms. Store your loot, and find that splendid courtyard for a stolen kiss before dinner.

DAY ONE: evening

DINNER

Stay casual tonight. **Galaxie Diner** (4801 rue St-Denis; 514–499–9711; station Laurier; inexpensive) is an old-fashioned eatery capitalizing on the nostalgic longing for a less complicated time. And it is the perfect place for antiques hunters. The stainless-steel diner is the genuine article. Built in the early 1950s, it was transported here from Boston and restored. Gum-chewing waitresses are part of the retro atmosphere, as are the red vinyl booths, Formica counters, and the jukebox at each table. The memorabilia here look like they come from the shops you visited today. Probably did. The burgers, onion rings, and malts are great. Pretend you're back on the college campus—or in your old high-school hangout. Put a quarter in the jukebox and play the oldies you adored once upon a time. The Platters, Elvis, Ben E. King, the Temptations, the Supremes—the selection dates back forty years. When you finally wrench yourselves away from the familiar tunes, you might want to head back to the guest house and make your own music.

DAY TWO: morning/afternoon

BREAKFAST

The courtyard where you embraced last evening is the same romantic place where you'll be sipping a café au lait in the morning.

Breakfast in the courtyard is a special affair. Fresh bread is baked on the premises (except, the hosts admit, if they get lazy and pop out and buy fresh croissants). Fresh fruit and juice, plus an assortment of cereals, complete the meal. The pleasant atmosphere is so unhurried, you may want to hold hands and linger a bit before heading for the métro for another day of treasure seeking. After all, most of the stores don't open until late morning.

You'll be gone all day and won't return before dinner, but don't fret about dressing up. You'll dine this evening where casual clothing is the norm.

Take the métro directly from the guest house to Lionel-Groulx station. Head south when you exit and walk to rue Notre-Dame, where you'll immediately find the district dubbed Antiques Alley. Almost forty shops along the stretch hold something for everyone and offer utter contrasts in content and style. You'll shop the length of the street up until rue Guy—and don't worry if you don't see a store for a few blocks between Vinet and Canning Streets. Some residential units interrupt the flow, as does Parc de l'Encan, where horses were auctioned in days gone by. Just keep walking. The shopping begins again.

Near the beginning of the stretch is the famous **Napoléon Antiques** (2509 rue Notre-Dame Ouest; 514–932–6844), where treasure was found a few years ago. The shop specializes in the Napoleonic era. It keeps a limited schedule, however, and may not be open when you arrive. No matter. More than three dozen other shops are here to discover. Fine examples of Québec pine furniture are sold at **Pierre St-Jacques** (2507 rue Notre-Dame Ouest; 514–933–9293). One of the loveliest shops on the street—and one of the priciest—is **Grand Central** (2448 rue Notre-Dame Ouest; 514–935–1467) where the chandeliers are breathtaking. Some date from the 1890s and were originally meant to hold candles for illumination. They've been electrified by artisans at Grand Central, who are specialists in lighting restoration for businesses and private clients. Grand Central also carries stunning furniture made in New England from mahogany rather than the bleached pine more common in Québec.

When you leave Grand Central and continue your stroll on rue Notre-Dame, stop to see two old bank branches, both built in 1895. Worth a pause just to gaze at their architecture, they are the

Bold Move

Rue St-Paul was the home of Elizabeth Begon in the 1700s. Born into a humble Montréal family, Elizabeth fell in love with Claude Michel Begon, a military officer from France, when she was sixteen and he twenty-nine. His parents, members of the French aristocracy, opposed the match, but the couple went ahead and married anyway without permission. They arrived in church one Sunday morning in 1718, declared their love, and engaged themselves in front of the priests. The priests accepted their declaration, raised glasses of wine in celebration, and thereby performed what was then called "Mariage à la Gaumine" —named after a monk who lived in the sixteenth century and accepted marriage without an official witness. With Elizabeth at his side, Claude Michel went on to become governor of Trois Rivières, Québec. After his death, Elizabeth moved back to Montréal and lived in a big house on rue St-Paul, in the spot where Bonsecours Market is today.

Merchants Bank of Halifax building (1870 rue Notre-Dame Ouest), the work of designer Edward Maxwell, and the red sandstone former branch of the **Bank of Montréal** (1850 rue Notre-Dame Ouest), designed by Sir Andrew Thomas Taylor.

About this time, you'd probably welcome a cup of tea and a light snack. It's no coincidence that at this point in your journey, a tea salon is steps away.

TEA or SNACK

Collapse into a chair at **Ambiance Tea Room** (1874 rue Notre-Dame Ouest: 514–939–2609; inexpensive). If you like the chair you are sitting in, you can have it—for a price. Almost everything at Ambiance is for sale, so while you're having a snack, eye the goods at this combination antiques store and restaurant, and hash over a potential purchase. Better yet, hash over the wonderful menu, which, in addition to tea, includes wine sold by the glass, cocktails, and beer. Salads and sandwiches are exceptional. So are the homemade soups and a variety of home-baked pies and cakes. Why not order a steaming cup of tea and then share a curried chicken sandwich on Russian black bread? Have another cup of tea—and order two forks—for the slice of pumpkin pie you've requested served with a dollop of fresh whipped cream on top.

Now you're amply fortified to continue the rest of your treasure hunt. On the next block, gold-lettered signs identify **Antiquités Claude Blain** (1752 rue Notre-Dame Ouest; 514–938–9221), a shop where an episode of the TV series *Hart to Hart* was filmed. Another favorite of film crews is **Antiquités Michelle Parent** (1650 rue Notre-Dame Ouest; 514–933–9435), a classic shop that looks straight out of the movies—and was used in *Snakeater's Revenge* with Lorenzo Lamas. Crystal chandeliers hang from the ceiling here and sprinkle light over a mix of English and French furniture. Between these two shops is **Le Village des Antiquaires** (1708 rue Notre-Dame Ouest; 514–931–5121), which houses under one roof ten dealers specializing in everything from canes and hatpins to silver and porcelain.

When you have thoroughly combed the offerings here (and surreptitiously purchased a piece of jewelry for your love), you're ready to enter the oldest part of town. Walk along rue des Seigneurs (found between the 1800 and 1700 block on rue Notre-Dame) south to the canal footpath and continue hand in hand along the St-Lawrence River into Old Montréal. It's about a half-hour walk east to rue St-François-Xavier, where you'll walk north and rejoin rue Notre-Dame.

Since you're intrigued by antiquity, you'll want to visit the oldest building still standing in the city of Montréal. The **Old Saint-Sulpice Seminary** (130 rue Notre-Dame Ouest) was built in 1685 as a residence for the Sulpician priests, a religious order that managed the Seigniory of Montréal Island for generations. Today, retired priests live here, and visitors are not allowed inside. That rule doesn't prevent you from peeking through the iron gate or noticing the clock outside the entrance. It dates back to the early 1700s and is the oldest of its type in North America. The fieldstone edifice will surely enchant lovers of antiquity. When you've admired the beauty, retrace your steps a few blocks to rue St-Paul.

DAY TWO: evening

DINNER

If you have done the antiques district right, and enjoyed your long walk, you're probably ready to drop. **Le Petit Moulinsard** (139 rue

St-Paul Ouest; 514–843–7432; inexpensive; $20 for a three-course table d'hôte) is a warm and friendly Belgian bistro that specializes in *moules*—or mussels—and French fries, traditional Belgian fare, and other daily specials as well. The retro theme of yesterday is carried over here. The wood walls are a showcase for the characters of Georges Rémi Hergé's *Tintin* comic strip, beloved by a generation of French-speaking kids who grew up in the 1950s and have now passed their love of the character along to their children. Most Québecers my husband's age followed the adventures of the ageless Tintin, his white scottish terrier, Milou, and Capitaine Haddock, a rich sailor who liked to drink. Now my daughter is familiar with the adventures of Tintin as well—on video.

What should you order here? Start with a beer. The lively bar offers more than 150 brands from around the world. Then try the Capitaine Haddock salad. It's delicious. You decide whether to try a daily special or the house favorite from the sea. The bistro atmosphere here makes for a joyous evening—perfect for reliving your adventures and for admiring the piece of antique jewelry you tucked away earlier and have just presented to your love.

If you don't want to call it a night after dinner, head for an antiques-filled environment a few doors down that also offers live jazz. At **L'Air du Temps** (194 rue St-Paul Ouest; 514–842–2003), an ancient rocking horse hangs from the ceiling and melds nicely with a wood bar that extends the length of the club. It's easy to unwind and get cozy in the sultry atmosphere. Why not linger? Tomorrow morning, after a delicious breakfast, you'll exit—packages in hand.

FOR MORE ROMANCE

If your budget allows—or even if it doesn't, and you just admire lovely things—visit one the most beautiful antiques shops in the city. **Le Petit Musée** (1494 rue Sherbrooke Ouest; 514–937–6161) means "little museum," and this store is precisely that. Spread over four floors, some 10,000 pieces are displayed with the fine touch of a master curator. Clients come from around the world to seek the antiques that have made Le Petit Musée a fixture for forty-five years.

I've still got my eye on a grandfather clock there—if I win the lottery.

Another suggestion for antiques lovers (with a car): take the fifty-minute trip to the village of Hudson to scout Finnegan's Market, open only on Saturdays from May to October. Refer to the "Saddle Up" itinerary for more information on antiquing in this mainly English village.

Pampering Yourselves the French Way

IF YOU NEED PAMPERING, *MES AMIS*, here's the prescription: Go directly to the French side of town and play in the Plateau. On this frisky itinerary designed to restore *joie de vivre*, every move you make leads to pleasure. Slip onto a heated massage table. Shop on the liveliest street in Montréal. Sip tea in a cozy salon. Savor food prepared by fine French chefs. Sleep in—and don't tell.

Spoil yourselves utterly in a place where the nights are designed for love—and so are the mornings. The afternoons? On the French side of town, *l'amour* is the main theme any time.

PRACTICAL NOTES: Start your itinerary on Friday, when stores are open late. (On Saturday, they close between 5:00 and 6:00 P.M.) Although this moderately priced itinerary works year-round, it is more fun (and less expensive) in the off-season, when rates at the inn are lower and the spa is less crowded.

DAY ONE: morning/afternoon

A silver cupola distinguishes **Auberge de la Fontaine** (1301 rue Rachel Est; 514–597–0166; station Mont-Royal; $125 to $200, continental breakfast and parking included), a stately private residence that was later converted to a discothèque. Jean Lamothe and wife Céline Boudreau bought the disco in the late 1980s and gave it new life. It now houses twenty rooms, two with balconies overlooking Parc Lafontaine, one of the city's largest greenspaces and a great place to

*R*om**a**nce
AT A GLANCE

◆ *Cocoon at **Auberge de la Fontaine**
(1301 rue Rachel Est; 514–597–0166), an
inn that offers terry-cloth robes and Jacuzzi
tubs. But before you get cozy, stroll to
Laloux (250 avenue des Pins Est; 514–
287–9127) for an elegant lunch at a lovely old-
world bistro, followed by an afternoon spent window-
shopping at designer boutiques along rue St-Denis.*

◆ *Pamper yourself with a rejuvenating rain massage at **Aqua-Cité** (666 rue
Sherbrooke Ouest; 514–845–8455), where the staff specializes in balneother-
apy, turning you onto the marvels of water. Every drop of weariness disinte-
grates as you relax after your treatment in a lounge looking over Mont-Royal,
sipping herbal tea and ultimately drifting off into sleepy oblivioun on comfortable chairs.*

◆ *Journey to the south of France when you dine at **Le Club Des Pins** (156
avenue Laurier Ouest; 514– 272-9484), where the warm blue-and-yellow
decor and robust French food transport you across the Atlantic.*

bike or stroll through. **Cycle Pop** (1000 rue Rachel; 514–526–2525)
is just steps from the inn if you'd like to rent a bike—or in-line skates.

Choose a room with a Jacuzzi tub for your romantic weekend.
You'll find terry bathrobes near the tub. The rooms are spacious and
nicely decorated and impart a sense of calm as soon as you enter. If
your room is not yet available, leave your bags and walk west on rue
Rachel to rue St-Denis. Walk south on rue St-Denis to the corner of
Pine. Here you'll find the most wonderful French bistro in the city.

LUNCH

Dubbed "Paris on Pine," **Laloux** (250 avenue des Pins Est;
514–287–9127; station Sherbrooke; lunch Monday through Friday;
moderate; table d'hôte, $10 to $16) is a visual, auditory, and gustatory
experience. Simply put, Laloux works on all your senses. The ambience
is Old World bistro—a striped awning outside, sheer curtains and mirrors in a light-filled interior. It's elegance in a simple manner. The food
is the same. Chef André Besson, whose father was a butcher and whose
mother inherited a bistro near Lyon, France, never thought of straying
far from the kitchen. In Paris, he worked with Paul Bocuse. He has car-

ried the French tradition to Montréal, where you are the beneficiary today. Have a glass of wine and savor the flavors.

When you have fortified yourselves for an afternoon of browsing, exit the restaurant, turn right and begin your shopping spree by walking north on rue St-Denis. Once a residential street for the well-to-do (you can spot the entrance for servants on the street level of these former homes), rue St-Denis is best known now for shopping and café hopping. You'll find restaurants, tearooms, bookstores, game emporiums, antiques stores, and craft galleries—and some of the hottest fashion designers in Québec, who have chosen to work and sell in what they call an atelier-boutique. These combination workshop/stores include **Chapofolie** (3944 rue St-Denis; 514–982–0036) for imaginative hats; **Dubuc: Mode de Vie Inc.** (4451 rue St-Denis; 514–282–1424; boutique, 514–282–1465) for the latest in menswear; and **Muse** (4467 rue St-Denis; 514–848–9493), for stylishly original jackets, skirts, and pants.

The most fabulous kitchenware is at **Arthur Quentin** (3960 rue St-Denis). **Giraffe** (3997 rue St-Denis) carries a wide selection of artifacts from Africa. Make sure to duck into the Société des Alcools du Québec (4128 rue St-Denis) to pick up a bottle of wine for dinner. You're going to a restaurant tonight where BYOB (bring your own bottle, or *apportez votre vin*) is the rule—and a much-beloved rule in these parts. You may want to pick up an aperitif to enjoy in your room before you go to dinner.

Continue now with your shopping. If you pine for pine, stop at **Antiques Puces-Libre** (4240 rue St-Denis) with three floors of nineteenth-century French-Canadian country collectibles. **Champigny** (4380 rue St-Denis), a huge French bookstore, carries newspapers and magazines from around the world. At the corner of rue St-Denis and rue Marie Anne is the Chinese Catholic church. Across the street, at 4350 rue St-Denis, is the former Montréal press club. **Le Valet D'Coeur** (4408 rue St-Denis) sells games of every kind.

AFTERNOON TEA

When you need a break, backtrack a bit to **Le Daphné** (3803 rue St-Denis; 514–849–3042; inexpensive), where you can sip a cup of tea or coffee or a glass of wine, for that matter, in a tea salon setting that is more French than British in style. You won't be able to resist the ice cream parfaits with marvelous names like La Dame Blanche, La Divine, and Le Diable Rose.

Walk back to your lodging now, purchases in hand. Open the bottle you just bought when you get back to the room. Cocktail hour begins with a soak in the Jacuzzi. It continues when you put on your bathrobes and sneak under the covers. When will it end? That's up to you to decide.

DAY ONE: evening

DINNER

When the cuddling has concluded, the coddling begins again. Dress up, and when you leave the inn, don't forget your bottle of wine. Stroll over to **Le Flambard** (851 rue Rachel Est; 514–596–1280; station Mont-Royal; moderate), where almost all the tables are meant for two. With a green and white dotted swiss cloth on the table, eucalyptus leaves lining the walls, and a chanteuse on the stereo, this tiny hole-in-the-wall bistro offers delicious French food at extremely reasonable prices. Start with rich tomato soup, then choose a lush salad made with Québec's noted frissée lettuce, and then move to salmon with mustard sauce. Service is so pleasant and the ambience so cozy, you won't want to leave. The waiter will pour you another glass of wine. You're in no rush. Life is finally slowing down.

After dinner walk a few short blocks to **Le Sofa Bar-Porto** (451 rue Rachel Est), a sultry spot that features live soft jazz Wendesday through Sunday nights. It stays open until 3:00 A.M. I'll leave you here. *Bonne nuit.*

DAY TWO: morning

BREAKFAST

Breakfast at the auberge is a do-it-yourself affair in a combination sitting/dining room with a view of the street. Cereal, fresh-baked bread,

Love Songs, the French Way

If any of these French-Canadian singers are performing while you're in Montréal, buy tickets! You'll love the music even if you may not understand the words.

* *Ginette Reno: An oldie but goodie with a goddess's voice and a warm stage presence.*

* *Daniel Lavoie: A sultry voice, beautiful songs, and smoldering good looks.*

* *Céline Dion: The best-selling French-speaking artist of all time and the featured singer in Atlanta at the opening ceremony of the 1996 Summer Olympics.*

* *Luc de Larochellière: A songwriter-singer whose savvy lyrics and urban music captivate.*

* *Daniel Bélanger: A noted lyricist whose catchy tunes are engaging.*

muffins, and yogurt are offered buffet style. Watch the world go by, then take the métro or a cab to ultimate pampering.

Both of you are scheduled for a rejuvenating session at **Aqua Cité** (666 rue Sherbrooke Ouest, sixteenth floor; 514–845–8455; station McGill, $89 each for the mini-program), where you'll find a quiet oasis perched high above the city streets and affording a view of Mont-Royal. Owner Jocelyna Dubuc, a health-and-fitness maven, has operated a bucolic center for health and well-being in the Eastern Townships for over twenty years. She has transferred her knowledge to the city, where her appreciation of the revitalizing effect of water is put to full use. Choose a mini-program in balneotherapy, perhaps, which has you massaged in the tub—or on a table under a warm shower. Absolutely energizing. For those who don't care to get wet, Aqua Cité has conventional massage, lymphatic drainage treatment, and pressotherapy, to name a few services. Hands in bad shape? Feet hurt? Sign up for hand or foot care; you'll get a soothing massage, removal of dry skin, and a mineral pack and heat treatment. Oooh la la. Chill out in terry bathrobes on lounge chairs in the after-care room. Sip herbal tea, enjoy the calm, and drift gently away. After a short nap, every scintilla of stress has vanished. Now, isn't it time for lunch? Grab a cab and get ready to indulge.

LUNCH

Toi, Moi & Café (244 avenue Laurier Ouest; 514–279–9599, open 8:00 A.M. to 12:30 A.M. on weekends; inexpensive; lunch from $7.00) is designed for couples. Coffee is roasted on the premises, overnight, in the huge roasting device at the entrance. More than fifty varieties are offered from around the world and then brought to your copper-topped table in a two-cup French press. Waffles are specialties here and are served until 4:00 P.M. on the weekends. Topped with mountains of whipped cream, layered with banana, kiwi, and other fresh fruit, and drizzled with chocolate sauce, they are perfect for pampering your tastebuds while you listen to B. B. King, muted, on the stereo. Decadent.

Finish your afternoon shopping on avenue Laurier, one of the toniest streets in the city and the place where wealthy Québeçois enjoy dropping a few (or more) dollars at art galleries and clothing boutiques. You'll find Italian menswear at **Valérie Simon** (366 avenue Laurier Ouest; 514–272–0618); women's fashions at **Amelis** (1066 avenue Laurier Ouest; 514–277–2116); and, if you're looking to bring a gift to any little ones you left behind, children's clothing at **Jeunes d'ici** (220 avenue Laurier Ouest; 514–279–9129). Before you leave the neighborhood, stop for a visual experience at **Exotika** (400 avenue Laurier Ouest; 514–273–5015), a multilevel eatery/bar/club that proposes to take patrons on a "voyage" to Europe, Africa, and India. You'll find a cobblestone floor, sandstone walls, and a Mediterranean feel on the street level. A few paces away, in a space designed like an airport lounge, you can sip a cappuccino at the espresso bar and slip on headphones to sample snippets of an international selection of CDs. When you find the music that turns you on, share it with your partner. Maybe you'll discover a new group together.

If the earphones interfere with your intimate mood, you might want to check out the wall of magazines and head for the sofa with your selections. Linger here over your copy of *Paris Match*. What's the hurry? Stress is a word that's no longer part of your vocabulary. Float back to the inn when the spirit moves you.

DAY TWO: evening

DINNER

Dress for dinner, but keep the pace slow. You're heading for the south of France tonight at **Le Club Des Pins** (156 avenue Laurier Ouest; 514-272-9484; station Laurier; closed Sunday; moderate to expensive), where you'll be instantly transported to a Mediterranean setting by the cheery blue-and-yellow tablecloths, brightly colored plates, and stencils of fruit and fish on the wall. The restaurant is a neighborhood favorite and no doubt you two will be charmed by a robust French cooking style built around fresh vegetables, fish, and olive oil. Start with heavenly asparagus dressed with oil and basil, or try a mouth-watering terrine of cod and potatoes. For the main course, perhaps choose duck or lamb. The wine list here, by the way, is intriguing—and reasonably priced. Toast each other and bask in the sunny south. When the last morsel of the chocolate cake is gone from the plate, head back to the inn for your final night of amour.

FOR MORE ROMANCE

While you're on avenue Laurier in the afternoon, consider buying your love a flower (or two). Stroll over to the east side of Laurier, where you'll be charmed by the flowers, plants, and objets choisis (unusual gift items) at **Fleuriste Marie Vermette** (801 avenue Laurier Est; 514–272–2225). You're certain to leave with a package or a bouquet.

Pampering Yourselves the English Way

HEN BODIES AND MINDS desperately need pampering, you two will find everything to regain your balance in an English-speaking enclave radiating from Montréal's Fifth Avenue.

Rue Sherbrooke is where English-speaking Montréal cuts deals, does lunch, gets culture, sips tea, proposes toasts, and shops like crazy—and it's where your fun-loving escape will be based.

You'll find an international flavor in this elegant neighborhood today, since those British, Scottish, and Irish folks who left an enduring mark here have now been joined by other English-speakers from different parts of the world—and by French-speakers as well. But the British feel and the English language come through loud and clear in this part of town— directing you to forget your wordly cares and have a jolly good time!

PRACTICAL NOTES: This romantic getaway works better in the off-season, when the hotel offers promotional rates. Start your itinerary on Friday, when stores stay open late. And plan to stay for Sunday brunch, since the magnificent Mount Stephen Club is open to the public on that day alone.

DAY ONE: morning/afternoon

If indeed you arrive in a state of exhaustion, just drop your bags in the austere but elegant lobby of the **Hotel Omni Montréal** (1050 rue

Romance AT A GLANCE

◆ Stay at the **Hotel Omni Montréal** (1050 rue Sherbrooke Ouest; 514–284– 1110), where the concierge is accustomed to meeting absolutely any request—within legal bounds. After lunch in the hotel restaurant that fronts the street, visit the department store where British royalty loved to shop for fur. **Holt-Renfrew** (1300 rue Sherbrooke) was selected to make a mink coat for Queen Elizabeth II as Canada's wedding gift to the then princess.

◆ Swim in a rooftop pool at the hotel that stays open even when it's snowing, then schedule a massage in a low-lit room near the pool. After a morning devoted to fitness and relaxation, shop for a few hours on trendy Greene Avenue, capping the afternoon with high tea and scones at the **Ritz-Carlton** (1228 rue Sherbrooke Ouest; 514–842–4212).

◆ Make reservations for a very special brunch. The **Mount Stephen Club** (1440 rue Drummond; 514–849–7338), open to the public only on Sundays, is an architectural masterpiece built by Lord Mount Stephen in the 1880s. Today it's a historical site where you'll enjoy a sit-down brunch accompanied by classical music followed by a tour of the opulent former home. Weddings of the rich and famous often take place here.

Sherbrooke Ouest; 514–284–1110 or 800–228–3000; station Peel; $259 to $279 a night) and prepare yourselves for special attention. The concierge staff here can meet any demands—after all, staffers had to locate eighteen different kinds of spring water for Cher, who arrived with three pages of requests. And she's not the only one who merited special treatment. Céline Dion had her wedding reception here. Bette Midler and Rod Stewart slept here (but not together), as did Luciano Pavarotti, Elton John, Aretha Franklin, Michael Jackson, and Madonna. All of them received star treatment, and so will you. For instance, if there's a play you'd like to see tomorrow night at the **Centaur Theatre** or the **Saidye Bronfman Centre**—the English-language theaters in town—just ask. Tickets will be secured.

The Omni has 300 rooms spread over thirty-one floors. You'll request a corner deluxe room facing the mountain, perhaps No. 2602. It provides a panoramic view of prestigious McGill University and the rich gray stone buildings in the Golden Square Mile, where most of Canada's wealth was concentrated in the 1800s. The view of Mont-Royal is so tantalizing, you can almost touch it. Your king-size bed is separated from the cozy living room by a French door. If you can't check in to your room just yet—check-in time is generally 3:00 P.M.—then have your bags safely stowed at the front desk and unwind over lunch.

LUNCH

Eat on the street—well, almost. The Opus II dining room, at the edge of Sherbrooke and Peel, has a greenhouse aspect to maximize people-watching potential. Have a cocktail and watch the business-people scurry. Pity them. You're here to relax. Order from the Mediterranean-based menu. Your great escape begins.

After lunch, your escape route leads to a shopping excursion just three blocks west of the hotel. **Holt-Renfrew** (1300 rue Sherbrooke; 514–842–5111; open every day) was founded more than 150 years ago in Québec City under the name Henderson, Holt, and Renfrew Furriers. The store made its reputation by supplying fur to British royalty—and was selected to make a Labrador wild mink coat for Princess Elizabeth, (now Queen) as Canada's wedding gift to her. The Montréal outlet, an art deco building that opened in 1937, still prides itself on the fine furs sold in the Birger Christensen salon. Today, however, the store has expanded its repertoire and its reach, showcasing designer boutiques behind a series of restored gray stones to the west of the original building. Spread over four floors, you'll find Calvin Klein, Bottega Veneta, Chanel, Donna Karan, Giorgio Armani, and Holt-Renfrew's own private label for men and women. And while you're in a spending mood, why not stop by the Tiffany boutique in the store? It's a great spot to purchase a prized bauble to commemorate your trip.

Two blocks west of Holt-Renfrew, you'll find a statue of Jean d'Aire, Burgher of Calais. One of Montréal's most valuable sculptures, it's guarding the entrance to **Galerie Dominion** (1438 rue Sherbrooke Ouest; 514–845–7471; open Monday to Friday; 10:00 A.M. to 5:00 P.M.). Fashioned by Auguste Rodin in Paris, the statue sits outside a gallery known for its collection of bronzes. In business since 1941, Dominion Gallery initially carried only works by Canadians. Today, its four levels are filled with works from around the world—

and old masters share space with contemporary artists. Browse here for a look at what's new and old.

Men (and gift-giving women) love **Davidoff** (1452 rue Sherbrooke Ouest; 514–289–9118), which specializes in fine cigars and pipes, ties, wallets, and sunglasses. It even carries its own line of cologne. The store was founded by Zeno Davidoff of Geneva, and you're standing in the only Canadian outlet. Nearby you'll find **La Galleria** (1486 rue Sherbrooke Ouest; 514–932–7585), which carries an impressive collection of museum-quality pre-Columbian art as well as bronzes and ceramics from Southeast Aisia that date back to the Tang dynasty over 1,000 years ago. A few prized pieces sat in the emperor's summer palace in China and were brought to Montréal in the 1800s. Here is beauty, history, and antiquity in one shot.

Speaking of antiquity: It fills every inch of the **Le Petit Musée** (1494 rue Sherbrooke Ouest; 514–937–6161), a graceful and gorgeous antiques shop that looks more like a museum. Fine English porcelain is beautifully displayed and is just one of the reasons that lovers of antiquity come from around the world to scan the four floors filled with more than 10,000 items. End your shopping spree at **Cartier** (1498 rue Sherbrooke Ouest; 514–939–0000). If you haven't been seduced by the ancient artifacts on previous stops, you'll surely be seduced by the modern pieces here.

Take those packages back to the hotel now, gazing at the heritage homes, apartments, and churches as you stroll. Scottish immigrants-turned-entrepreneurs settled near the mountain nearly 200 years ago, building imposing mansions on sprawling estates. Plaques outside some of the structures along rue Sherbrooke explain the history. Take your time walking to the Omni. Once you get there, stay put: the Omni just happens to house one of the finest restaurants in town. First, however, pamper your street-weary feet. A swim in the heated pool up on the roof before dinner will soothe your heels and ankles as well as your hearts and souls. Even if it's snowing, you won't shiver. Promise.

DAY ONE: evening

DINNER

Long before Great Britain relinquished control of Hong Kong to the Chinese in 1997, many of Hong Kong's residents had already decided to leave that island city for this one. Thousands of Chinese raised under English rule emigrated to Montréal, including many who entered the restaurant business and brought a new awareness of Asian dining to the city. With its minimalist decor, **Zen** (lower lobby, Omni; 514–499–0801; moderate) is without a doubt the most adventurous dining experience in town when it comes to representing foods from the Pacific Rim. The Zen Experience is an all-you-can-eat array of more than forty dishes, wild and tame, selected by Zen chefs in London, Hong Kong, and Montréal. Choose as many as you'd like. They'll be brought to your table by efficient staff, in any order requested. Start with sweet corn soup with chicken. How about two appetizers each? Cuttlefish cakes and steamed dim sum, perhaps. Your main course might be crispy, aromatic duck served with a crepe or ravioli Hunan with peanut sauce. How about a side dish of sautéed noodles and bean sprouts? That's what I'd choose—now you two discover your own delights.

Such Suite-ness

Singer Céline Dion held her wedding reception at the Omni a few days before Christmas in 1994 and spent her honeymoon in its suite on the thirtieth floor. The bath, as big as a bedroom, features a marble tub overlooking the mountain, matching double sinks, a Persian throw rug on the marble floor, and a toilet enclosed by frosted glass. You can stay here, too— for a mere $1,499 a night.

Head for your suite after dinner. From your living room, watch the city at night and the hulking mountain that faces your window. Admire your purchases. Admire each other.

DAY TWO: morning

BREAKFAST

Devote your day to restoring the body as well as the mind. To that end, why not enjoy breakfast while you're resting and relaxing in bed? At the hour you specified on a tag you attached to the doorknob last night, a waiter will knock and announce that breakfast has arrived. Cereal, muffins, juice, fresh fruit, and coffee or tea (for $12 per person) will be wheeled up to the bedside to help you face the day gently.

After breakfast, take advantage of one of the hotel's best features. Gymtech in the Omni might be the finest health club in any Montréal hotel, and its services (except for massage) are included in your room rate. Workout clothes are provided in case you don't have any with you. You'll find free weights, Keiser machines, bikes, Stairmaster, and treadmills. Classes are given in aerobics, yoga, and toning. (Get the schedule in advance of your stay so you can plan accordingly.) You may have already discovered the heated outdoor lap pool on the roof. Now discover the massage rooms tucked away near the locker-rooms. Book a relaxing massage in a low-lit environment, and let the tensions melt. After the massage, a steam room and showers beckon. Pure bliss.

After your workout, return to your room and dress for a casual afternoon of strolling west as you dig deeper into the English roots of Montréal. When you exit the hotel, turn left and walk along rue Sherbrooke about a mile until you reach avenue Greene. The English equivalent of avenue Laurier (on the French side of town) is a charming brick-paved lane lined on both sides with boutiques, antiques shops, galleries, bookstores, and restaurants. Here's where you'll pause for lunch and spend most of the afternoon shopping.

DAY TWO: afternoon

LUNCH

Bistro On The Avenue (1362 avenue Greene; 514–939–6451; inexpensive) is a cozy spot to see-and-be-seen—and a good perch to catch the action on Greene, where the shops attract luminaries like Mila Mulroney, wife of Canada's former prime minister, Brian Mulroney. Specials at the Bistro change every day, but be assured that pasta, fresh fish, and an array of salads will be on the menu whenever you arrive.

Energy renewed after lunch, you're now eager to explore both sides of the avenue. Don't miss **Galerie Kastel** (1368 avenue Greene; 514–933–8735), noted for its fine collection of Canadian paintings and sculpture. Beautiful gift items, housewares, and women's wear can be found in **La Cache** (1353 avenue Greene; 514–935–4361), founded by a Montréaler who now has opened outlets stretching from Prince Edward Island to British Columbia. Climb a flight of stairs to browse in **Double Hook Book Shop** (1235A avenue Greene; 514–932–5093), dedicated to Canadian books only.

Behind avenue Greene, you can't miss a hulking, black metal building with trademark tinted glass. Architect Ludwig Mies van der Rohe, head of the Bauhaus movement in Germany, designed **Westmount Square** (514–932–0211) in 1964. It contains offices, apartments, and a small, exclusive shopping arcade. In the arcade, you'll find **Sergio L'Uomo** for men and **Lily Simon** for women. At **Ma Maison**, you'll see and covet everything you ever wanted to buy for your table. You'll also find an **SAQ Classique**, which sells fine wine. Pick up a bottle to take back to your suite so you can create your own cocktail hour this evening. At **Le Marché Westmount Square**, pick up some cheese, a baguette, and a few pieces of what some swear is the best sushi in town—to enhance your enjoyment of the wine, of course. Before your thoughts turn to the design of your evening, however, it's high time to make time for high tea.

AFTERNOON TEA

Grab a cab to the **Ritz-Carlton Hotel** (1228 rue Sherbrooke Ouest; 514–842–4212), where the ladies once wore white gloves and hats. Some still do, especially for afternoon tea (served from 3:30 to 5:00 P.M.; $14.95). Out comes the silver service as the vaunted English ritual unfolds. Select from more than fifteen types of tea —accompanied, of course, by a multitiered tray filled with cucumber, egg salad, and smoked salmon sandwiches, and with petit fours and scones served with Devonshire cream. In summer, tea is served in the outdoor Ritz garden. In colder weather, it moves to the Palm Court, where you'll cozy up and enjoy your steaming cup near the fireplace.

Stroll back after teatime to your hotel, where the concierge informs you that you do, indeed, have tickets for a play tonight. Relax in your room for an hour or so before getting dressed for the evening. Savor your seclusion in whatever way you choose, remembering to open the wine and enjoy the treats you bought earlier at the market. They'll tide you over until you return from the theater. When you have gussied yourselves up in theater clothes, head out into the evening. Enjoy the show.

DAY TWO: evening

When the final curtain falls, it's probably about 10:00 P.M., and the theater crowd is streaming out into the street. You loved the play—and now you're in the mood to play around. The English side of town has an equivalent to rue St-Denis (on the French side) when it comes to nightlife. It's called rue Crescent. Take a cab to a pub where you'll eat, drink, and be merry.

DINNER

Sir Winston Churchill Pub (1459 rue Crescent; 514–288–0616; inexpensive to moderate) has been offering food, drink, and a good time from the same location for roughly thirty years. In summer, you'll find the outdoor terrasse jammed, so you might want to call ahead for a reservation. In colder weather, the action moves inside to the comfortable pub, where you'd be wise to secure a booth for dinner. Menu selections are wide and varied —from burgers to pepper steak—and the chef here specializes in Cajun dishes, so you won't go wrong with blackened fish or chicken. If you're not interested in a full meal at this time of night, you might consider a salad—or you might want to share a main course.

After dinner, move upstairs to the tiny dance floor, where the disco-style music doesn't stop until 3:00 A.M. I'll say toodle-oo here and now.

DAY THREE: morning

BRUNCH

You returned to the hotel in the wee hours, so you're luxuriating in bed this morning. When you finally awaken, pack your bags, and get ready to see how the wealthy lived a century ago. Leave your luggage with the bellman. You're bound for the **Mount Stephen Club** (1440 rue Drummond; 514–849–7338; open to the public Sundays only, between 11:00 A.M. and 1:30 P.M.; reservations required; $25), where you'll have brunch in a magnificent Renaissance-style mansion built in the 1880s by Lord Mount Stephen—who began life humbly enough as George Stephen of Stephen Croft, Scotland, and who lived, as luck would have it, around the corner from your hotel.

Walk to the mansion, which craftsmen from Europe spent three years constructing for Stephen, who was president of the Canadian Pacific Railway and the Bank of Montréal. Exotic woods from Cuba and Ceylon were used in the interior. The staircase alone will take your breath away. The home was declared a historic site by the Canadian government in 1920 and then bought as a private club. Members recently opened it to the public on Sundays only for a sit-down brunch, accompanied by live music from a chamber orchestra or perhaps a jazz ensemble; the music changes weekly, but it's always refined.

After you dine on a bounty of hot and cold selections, you'll be given a tour of the premises and a behind-the-scenes peek at Scottish opulence. Note the antique clock in the main lounge—which used to be the greenhouse. Made of wood from Cuba, the clock still keeps the hour. Also in fine working order is the grand piano, made of wood from Ceylon. In the second-floor bedroom, each of the stained-glass windows represents a scene from a Shakespearean play. There's even stained glass in the men's bathroom on the second floor.

After your tour, bid farewell to the English side of town. As you leave Lord Stephen's mansion, gaze up at the message above the entrance. It was penned by the Bard: "True friendship's laws are by this rule expressed/ Welcome the coming, speed the parting guest."

FOR MORE ROMANCE

Stash some sweetness in your luggage before you dash off. You'll be drawn like a magnet to the truffles at **Divine Chocolatier** (1454 rue Drummond; 514–282–0829), named the best maker of chocolate truffles in the Montréal region by the *Gazette* newspaper in 1999. Divine offers four kinds of truffles: classic, dark chocolage, or flavored with lemon, peanut butter, or champagne. It's hard to choose, so try them all! (And bring some back home.)

Day Tripping

⊙riental Air

CHINATOWN AND THE CHINESE GARDEN

ONTRÉAL'S CHINATOWN MAY BE SHRINKING in population, but it nevertheless symbolizes the durability of a community that planted roots in Canada in the late 1800s. Chinese workers arrived in the West at that time to help build the Transcontinental Railway, and they later migrated east in search of opportunity in Montréal, then Canada's largest city. Only about 400 Chinese people live in Chinatown today, a sliver of the 85,000-plus Chinese scattered around Montréal and its suburbs. Even so, many Chinese return to Chinatown to dine, to shop, and to reconnect with their past.

You and your companion can connect—or reconnect, as the case may be—with your gentler, spiritual nature on an East-meets-West itinerary filled with beauty and serenity. You'll feel peaceful, harmonious—and full of love.

PRACTICAL NOTES: Although a romantic destination year-round, the Chinese Garden takes on an uncommonly lush aspect during La Magie des Lanternes, the Chinese Lantern Festival, held for seven weeks every autumn. More than 700 lanterns from Shanghai are strung around the Garden and create an exquisite scene as evening falls. A life-size dragon—actually a lantern—floats on Dream Lake. Monkeys, dogs, tigers, and pigs—all lanterns crafted of silk—pop up around the pavilions to surprise, enchant, and light up the night. If possible, time your visit to coincide with this unforgettable event.

The East-meets-West brunch at Chez Chine is held on Sunday only. If you want to do this itinerary on another day, go to Chez

$\mathcal{R}$**omance**
AT A GLANCE

◆ Begin your exploration of the city's Asian roots in **Chinatown**, where you'll pass under a ceremonial archway crafted by local artists, taste the work of a dragon candy-maker, visit a traditional Chinese herbalist, and spend a few contemplative moments in **Dr. Sun Yat Sen Park** surrounded by symbols of peace and harmony.

◆ Admire a rainbow of exotic fish swirling in a miniature lake as you're escorted to your table at restaurant **Chez Chine (99 avenue Viger Ouest; 514–878–9888)**, where you'll dine on dim sum and other oriental treats at an East-meets-West brunch.

◆ Spend the afternoon in true tranquility at the largest Chinese Garden outside Asia (4101 rue Sherbrooke Est; 514–872–1400), where you'll explore seven pavilions surrounding a man-made lake, then stroll over to the **Japanese Garden** to catch a spectacular display of bonsai trees and a traditional tea ceremony. Finish your Oriental exploration with a taste of Japan— dine at the very minimalist **Sushi Maki (1240 rue Crescent; 514–861–2050)**.

Chine for lunch instead, where you'll find a similar, though not as elaborate, blend of East and West on the menu.

DAY ONE: morning

Rue de la Gauchetière, between boulevard St-Laurent and rue Jeanne-Mance, is the heart of Chinatown (station Place d'Armes). Before the Chinese claimed the area in the 1920s, it was home to a number of ethnic groups. Today, newcomers from Vietnam, Korea, Laos, and Cambodia have contributed to the oriental flair, as you can see in the restaurants and grocery stores.

The street was redesigned as an outdoor pedestrian-only mall in the 1980s. Two ceremonial archways crafted by local artists and architects mark the passageway. In the brick pathway between the arches, six inset bronze medallions are inscribed with dragons—traditional Chinese symbols of life, fortune, and strength.

Visit food stores, craft shops, and traditional Chinese herbalists along rue de la Gauchetière, and on district side streets like rue Clark, rue St-Urbain, and boulevard St-Laurent. When you're finished browsing, wander into Dr. Sun Yat Sen Park (at the corner of de la Gauchetière and Clark), named after the father and first provisional president of the Republic of China (Taiwan). There are no swings or slides here, just benches and a mound of rocks—symbols of peace and harmony to the Chinese. The park is a perfect place to people-watch before brunch.

BRUNCH

Elegant **Chez Chine** (99 avenue Viger Ouest; 514–878–9888; moderate) serves an East-meets-West buffet on Sundays from 11:30 A.M. to 2:30 P.M. The restaurant is housed in the **Hotel Jardin Sinomonde**, a real blend of East and West. Jardin Sinomonde is actually a thematic Holiday Inn topped by twin pagodas and adorned with calligraphy created by the brother of the last emperor of China. The restaurant inside this unusual Holiday Inn is designed as a serene Chinese garden, with exotic fish darting under a network of bridges positioned over a miniature lake. The menu is also a blend—half continental, half oriental. At Chez Chine, you'll sample duck, pork, rice, and dim sum (small dumplings filled with meat, fish, or vegetables), but you can also partake of pasta, potatoes, beef, and fish as well.

Dim sum is the perfect food for lovers. It means "delight of the heart."

DAY ONE: afternoon

An oriental air permeates the **Botanical Garden** (4101 rue Sherbrooke Est; 514–872–1400; station Pie IX; open 9:00 A.M. to 9:00 P.M.; $8.75 admission), where upon entry you'll receive a map of the 180-acre spread. You're now at the second-largest garden of its type in the world (the biggest is in London), and a red mini-tram, or *balade*, shuttles you, free of charge, to the various venues. Your first stop is within easy walking distance of the gate: the Exhibition Greenhouses.

Head for the third greenhouse in a string of ten. It houses the orchids. You'll learn, as you enter the tropical setting, that there are nearly 30,000 species of orchid worldwide—even in the chilly clime of Québec, forty-eight types of orchid grow. The majority of orchids are epiphytic, which means they grow on other plants solely as a mean of support. Imbibe the fragrance and color, then head back to the tram. There's more to follow.

Take the tram shuttle to the Japanese Garden and Pavilion, where exhibits range from calligraphy and decorative pottery to home furnishings and the art of tsutsumu—which means wrapping packages with refinement. Japanese bonsai are exhibited here in the summer.

An hour or so before sunset, make your way to the Chinese Garden. Created in China—and built here by Chinese workers—the Montréal-Shanghai Friendship Garden, as it is formally called, is the largest such attraction outside Asia. The six-acre garden became an instant smash when it opened in 1991. Linked by winding pathways and set around a lake, seven pavilions provide varying vistas and quiet sanctuary. When it's all aglow for the Chinese Lantern Festival, the garden is particularly stunning.

DAY ONE: evening

In keeping with the theme, you'll want to end the day in a minimalist fashion.

DINNER

Sushi Maki (1240 rue Crescent; 514–861–2050; open every day; moderate) provides a simple menu that is simply delicious: sushi and sashimi prepared just as you would eat it in Japan. A little gem, Sushi Maki is frequented by locals who appreciate the minimalist approach. It's the perfect place to end your oriental outing.

FOR MORE ROMANCE

If time permits at the Botanical Garden, stroll in the Arboretum, where traffic is light. You'll walk in near seclusion amid blue spruce and long-needled pine, insulated from the sounds of the city. Steal a kiss in virtual privacy. Because the Arboretum features so many varieties of evergreen, it is beautiful to behold any time of year.

Taste of Québec
A Sampler

WHERE DO QUÉBEÇOIS LIVE, EAT, WORK, SHOP, PRAY— and play? Take the pulse of the city on this sampler. Discover people, places, and things typically French-Canadian—all in one day. A romantic carriage ride in Old Montréal starts your outing. Snuggle close. The ride sets the tone for other intimate encounters. Time-travel through centuries guided by French-Canadian artisans, designers, chefs, and musicians. Delight in aspects old and new, spiritual and worldly, physical and emotional, and as you do, delight in each other.

PRACTICAL NOTES: Although this itinerary is workable any time of year, make sure to phone ahead if you'd like an appointment in a particular design studio.

DAY ONE: morning

Grab breakfast at home or at your hotel so you are ready to roll, literally, through the cobblestone streets of Old Montréal. Take the métro to Champs de Mars and commission a horse-drawn carriage on Place Jacques-Cartier between rue de la Commune and rue Notre-Dame. Winter or summer, *calèche* drivers squire visitors around the Old Quarter, providing blankets when it's cold. As the horses clip-clop, you'll see some of the oldest and grandest structures in the city.

Notre-Dame Basilica was built in the 1820s by a Protestant architect who converted to Catholicism during the project. The revered church is favored by prominent Québecers as the site of

♦ Take a horse-drawn carriage through the cobblestone streets of **Old Montréal** as you begin a day devoted to people, places, and things uniquely Québeçois.

♦ *Debark from your carriage at the exact spot where the city was founded in 1642, at the edge of* the St-Lawrence River, and begin your voyage of discovery at *Pointe-à-Callières museum (350 Place Royale; 514–872–9150).*

♦ *Shop in the ateliers of Québec's top designers and artisans along trendy* **rue St-Denis**, *where you'll find unusual clothing and jewelry to bring home as gifts—or keep for yourself!*

♦ *Lunch on traditional Québec tourtière and feve aux lards at* **La Binerie Mont-Royal** *(367 avenue Mont-Royal Est; 514–285–9078), a family-owned restaurant in operation for almost 50 years. Then spend the afternoon touring Montréal's most famous neighborhood,* **the Plateau**, *where you'll be enchanted by the trademark corkscrew staircases on turn-of-the-century homes.*

grand weddings—and grand funerals. Bonsecours Market, with its tapered cupola, only recently resumed its original function as a public market. It was once City Hall. Pointe-à-Callières is an archaeology and history museum built on the very spot where the city was founded in 1642. Debark here to see the St-Lawrence River and the longest street of row houses in North America along rue de la Commune.

You won't tour the museum at **Pointe-à-Callières** (350 Place Royale; 514–872–9150; closed Monday), but do visit the museum boutique. It's a good place to pick up Québec maple products. Québec produces 75 percent of the world's maple syrup, and French-Canadians make a ritual out of springtime sap-gathering even today. Choose the Héritage Yamaska brand of syrup for its innovative packaging—a bottle of syrup comes in a braided Native-style pouch.

Don't leave Old Montréal without detouring a few blocks west on rue de la Commune and stopping at **Vermeil** (90 rue Prince; 514–878–9302; open every day from 9:00 A.M.; call in advance to make sure you'll see artists at work). Glass artisans Luc Taillon and Mario Paré make utilitarian objects as well as decorative and delicate pieces.

If you are interested in visiting **Lili-les-Bains**, designer Louise Daoust's bathing suit and resortwear workshop and boutique, do it now because it's not far (see the sidebar on designers in this chapter).

Otherwise, retrace your steps to the métro and take it to station Mont-Royal. Walk west on avenue Mont-Royal. It's time for lunch.

DAY ONE: afternoon

LUNCH

Traditional French-Canadian food is rarely served at restaurants in favor of more sophisticated French fare. But you can taste dishes that are still served in French-Canadian homes—authentic dishes that once helped very large families get through very long winters (not to mention meatless Fridays)—at **La Binerie Mont-Royal** (367 avenue Mont-Royal Est; 514–285–9078; inexpensive), a family-owned business operating from the same hole-in-the-wall locale since 1940. I went to the tidy little eatery with a woman whose mother sent her there every Friday when she was a kid to get a carton of baked beans for those meatless nights in Catholic households. Needless to say, baked beans (*feves au lard*) are still on the menu. So is yellow pea soup (*soupe aux pois*), meat pie (*tourtière*), and unemployment pudding (*pouding chomeur*), a cake soaked in a brown sugar sauce that dates from the Depression. Best-selling French-Canadian author Yves Beauchemin used La Binerie as a source of inspiration for his book *Le Matou*. The food is good, and so is the service. A main course with soup, beverage, and dessert will set you back less than $8.00.

Now it's time for a stroll along a residential street in the Plateau, a neighborhood that is very French, very working class, and very charming. Rows of triplexes that seem never-ending are distinguished by outdoor staircases that saved space for big families in days gone by. Take a right on rue St-Hubert, where houses were built in the late 1800s for the upper middle class, including Montréal mayor Camilien Houde. Notice the signs of wealth: balconies, elaborate cornices, stained-glass panels in the windows. Continue walking until you hit rue Rachel. Turn right and continue east to rue St-Denis.

A former residential street for the wealthy, rue St-Denis is now the trendiest street in the city, day and night. Here you'll find some of Québec's top clothing and jewelry designers, who have both their workshops and stores in the same place. Pick and choose from the

Be Original

What are the best places to shop for designer clothing in Montréal? A designer provided her private list of the best Québec designers in town:

Women's wear:

✳ Lili-les-Bains (1336 rue Notre-Dame Ouest; 514–937–9197): Designer Louise Daoust crafts bathing suits and resortwear for all sizes but works special magic for large-busted and large-sized women.

✳ Muse (4467 rue St-Denis; 514–848–9493): Christian Chenail designs beautiful jackets, skirts, and pants in this funky art deco shop.

✳ Hélène Barbeau (3416 avenue Du Parc; 514–849–4010). Petite women, particularly, will love the soft and fluid dresses.

✳ Marie Saint-Pierre Boutique (2081 avenue de la Montagne; 514–281–5547): Are you searching for the right outfit for a very special occasion? Formalwear is Marie Saint-Pierre's domain.

Men's wear:

✳ Dubuc: Mode de Vie Inc (4451 rue St-Denis; 514–282–1424; boutique 514–282–1465): Designer Phillippe Dubuc creates very trendy clothing for up-and-coming businessmen.

Hats:

✳ Le Sieur Duluth (4107 rue St-Denis; 514–843–8933): Berets, rain hats, and other chapeaux designed by twenty Montréal artisans are here.

✳ Chapofolie (3944 rue St-Denis; 514–982–0036): Local designers display hats and other fashion accessories in this boutique.

Jewelry:

✳ Kamikaze (4156 rue St-Denis; 514–848–0728): Unforgettable jewelry. Wild and crazy designs from Montréal artists (and a few from Toronto). In the evening, believe it or not, the jewelry store transforms into a bar. Le Passeport is open every night for dancing from 10:00 P.M.

✳ Kyoze Boutique (1455 rue Peel in Les Cours Mont-Royal; 514–849–6552; plus two stores in the World Trade Centre at 393 rue St-Jacques Ouest; 514–847–7572): Carrying original designs from Québec and Canadian artisans, Kyoze (a play on the French term for "those who dare") carries both jewelry and clothing at its three locations.

list of designers in the "Be Original" sidebar. Not all of them are located on St-Denis, but those that aren't are close by. Maybe you'll leave Montréal with a made-to-measure outfit or an off-the-rack hat. I'll leave it up to you. Shop until dinner.

DAY ONE: evening

DINNER

You'll travel from one extreme of French-Canadian cuisine to the other when you dine at **Toqué!** (3842 rue St-Denis; 514–499–2084; reservations required; expensive), where chef Normand Laprise is reinventing French-Canadian cuisine by glorifying regional products and giving them a new spin. The name of the restaurant means "nuts"—as in crazy, which can refer to the food—completely original in both taste and form—or the chef. Laprise insists that you not call his food French. It is Québeçois, he says. It is also wonderful. Salmon tartare served with avocado purée. A main course of fois gras, pheasant, or tender venison. A decadent chocolate dessert. Some critics say this is the best restaurant in town. What a way to end the day—almost.

After dinner you'll finish your adventure where it all began—in Old Montréal. Remember Woodstock? Remember the musical happenings of the late 1960s and early 1970s? Québec throws a musical happening every weekend at **Aux Deux Pierrots** (104 rue St-Paul; 514–861–1270), where up to 800 people dance and groove every Friday and Saturday night to a mix of French-Canadian songs and contemporary music from artists like U2. Has it been a while since you've seen hundreds of folks clapping hands to the beat—or dancing on tables? Don't wait any longer. Let loose and start dancing—table dancing is optional.

FOR MORE ROMANCE

Montréal's development as a commercial center began with the fur trade. Montréal's fur district includes not only shops but factories and is concentrated in an area bounded by rue City Councillors, rue Ste-Catherine, boulevard de Maisonneuve, and rue de Bleury. At **Fourrures Bourkas** (429 rue Mayor; 514–849–4294), you'll find Canadian-made furs at manufacturer prices. **Fourrures Naturelles** (400 avenue de Maisonneuve Ouest; 514–842–9005) is one of Canada's oldest makers of fine quality furs. You'll find both classic and contemporary styles.

King and his Queen
The Castle in St-Antoine

ROLE-PLAY ON A GRAND SCALE WHEN YOU DINE in a castle so sumptuous you'll feel like Napoleon and Josephine. Red-carpeted stairs lead to a castle where secret rendezvous are held with regularity and utmost discretion—romantic and otherwise. Here Bill Clinton dined, surreptitiously, with members of the Canadian military before his inauguration as president in 1992. His entourage landed their helicopter in a nearby church parking lot.

Your royal dinner won't be quite as hush-hush, but it will be every bit as grand. So will the prelude to this momentous occasion. The build-up is almost as enticing as the main event. And why not?

Let me tease you gently now as you prepare to dine in St-Antoine-sur-Richelieu, commonly known as St-Antoine, birthplace of Georges-Etienne Cartier, onetime prime minister of Canada. It was Sir Georges-Etienne Cartier's younger cousin, Louis-Joseph, who built the combination Moorish-Victorian castle where you'll be King and Queen for a night.

PRACTICAL NOTES: Save your pennies—and dollars—for this itinerary. The *menu gourmand du patron*, suggested by the chef, is $105 per person without wine, tax, or tip. The least costly bottle of wine here is $35. For most people, that price constitutes a splurge—which makes the Château St-Antoine a perfect choice for a special wedding anniversary or birthday.

Although the Château is open year-round Tuesday through Saturday, this itinerary works best from April to November, when the ferry operates and when walking is a joy. I've included a lovely B&B in St-Denis as a possible resting spot if you don't feel like driving

Romance AT A GLANCE

◆ Venture to the tiny village of St-Denis, where you'll retrace the only battle won by the French patriots who rebelled against British rule in 1837. Learn about the turbulent history of Québec's patriots at **La Maison nationale des Patriotes** (610 chemin des Patriotes; 450–787–3623) and see the church steeple where the liberty bell that called the patriots to arms is stored.

◆ Take a miniature ferry ride across the Richelieu River from St-Denis to St-Antoine-sur-Richelieu—a four-minute trip—and debark near a cemetery where the history of the village is virtually written on the tombstones. Former residents of St-Antoine-sur-Richelieu include Sir Georges-Étienne Cartier, one of Canada's founding fathers.

◆ Walk up a red carpet—and into the majesty of **Le Champagne** (1000 rue du Rivage; 450–787–2966), a restaurant set in an authentic Moorish castle built by Georges-Etienne's cousin, Louis-Joseph Cartier. Chef Yves Raymond and his wife Nicole own the castle now, and serve in elegant style at only nine tables, each in a different room. Canada's rich and famous flock here to enjoy outrageous food and drink in total discretion; Canadian military officials brought Bill Clinton here before his inauguration in 1992. He probably hasn't forgotten the place; nor will you.

back to Montréal after dinner at the castle. Of course, you'll have to make that decision in advance so you can book a room at Auberge St-Denis-sur-Richelieu on the river's edge.

DAY ONE: afternoon

Leave Montréal after brunch or lunch, wearing clothing that will be appropriate for dinner in a very nice restaurant. You'll want to wear comfortable shoes for the first part of the itinerary—and take along a nicer pair for your dinner date. To begin the half-hour trip, cross the St-Lawrence River via the Jacques-Cartier Bridge. Follow signs for Québec (132 Est/20 Est). On 20 Est, exit just after the bridge on the Richelieu River (133). Turn right on 133 Nord, and, if you're staying overnight, drop your bags at **Auberge St-Denis-sur-Richelieu** (603 chemin des Patriotes, St-Denis; 450–787–4078 or 800–789–5819; $75 to $95), a precious B&B in a refurbished home overlooking the Richelieu River.

Begin your exploration of the history of the town at **La Maison nationale des Patriotes** (610 chemin des Patriotes; 450–787–3623), an interpretation center housed in a private home built by Jean-Baptiste Masse in 1809. Here you'll learn about the turbulent history of Québec's patriots, who rebelled against English rule in the 1830s. Follow a pedestrian path that begins at Place du Bourg near the old church, leads to the **Cherrier House**, the oldest building in town, and ends at the battlefield where the Patriots were victorious.

A must-see spot is the **Église St-Denis** (450–787–3229 or 450–787–3623), built between 1792 and 1796. Although the facade was reconstructed in 1922, it still houses wood sculpture of great beauty. The church opens for tourists between 1:00 and 6:00 P.M. on weekends and asks that you donate $1.00 Off-hour visits must be specially arranged, and the price of entry will then be a minimum of $10.00.

She floats upon the river of his thoughts.
—Henry Wadsworth Longfellow

Continue exploring St-Denis, this time keeping art and artifacts in mind. Keep an eye out along chemin des Patriotes and Yamaska for a variety of shops specializing in antiques. Shop as long as you please, but allow yourself at least an hour before your dinner reservation to cross the river and explore St-Antoine in daylight. When you're ready, use the ferry to cross the Richelieu River. For $3.00, you'll get a four-minute trip on a ferry that can squeeze only four cars aboard. Once you have parked the car on the boat, get out and stand on the ferry to gaze back at the church steeple in St-Denis. The boat operates just six months a year. When the weather turns frigid and the river freezes over, commuters actually drive across an ice bridge to the other side, avoiding a 40-kilometer (25-mile) detour through the town of Sorel.

Turn left from the dock, and within a minute you'll find the **Château Saint-Antoine** and its restaurant **Le Champagne** (1000 rue du Rivage, St-Antoine-sur-Richelieu; 450–787–2966; open Tuesday through Saturday only for dinner and only with reservations; expensive). Louis-Joseph Cartier, who built the Château, was mayor of St-Antoine for nine years and ran a bustling import-export business that made him wealthy. He built his twenty-five room home in 1897 (there are twenty-seven rooms today) when he was almost fifty years old. Architect Kasimir St-Jean gave the house its exotic Moorish exterior. All the wood in the house is fir from British Columbia; the granite block foundation came from Mont-St-Hilaire and Mont-St-Bruno and was conveyed by river. The exterior walls are six bricks thick.

It took current owners Nicole and Yves Raymond three years to restore the castle after they purchased it in 1988. The townspeople were so attached to the place, some actually returned to the Raymonds photos or artifacts they knew belonged in the mansion. Even Cartier's descendants contributed to the restoration effort.

Before you enter the mansion, explore St-Antoine a bit. Artists, agricultureal producers, and antiquarians gather here each weekend to show off their wares. To get to know the village, begin with a visit to the graveyard behind the church. The history of this town (population 1,576) is virtually written on the tombstones. Sir Georges-Etienne Cartier is not buried here (he's on top of Mont-Royal), but there is a statue here to honor him. Next, take a walk along du Rivage Street and see the architecture of times gone by—architecture that is far different from the exotic castle you're about to enter.

DAY ONE: evening

DINNER

Sunset at the Château Saint-Antoine is magic. The floral gardens are glorious as you walk up the path to the house. Nicole Raymond, dressed discreetly in a black

Just Like Old Times

Waiter and greeter Gilbert de la Cathédrale says the most romantic event held in the Castle was a twenty-fifth wedding anniversary party where everyone dressed in eighteenth-century attire—even the waiters. Two footmen in white wigs greeted the guests, who were then invited to sip cocktails on the verandah. As evening fell, the twenty guests entered the Castle, which was lit only with candles and oil lamps lent for the occasion by the heirs of Cartier. The guests sat at one long table laden with flowers—a waiter behind each place setting ready to meet any need. Recalls de la Cathédrale: "It was like a painting."

suit, greets you warmly at the door. The railing on the wooden staircase ahead of you bears a carved C—whether that's for Cartier or Château is an unknown detail. The massive skylight on the second floor is original. The owners live on the second floor, which means most of the rooms on that level are closed to the public, but you can still explore the balcony—and look at the portrait of Cartier and his family that hangs there. Only nine dining tables are in the castle. Devoted patrons like to try them all.

To my mind, the most romantic one is the solo table in Le Salon Régence, originally Cartier's office. Only you two can fit in this little alcove. You can admire the original wood shutters in the office, ooh-and-aah over the fireplace that has been restored, sit on Louis XV chairs that are replicas of the originals, and gaze in each other's eyes in amazement at your surroundings.

Lace tablecloths showcase Christofle silver and porcelain rimmed in twenty-two-carat gold. Candles light every table, and fresh flower arrangements abound. Yves Raymond, who ran a restaurant on Bishop Street in Montréal for nine years, is such a stickler for fresh food he doesn't even have a freezer in the kitchen. He shops daily and draws heavily from a vegetable and herb garden behind the castle.

In this restaurant, you are never rushed. It's not the type of place where people hurry through dinner to get to the theater—though the meal itself unfolds just like a play. A waiter in white gloves brings your champagne (what else at a restaurant called Le Champagne?) and a loaf of olive bread. From there, your choice is fish, meat, or fowl—with a heavy emphasis on fish. Clam soup, fresh lobster with asparagus points, fresh tuna marinated in olive oil—that's just the prelude. Rack of lamb with thyme or Barberry duck comes next. As the wine in the glass decanter at your table disappears, you'll feel as if you rule the world.

For More Romance

Anything else pales next to what you've just experienced. Return home (or to the Auberge) and recall the memories again and again.

Down by the Old Mill Stream

OLD TERREBONNE

HISTORY TAKES A ROMANTIC TURN in Old Terrebonne, where old stone mills that once ground flour for biscuits have been given new life in our modern world while retaining their original beauty.

In Old Terrebonne you'll discover deep French roots but also a Scottish limb on the tree—the fur traders who helped build the town. Washington Irving drew inspiration for a novel about the fur trade here. Today, his books can be found in a modern public library housed in an old sawmill perched above a rushing river.

Old Terrebonne holds well-preserved treasure that is little explored even by Québecers. Make it your private world for an afternoon and evening.

PRACTICAL NOTES: Although you may drive a car, a car is not required for this itinerary since you can reach Old Terrebonne by métro and bus. Once there, you'll be glad if you've planned this itinerary in strolling season: May through October. Activities on Île-des-Moulins, such as guided tours and concerts, run from June 24 to September 1. Call to inquire about weekend programs (450–471–0619). For a map of notable homes, schools, and churches in the *quartier*, request the Circuit Touristique des Moulins from Tourisme Lanaudière (450–834–2535)—also available at City Hall (775 rue St-Jean-Baptiste; 450–471–4192) during the week.

♦ See where Washington Irving drew inspiration for his 1836 fur trade novel, *Astoria,* when you spend the day in **Old Terrebonne,** where nineteenth-century sawmills and flour mills have been beautifully preserved.

♦ While touring Île-des-Moulins (Island of Mills), pause to sit on a park bench and gaze at a floating statue entitled *La Dame Blanche; according to legend, she's desperately searching for her lover. Rent a bicycle and explore the narrow streets of Old Terrebonne, passing heritage homes, many of which now hold stores and restaurants.*

♦ *Cap the day by feasting on rack of lamb or sweetbreads with scampi in a private home dating back to 1760. At* **Le Folichon** *(804 rue St-Francois-Xavier; 450–492–1863), you can reserve a tiny private dining room set off by French doors if you call ahead.*

DAY ONE: morning

Have brunch in Montréal before getting under way. Some fine restaurants in Old Terrebonne don't serve lunch on weekends; that's why you're staying there through dinnertime.

If you don't have a car, Laval Transport bus No. 25 leaves regularly for Terrebonne from the Henri-Bourassa métro station. Transfer to bus No. 8, which brings you to the old part of town.

If you're driving from downtown Montréal, figure on a forty-minute trip. Take Route 15 (North) to Route 440 (East) to Route 25 (North). Exit at No. 17. You'll pull off the highway, pass a glaring stretch of fast-food joints, follow the signs to Île-des-Moulins—and suddenly leave modernity behind.

DAY ONE: afternoon

Parking is free in a lot beside Île-des-Moulins. Cross the pedestrian bridge that traverses Rivière des Mille Îles and leads onto the island. Lean over the wood railing and observe the wildlife on the river beneath the overhanging trees. You might spot a graceful crane.

On your right is a most unusual public library, where you may see a bird's nest near the entry. But that's not what makes the library special. It is housed in two old mills—a flour mill built in 1846 and a sawmill built in 1804. Enter and head for the stairs. From windows on the landing, you can see Rivière de Mille Îles rushing underneath the building, which is perched above the river.

Scottish fur baron Simon McTavish established some of the mills here as well as the old bakery farther along, which now houses a snack bar and an art gallery. McTavish's successor in the fur business, Roderick McKenzie, invited author Washington Irving for a visit, and the writer gathered material here for *Astoria*, his novel about the fur trade.

Across from the library you'll see the ancient seigneurial office of Joseph Masson, who owned most of Île-des-Moulins in the early 1800s. He was vice president of the Bank of Montréal and became the first French-Canadian millionaire. He and wife Geneviève-Sophie Raymond are buried, along with other Terrebonne notables, in an indoor cemetery in the basement of **Église Saint-Louis-de-France de Terrebonne** (corner rue St-Louis and boulevard des Braves). The Masson home is nearby at No. 901 rue St-Louis.

Explore the mills, then explore the rest of Île-des-Moulins on the walking trails that cross it. You'll find ten sculptures on the grounds—and in the river— including *La Dame Blanche*, a hulking white figure who is said to be searching for her lover (see sidebar). Sit on a bench and observe. You can almost feel her anguish. All through the summer, concerts ranging from blues to big band are offered at the Agora, an open-air stage, on the island.

If you'd like to explore the rest of Old Terrebonne by bike, you can rent one at **Cycles Évasion** (197 rue St-André; 450–961–9791). A good

"Louis, Where Are You?"

That's what La Dame Blanche *is supposedly shouting into the river as she searches for her fiancé, Louis Gauthier, who died in battle near Montmorency Falls near Québec City. According to legend, Rose— La Dame Blanche—never recovered from the shock of Gauthier's death and continued to search desperately for her lover around water.*

place to start retracing history, whether on two feet or two wheels, is rue St-Louis, where in addition to the two sites mentioned above, you'll also find an English school (No. 1228), a string of splendid Victorian-style private homes that once belonged to the wealthy bourgeoisie (Nos. 997, 969, 971, and 963), **Maison McKenzie** (No. 906), which dates back to 1807, and the first school established in Terrebonne (No. 696).

Weave along the narrow streets in the *quartier*. The oldest homes date from the 1700s. Many old homes are now occupied by restaurants, boutiques, a bookstore (La Librairie Lincourt, at 191 rue St-André), and even a cyberspace café (Pl@net.Café at 819 rue St-François-Xavier).

When you've explored the old homes and their new functions, return your bicycles. You are about to begin an intimate experience in one of those homes that has a new function—a restaurant.

DAY ONE: evening

DINNER

Originally built in the 1760s as a private home, destroyed by fire with the rest of Old Terrebonne in 1855, and rebuilt five years later on the same foundation, the building that houses **Le Folichon** (804 rue St-Francois Xavier; 450–492–1863; closed Monday; inexpensive to moderate; three-course table d'hôte, $15) has enjoyed new life as a restaurant for the past nine years. Call in advance and reserve La Serre—a tiny room with French doors that is very private and very much in demand. The cozy restaurant, which seats ninety patrons over two levels, has a working fireplace, a hardwood floor more than one hundred years old, and a wine-colored ceiling that adds to the warmth. You'll choose from specialties like rack of lamb, calves' liver, and sweetbreads with scampi, all prepared by chef and co-owner Christian Ouellet, who has been with Le Folichon since its start. Enjoy your dinner. After a few glasses of wine, you can almost hear *La Dame Blanche* calling.

FOR MORE ROMANCE

If you drive to Old Terrebonne, exit Route 25 at boulevard des Mille-Îles for a taste of local bounty. Continue for about a mile until you see, on the left, **Fromagerie du Vieux-Saint-François** (4675 boulevard des Mille-Îles, Laval; 450–666–6810), where a few goats might be wandering near the simple cottage on the property. Here you'll find delicious yogurt and an array of fresh cheese made only from goat's milk. Sample the herb-flavored cheeses. It's hard to choose among the varieties, but you probably won't leave without a package of this dreamy, creamy cheese.

Sugar Sugar
THE SUGAR SHACK IN RIGAUD

*L*A *BELLE PROVINCE* IS NOTED FOR EXCEPTIONAL French cuisine. But Québec also has a homegrown cuisine forged by French-Canadian pioneers and refined by generations of Québecois who followed. French-Canadians, like my husband, grew up eating pea soup (*soupe aux pois*), meat pie (*tourtiere*), baked beans (*feves au lard*), and sugar pie (*tarte au sucre*). You won't find this unassuming fare in many restaurants today—but you will find the menu at a sugar shack, or *sucrerie*, which venerates traditional Québec cuisine at the same time it celebrates Québec's lucrative maple syrup industry.

This close-to-nature itinerary takes you about 70 kilometers (44 miles) outside of Montréal to the town of Rigaud, home of one of the most romantic sugar shacks in the province. A tranquil maple grove provides the backdrop as you turn the clock in reverse and step into a rural setting devoid of modern trappings. Experience the ways that a typical French-Canadian family lived one hundred years ago. Witness traditional methods of extracting maple sap from the trees that surround you. Sample maple syrup in all its incarnations—and kiss the sticky stuff from your partner's lips a few times during your visit.

PRACTICAL NOTES: The Sucrerie is open all year-round, but it is packed in March and April, when the sugar collection is in full swing. Plan to visit, instead, in summer or fall, when it's far quieter and more romantic and when management has more time to devote to each guest. You will still see a demonstration of sugar collection; these are conducted year-round. Always call ahead for

Romance AT A GLANCE

◆ *Start your leap back in Québec history at the imposing Sanctuaire Notre-Dame-de-Lourdes (20 rue Bourget in Rigaud; 450–451–4631), a shrine where miracle cures are said to have been granted by the Virgin Mother.*

◆ *Walk through fields of wildflowers in a maple forest. Watch bread baking in a wood-fired oven. See how maple sap is tapped and collected. Do it all at the Sucrerie de la Montagne (300 rang St-Georges in Rigaud; 450–451–0831), where you'll turn the clock back to experience the ways of a typical French-Canadian family living in the nineteenth century.*

◆ *At dinnertime, savor authentic Québec cuisine around pine tables at the Sucrerie, sip a potent brew called caribou (made from red, white, and blueberry wines with a pinch of white whiskey), listen to traditional French-Canadian folk music—and learn to play the spoons.*

reservations (and request a table for two in the dining room). If you decide to visit in winter, bring along snowshoes or cross-country skis to explore the woods.

DAY ONE: afternoon

Have brunch before you leave Montréal. You're aiming for a midday arrival at the **Sucrerie de la Montagne** in the town of Rigaud. Before you arrive at the Sucrerie, however, make a stop at the imposing **Sanctuaire Notre-Dame-de-Lourdes** (20 rue Bourget in Rigaud; 450–451–4631). Known as the Canadian Lourdes, this shrine has attracted pilgrims ever since the fall of 1874. Marvelous cures and extraordinary favors are said to have been granted by the Virgin Mother to those who journeyed here (see sidebar). The Sanctuaire is roughly an hour outside Montréal. Take Autoroute 40 Ouest in the direction of Ottawa. Exit at Rigaud, Highway 342 Est (rue St-Jean-Baptiste), turn left on Highway 325 Sud (rue St-Pierre), and left on Bourget Street to the Sanctuary. Look for blue Tourism Québec signs to guide you along.

The open-air sanctuary bears a resemblance in atmosphere to that of Lourdes in France for uplifting both mind and soul. Located on Mount Rigaud, which is 700 feet at its highest point, the site provides a striking view of the Ottawa River, the Lac des Deux Montagnes, and the surrounding meadows. The shrine is open year-round, but only from May through September is a guide in place to welcome you. It is also only in those months that the shrine's small chapel is open for prayer, but the Stations of the Cross and the iron cross on the summit of the mountain, which pre-dated the shrine, can be viewed year-round. During July and August, a sound and light show here evokes the death and resurrection of Christ.

After you absorb the peacefulness and the beauty here, back-track to Highway 325 Sud, turn left on rang St-Georges, and follow the signs to the **Sucrerie de la Montagne** (300 rang St-Georges in Rigaud; 450–451–0831). It's a ten-minute trip.

Park your car in the lot near the entrance. Walk to the farthest log structure on the property—the actual sugar shack, which is paneled with lumber from old barns. You may be greeted there by owner Pierre Faucher, a rugged mountain man with a bushy beard who dresses in traditional nineteenth-century garb. Faucher's father was a lumberjack, and his mother's recipes are used in the kitchen. The cabin itself was built more than a century ago. Have a drink of caribou at the bar before you venture into 110 acres of woods and forest trails that comprise the Sucrerie. In summer, the woods are filled with wildflowers; in autumn, maple leaves create a brilliant display of fiery colors. Explore on foot or go for a hayride. You—and your dear—may glimpse a deer along the way.

To understand what maple syrup means to Québec, consider that 75 percent of the world's production comes from the

It's a Miracle

On July 14, 1956, the French daily newspaper Le Devoir *gave the following eyewitness account of a favor obtained at the Sanctuaire: "Everybody was stunned to see the little Micheline Huard walking straight and firm. She it was, who had left her crutches at the shrine the year before, going to lay a wreath of flowers at the foot of the Virgin, in grateful remembrance."*

province. Sap is collected in March and April, but at any time of year at the Sucrerie, you can see a demonstration of sap collection. Faucher still taps trees the old-fashioned way with a spigot and a bucket on each tree—no fancy pipelines here. The sap is then boiled down to syrup. After the demonstration, you can wander over to the on-site bakery where the bread you'll be eating for dinner is made in a wood-fired oven. The highlight of the visit begins at 6:00 P.M., when the live music starts and dinner ($40 per person) is served.

DAY ONE: evening

DINNER

The menu is pure Québeçois: pea soup, fresh bread, potatoes, maple-smoked bacon, country sausages, meat pie, baked beans, homemade ketchup, and maple-glazed smoked ham. You must leave some room for maple sugar pie, maple candy, maple walnut ice cream, and dessert crepes slathered with (what else?) maple syrup. During the meal, a folk singer plays guitar and afterward teaches you, upon request, how to play the spoons. By tapping two ordinary culinary instruments together against your thigh, you'll produce a rhythmic clicking that is so infectious you'll be compelled to leave the spoons behind and get on the floor and square dance. Give in to your impulse and start dancing.

Give Me Some Sugar

Sweetness is hard to come by. Did you know that it takes between thirty and sixty years for a maple tree to mature enough to make tapping it worthwhile? That a high-yield maple tree produces only about twelve gallons of sap a season? That it takes forty gallons of sap to make one gallon of pure maple syrup?

FOR MORE ROMANCE

Stay overnight at the Sucrerie. Two very rustic and romantic log cabins on the premises smell of sweet cedar, have a working fireplace, oil lamps on the mantel, a queen-size bed carved from maple wood, and a private bath with a tub (no shower). The first cabin on your left as you face the sugar shack was built in 1875 for a family of twelve and moved intact to the Sucrerie from another location in Rigaud. Light a fire in your cabin, cuddle up in bed, and leave the modern world way behind. An overnight stay, including dinner and breakfast, is $90 per person.

If you find yourself craving some more authentic French-Canadian cuisine upon your return to Montréal, seek out **La Binerie Mont-Royal** (367 rue Mont-Royal Est; 514–285–9078; inexpensive). This little gem, only a counter and a couple of tables, has been in business since 1940, serving traditional Québeçois cuisine to neighborhood folk who used to flock there every Friday (when meat was still a no-no for Catholics) for pints of *feves au lard* to carry home.

ITINERARY 21
One day, one evening

Euʀopeaɴ Adventuʀe
A Multicultural Tour

HAVE YOU EVER DREAMED OF EXPLORING EUROPE together? Have you ever fantasized about visiting Athens or Rome or Lisbon as starry-eyed lovers? Don't get on a boat. Don't get on a plane. Put on your walking shoes and travel down boulevard St-Laurent to explore remnants of the ethnic communities that have settled in Montréal over the last century. You don't need a passport for the journey down the boulevard that is commonly called the Main. You just need an ardent desire for global adventure.

PRACTICAL NOTES: While this itinerary works any time of year, the flavor of the neighborhoods comes alive from May to October when the weather is warmer, the market is bustling, and the park benches are not covered with snow. You'll be walking from neighborhood to neighborhood, so wear comfortable shoes, but don't wear jeans, since you'll be lunching and dining in lovely restaurants.

DAY ONE: morning

BREAKFAST

Begin your European adventure by having breakfast in a sector of the city that was once Canada's answer to New York's Lower East Side. Not much remains of the vibrant Jewish quarter that spread east and west of boulevard St-Laurent from the turn of the century to the early 1950s, but a fixture there over the past half-century has been **Beauty's** (93 rue Mont- Royal Ouest; 514–849–8883; station Mont-

167

♦ *Explore Europe without ever leaving Montréal by taking a daylong journey down the Main, the nickname for boulevard St-Laurent. You'll visit Portugal, Greece, Italy, and parts of Eastern Europe— all in one day.*

♦ *Pause in an urban park where a rooster rules from a gazebo and watches over the Portuguese community. Sample a bagel that Jewish (and non-Jewish) Montréalers insist has no peer anywhere in the world at the* **Bagel Factory** *(263 St-Viateur Ouest; 514–276–8044). Visit a church in the Italian community where a mural once caused a huge scandal.*

♦ *Hash over the memories of your whirlwind European adventure when you dine and dance the night away at* **Casa Napoli** *(6728 boulevard St-Laurent; 514–274–4351). The restaurant's facade became a landmark to millions when it was featured in a popular Québec television series called* Omerta.

Royal; open from 7:00 A.M. during the week, 8:00 A.M. on Sunday; inexpensive). The restaurant is a ten-minute walk from the métro station, or you can grab bus No. 11 or No. 97, which will drop you off right in front.

A classic diner that has been modernized to keep it spiffy, Beauty's is the home of the mishmash omelet, a jumble of eggs, hot dog, salami, fried onions, and green pepper that was patented by restaurant founder (and still owner) Hymie Sckolnick. If the mishmash doesn't turn you on, a bagel sandwich will. Order yours with whipped cream cheese, smoked salmon, sliced tomato, and red onion.

The first Jews arrived in Montréal in the 1760s as civilians engaged by the British Army, which had conquered Québec. A congregation was founded in 1768, but the Jewish population grew very slowly. Fewer than 8,000 Jews lived in Montréal at the beginning of the 1900s. All that changed dramatically with the outbreak of World War I, when immigrants flocked to the city. By the onset of World War II, some 80,000 Jews lived in the city, most of them around boulevard St-Laurent. They came mostly from Eastern Europe; Yiddish was their common language. Today, visitors to Montréal are surprised to learn that the city has a growing segment of French-speaking Jews from

North Africa, who make up 20 percent of the current Jewish population of 90,000, and that Montréal also has the largest number of Hasidic Jews in North America outside New York. You'll probably see members of this religious sect as you wander through the neighborhood; the men wear fur felt hats and long black coats.

Today, the neighborhood radiating from both sides of boulevard St-Laurent is more Greek and Portuguese than Jewish. The Jewish community has spread to other parts of town and to the suburbs. You'll see a few remaining landmarks, though, beginning with **Beth Shlomo** (3919 rue Clark at the corner of rue Bagg), the last synagogue left in the quarter. A three-minute walk from Beauty's, the red-brick synagogue dates from the 1920s. Services are still held every Saturday morning and on Jewish holidays.

To get a feel for what the quarter was like in the first half of this century, walk east from the synagogue to the corner where St-Laurent links up with Napoléon. Two blocks farther east you'll see the **Colonial Turkish Steam Baths** (3963 Coloniale; 514–285–0132), a true vestige of times gone by. When homes had no hot water, residents went to the baths for cleansing. Today, a steam bath, sauna, whirlpool, and massage have been added to the operation as well. The Baths are open every day to men, except Tuesday, when it's ladies' day.

Now you'll backtrack and stroll along a stretch of the Main between Napoléon and Duluth. Here you'll find **St-Lawrence Bakery** (3830 boulevard St-Laurent), in business since 1912 and maker of the braided egg bread that Jews call challah; **Warshaws** (3863 boulevard St-Laurent), a supermarket; and **Chez Schwartz Charcuterie Hébraïque**, otherwise known as **Schwartz's Delicatessen** (3895 boulevard St-Laurent), where the faithful of all persuasions flock to worship the best smoked meat in the city. Just across the street from Schwartz's is **Bersons Monuments** (3884 boulevard St-Laurent), supplier of cemetery headstones for generations.

Continue north on boulevard St-Laurent for two blocks, where the neighborhood takes on a Latin flair. Sit for a moment on a bench in pretty **Parc Portugal** at the corner of boulevard St-Laurent and rue Marie-Anne. I'll tell you about the Portuguese community as you admire the tiled fountain and the weathervane shaped like a rooster —a traditional Portuguese good luck symbol. When the Jewish immigrants left the area in the 1950s, an influx of Portuguese immigrants replaced them. Now the area is filled with their stores, restaurants, and homes, which are sometimes decorated with brightly colored pictures of saints or other religious icons. The Portuguese were later joined by immigrants from Spain, Mexico, and South America. Steal a kiss under the rooster-topped gazebo and start exploring. Walk east to avenue Hotel de Ville and then one block south, where you'll find **Église St-Jean Baptiste** (309 rue Rachel Est). Built in the 1870s, it is now a meeting place for the burgeoning Latin community. The interior is breathtaking, so take a peek. Organ concerts are occasionally held here, and if you're fortunate, you'll hear the sound of music.

A Touch of Sweetness

For the uninitiated, Montréal bagels are quite a shock. They don't look or taste like any bagel you may have eaten in New York, Chicago, or Los Angeles. One reason? They're made with honey-sweetened water. Buy a few Montréal bagels to bring home at the Bagel Factory (263 St-Viateur Ouest; 514–276–8044). Don't rush to that address yet, though. The Bagel Factory is actually much closer to the Greek part of town, which you'll visit this afternoon.

Now return to the Main. Take a leisurely walk about a mile north to avenue St-Viateur, where you'll turn left and work your way into a neighborhood where many of the signs are lettered in Greek. As you head west along avenue St-Viateur, you can't miss an imposing brick building featuring an enormous front window that looks like a fancy lace doily. **St. Michel and St. Anthony's Catholic Community** (105 avenue St-Viateur) once served the Irish population (notice the shamrocks inset in the brick) but is now a Polish church. Mass is said every day in English—and in Polish on weekends.

Continue walking west toward Athens. You won't see the Acropolis, but Montréal is among the top ten cities in the world when it comes to a Greek presence. Before you enter the city's Greektown, stop in the bagel shop (see sidebar) for those honey-sweetened treats I promised you earlier. Tuck them away. You're having lunch on a Greek isle.

DAY ONE: afternoon

LUNCH

Some call it the best Greek restaurant in Canada. At **Milos** (5357 avenue du Parc; 514–272–3522; moderate to expensive), owner Costas Spiliadas may just offer the best Greek salad in the world—made with the finest olives and the freshest feta—and he bottles his own olive oil. Enjoy the Greek salad for lunch, along with an appetizer to share and a glass of wine—or maybe ouzo. Don't fill up here, though you might be sorely tempted by the fresh fish and seafood. Remember, in a few hours, you'll be dining in Rome.

The Greek quarter runs along avenue du Parc, roughly from avenue St-Viateur to rue Jean-Talon, where it veers off into an elongation of the neighborhood called Park Extension. An array of Greek restaurants, food stores, banks, boutiques, and businesses fill the area and form a lively and colorful enclave. Greeks have lived in Montréal since the mid-1800s, when they arrived to work at the port and in the fur trade. Today, more than 50,000 Greeks live in the greater Montréal area, and like many immigrants, they are trilingual—speaking English, French, and Greek.

If you've left a little room for dessert, why not stop at **Navario Bakery & Pastry Shop** (5563 avenue du Parc; 514–279–7725; open daily) for a sweet treat to munch while you hop in and out of the stores in the quarter. Be sure to browse a while in **Theo & Filles** (5112 avenue du Parc;

Read All About It

Montréal's Jewish quarter is the setting for Saul Bellow's book Herzog and Mordecai Richler's St. Urbain's Horseman and The Apprenticeship of Duddy Kravitz. The writer known as Trevanian (The Day of the Jackal) used boulevard St-Laurent as the setting for his novel The Main.

514–276–7443; open daily). Theo Kaklamanis operated in the same spot for more than three decades, making custom-made draperies and bedspreads. In 1994 his two daughters, Suzie and Effie, took over the operation, which now specializes exclusively in giftware and decorative items like vases and romantic ambience lamps, some of which are sold nowhere else in Montréal. Here's a good place to buy a carved wood duck, a small jewelry chest, or a beautiful candleholder to bring home to your mother-in-law.

As you roam the quarter, old Greek women dressed in black from head to toe cross your path, as do Hasidic families out for a walk. You're in another time and place. Europe in the 1800s? Keep going. One more country remains on your itinerary.

Walk north along avenue du Parc through the Greek quarter. When you cross under an overpass, the first street you'll see is rue Beaubien. Take a right and walk less than ten minutes to boulevard St-Laurent, where you'll turn left. Like magic, you're in Italy. Say hello to Rome and Florence.

More than 200,000 Italians live in Montréal and its suburbs, and the city's largest ethnic group has a presence on the Main proportionate to its size. Italian restaurants, bakeries, groceries, espresso bars, and pizzerias are scattered around the Main and the streets radiating from it between rue St-Zotique and rue Jean-Talon. A huge public market dominates the quarter and attracts Italians and non-Italians in droves. Make your first stop the magnificent **La Madonna Della Difesa**—Our Lady of Protection—on the corner of rues Dante and Alma. Founded in 1910, the church was designed by Guido Nincheri, a native of Florence, who also painted the magisterial ceiling fresco tracing the history of Catholicism back to Adam and Eve. On the right, as you face the altar, you'll glimpse the fresco's most famous subject—and most scandalous. It's Mussolini on horseback, painted at a time in the early 1930s when the dictator was widely regarded as a hero. During World War II the mural was covered up by the Royal Canadian Mounted Police. You can enter the church every day and lose yourselves in the beauty of the twelve stained-glass panels, the marble altar, and that fabulous fresco.

A public park sits alongside the church. Spend a moment in **Parc St-Jean de la Croix**, with its statue honoring victims of war, before returning to boulevard St-Laurent. At the corner of rue Dante and boulevard St-Laurent you'll see **Trattoria dai Baffoni** (6859 boulevard St-Laurent; 514–270–3715), a neighborhood fixture where all the waiters have mustaches—or baffoni. Head north along boulevard St-Laurent, where you'll spend time in **Libreria Italiana** (6792 boulevard St-Laurent; 514–277–2955; closed Sunday), which carries newspapers and magazines from Milan and Rome and an impressive selection of books, music, and videos imported from Italy; and in **Milano Fruiterie** (6884 boulevard St-Laurent; 514–273–8558), which started out nearly fifty years ago as a fruit store but now stocks delectable Italian chocolates, olive oils, pasta, and canned goods from Italy. The smells from the appetizing counter are tantalizing— and so hard to resist. You just might have to buy something to tuck in your luggage for the trip home. Maybe a bottle of olive oil for your own table? Milano carries about a dozen brands.

When you've purchased your goodie, head for the **Marché Jean-Talon** (7075 avenue Casgrain), accessible by walking east on avenue Mozart. Some food experts consider Jean-Talon the best market in the city. Designed like a square and encompassing several blocks, it has open-air stalls that operate in summer and fall and are surrounded by permanent shops that operate all year long. You'll find butchers, bakers, and cheese purveyors in the exterior shops. In the interior, when weather permits, the stalls are jammed with vendors selling flowers, fruits, vegetables, herbs, eggs from local farms, and locally produced honey and maple syrup.

When you've sniffed and smelled and tasted just a little bit— some vendors let you sample—you're finally ready for a complete Italian meal. Is your mouth watering?

DAY ONE: evening

DINNER

You undoubtedly noticed **Casa Napoli** (6728 boulevard St-Laurent; 514–274–4351; moderate to expensive; reservations required) as you strolled along the Main. You can't miss the statues in front of the restaurant—they recall Italian architecture in ancient Rome—and the setting is so authentic it was used in the wildly popular Québec television series *Omerta*, which detailed the lives of Montréal's mafiosi. Inside, stone caves with wrought-iron gates lend an old-world ambience to match the old-world cuisine heavy on fish and grilled meats. In a traditional touch, pepper steak, rack of lamb, and duck are prepared flambé-style at your table. Ask to be seated in La Grotta, a table for two in a cave. It's hard to get more intimate—in a restaurant, that is. Casa Napoli has one of the finest wine lists in the city (see sidebar in "Clinking Glasses" itinerary), and, from Thursday through Sunday, live music is the perfect enticement for slow dancing. As you hold each other close on the dance floor, think of what you've accomplished together. You've traveled through Europe—and it only took a day!

For More Romance

Now that you've toured Europe, you may also want to see the Orient while you're in Montréal. Set aside a day for the "Oriental Air" itinerary.

Make a Date

$\mathcal{B}ig\ \mathcal{G}rin$

The Just For Laughs Festival

ESIEGED BY A BRUTISH WINTER that routinely runs from November to May, Montréalers ecstatically celebrate even the slightest crack in the deep freeze. On the first warm day in early April, for example, restaurateurs fling open their terraces for alfresco dining (never mind that a blizzard is likely waiting in the wings), and Montréalers shed hats, gloves, scarves, and coats in gleeful anticipation of summer.

Spring is just a blip on the weather map in Montréal, a mere handful of days in late May and early June. Summer, on the other hand, is a season. When the last snowbank finally melts, Montréalers are more than ready to throw a big party. They do it in almost ritualistic fashion with a series of festivals that stretch all summer long.

The light-heavyweight in the series is undoubtedly a playful affair (it turns eighteen in 2000). The Just For Laughs Festival (or *Juste Pour Rire*) is the world's largest celebration of humor. The *Hollywood Reporter* calls it the Cannes Festival of the comedy world. Blockbuster talents like Bob Newhart, Sinbad, Tim Allen, Drew Carey, and Dame Edna Everage are here, as are virtual unknowns longing to be discovered. Lucky breaks do happen, and talent scouts are as thick as flies.

Because the comedy acts are scattered around town, this itinerary allows you to experience a slice of life in several parts of the city. I'll take you to indoor and outdoor venues, keeping a moderate budget in mind. Giggles, chuckles, or rollicking hee-haws are strongly encouraged at every point along the way.

$\mathcal{R}$omance
AT A GLANCE

◆ Drop your bags at a century-old B&B located just blocks from the heart of the **Just For Laughs Festival,** the world's largest celebration of humor, and spend the day getting in the mood to laugh. Have your funny valentine's smile captured by a street artist in **Place Jacques-Cartier** and later watch an astounding fireworks display from the Old Port.

◆ Tour the only international humor museum in the world, then stroll over to Festival headquarters on rue St-Denis. An inflatable green Devil with a wicked grin bids you welcome to humor headquarters, where you'll catch live performances on the street all evening.

◆ After dinner at **Maestro S.V.P.** (3615 St-Laurent; 514–842–6447), a cozy seafood restaurant with the most extensive oyster bar in town, snuggle up for an intimate evening of love and laughter at the **Comedy Nest** (in the Nouvel Hotel, 1740 boulevard René-Levesque Ouest; 514–932–6378).

PRACTICAL NOTES: The Just For Laughs Festival stretches over eleven days in July, the heart of tourist season, so make your hotel reservations in advance. For the latest information on schedules and performers, call the Festival Hotline (514–845–3155) or check the Festival Web site (www.hahaha.com). Secure tickets to the large headliner shows in advance; for ticket prices and reservations, call 514–790–HAHA after May 31 when the festival lineup will be set. The shows take place at the following venues: Théâtre St. Denis, Salles du Gesu, and Club Soda. Thematic shows routinely include: The Relationship Show, the X-Rated Nasty Show, the Late Night Danger Zone, and the Bar Mitzvah Show of Jewish Humor.

Casual attire works well for all parts of this itinerary. So do wear comfortable shoes. You'll be walking a lot in pursuit of laughter, and sore feet aren't funny. **Rue St-Denis,** Montréal's liveliest street, serves well as the festival's outdoor stage—and your headquarters for laughter and love. Admission to this outdoor stage is nominal (about $4.00), making it a potent draw for budget-minded folk. Indoor shows, by contrast, are set in large theaters and in small clubs around the city. These demand advance ticket purchase, and the prices are higher.

Two shows of the four-week **Benson & Hedges International Fireworks Competition** (800–361–4595) coincide with the Just For Laughs Festival. Skilled pyrotechnicians from as far away as Spain, Germany, and Australia compete on different nights. Set to music, the shows are an absolute treat to view wrapped in each other's arms in the **Old Port**—and they are free, no less, from that vantage point. If you can plan your Just For Laughs holiday for a weekend, you should be able to see the explosive display, and sparks will fly.

DAY ONE: morning

Sparks begin to ignite the moment you enter the Victorian row house you'll call home this weekend. Built in the 1870s, **Angelica Blue B&B** (1213 rue Ste-Elizabeth; 514–844–5048, 800–878–5048; station Berri-UQAM; from $65 to $125) features old pine floors, 11-foot-high ceilings, and exposed brick walls in every room. You might request the Victorian suite for lovers, which has a king-size bed and a claw-foot tub. Other rooms are organized along thematic lines: a Mexican room, Oriental room, and Safari room reflect the passions of your hostess, a former cruise line employee. Set your bags down in your space of choice, and change into comfortable clothing for a daylong laughfest. You won't be coming back before midnight, but one of the best features of your B&B is location. It's not only just paces from the Just For Laughs Festival site, but it's also a short walk from the city's leading tourist attraction—the **Old Port**—where you'll be spending the afternoon sightseeing and getting wacky.

DAY ONE: afternoon

Stroll over to **Place Jacques-Cartier** (174 rue Notre-Dame Est; métro Champs de Mars), perhaps Montréal's most photographed spot. Lined with flowers and cafés and shops, Place Jacques-Cartier is home to mimes, magicians, and street artists who'll paint your portrait with a definite eye for the droll detail. A street artist in Jacques-Cartier Square sketched a remarkable likeness of my husband, an air-traffic controller, landing an airplane in a champagne glass. Sit for a portrait; it's a wonderful keepsake. Then head for the silver dome rising up at the edge of the Old Port.

LUNCH

Bonsecours Market, under that silver dome, dates from 1849. It originally housed city hall, and, at the same time, farmers' stalls. It also housed the Parliament of the United Canadas for six years after the original parliament burned down. After many incarnations, it was refurbished for Montréal's 350th birthday celebration in 1992. On the port side, you'll find vendors selling fine local produce. Pick up some sandwiches and fruit (and a delicious glass of fresh-squeezed carrot juice) so you can picnic at the Old Port right in front of you.

Location is Everything

A hotel may appear to be a strange place for a comedy club, but as Comedy Nest owner Ernie Butler cracks, nothing beats the club's location for romance: The bedrooms are just steps away.

Now get ready for a rollicking good time. Stroll from the Old Port to the Festival site on rue St-Denis. You can't miss it—an inflatable green devil with a wicked grin bids welcome with open arms, hinting slyly at the good time ahead. During the festival the street is open to pedestrian traffic only, so amble down this commercial corridor freely and window shop along the way. Scope out the location of stage shows on the street, choose one that seems appealing, and get into viewing position. The shows begin when the workday ends (around 6:00 P.M.) and they run until midnight. Laugh your heads off—and don't stop until your stomach says that hunger is no laughing matter.

DAY ONE: evening

DINNER

Spirits high, walk back to the city's Old Quarter, where you'll experience a change of scene and an intimate dinner at **Le Grill** (183 rue St-Paul Est; 514–397–1044; moderate), a charming and bustling restaurant with an eat-in courtyard that is surrounded by stone walls dating back to the 1700s. The fare is French-Continental (kidneys and seafood fettuccine both share the menu), and there's a table d'hôte each night that includes three courses.

After dinner, head to nearby Jacques-Cartier Pier for thirty minutes of fireworks at 10:00 P.M.—that is, if the International Fireworks Competition is scheduled. Just follow the crowd to the clock tower at the end of the pier and marvel at the delicate shapes of colored light that blossom against the velvet night. Every pyrotechnic extravagance is better than the one before. When the fireworks reach a crescendo, you'll find your excitement level at a peak. Keep it that way. After the show, you'll walk slowly back to your B&B.

DAY TWO: morning/afternoon

BREAKFAST

Take your time this morning. You'll find a full buffet breakfast awaiting either in the café bistro or on the patio, depending on the weather. Choose from fresh crepes or waffles, delectable breads, fresh fruit and juices, and coffee or tea. Linger over your meal, and share a private joke before a new round of laughter begins.

Now you're ready to hit the Main, the moniker conferred on boulevard St-Laurent, the great divide, the street that splits the city east and west geographically and along linguistic lines as well. The English have traditionally lived west of St-Laurent; the French have lived east. To get there, you'll take a leisurely stroll along rue Ste-Catherine, a few blocks north, pausing to window-shop on one of the city's liveliest corridors. Rue Ste-Catherine caters to the young and young-at-heart. You'll find contemporary clothing boutiques, record stores, French and English bookstores, and many quality shoe stores. The short walk can easily stretch into an hour or two. Let it. Have fun exploring.

You're heading for a former brewery. Not a drop is served in the old Ekers brewery, a landmark building, which is now the home of **Just For Laughs Museum** (2111 boulevard St-Laurent, between

Ontario and rue Sherbrooke; 514–845–2408; open seven days a week during the festival, 1:00 to 8:00 P.M.). Merely looking at the building from the street is a kick. The design is sure to elicit a laugh.

An offshoot of the Just for Laughs Festival, the museum is the only one in the world devoted to humor. It documents the history of laughter around the globe and through the ages, from Greek satire to Shakespeare's court jesters to the Marx Brothers to TV sitcoms. Special exhibits created just for the festival are offbeat, often interactive, and always designed to put the visitor in another realm. When you're finished chuckling over the newest offering, the laughter doesn't stop. Walk to rue St-Denis, where you'll catch an the action at the festival before dinner. In between chuckles, have a beer and a light snack at concession stands on the festival site. Be prudent. You're saving your appetite for an early dinner.

DAY TWO: evening

DINNER

Tell a joke linking oysters with sexual prowess and you'll get lots of laughs. But is the humor justified? You two will test those punch lines tonight at **Maestro S.V.P.** (3615 St-Laurent; 514–842–6447; moderate), a cozy seafood restaurant with the most extensive oyster bar in town. Owner Ilene Polansky has blended romantic decor, good food, and irresistible humor into an intimate package. Blink and you'll miss her place, but the tiny restaurant, located on the hottest strip of the city (once the sun goes down), is just perfect for couples. Have a blast—and let me know if those oysters do the trick.

If you don't have a ticket for one of the festival's blockbuster shows, a wonderful alternative (cheaper and more intimate, too) is the **Comedy Nest**, securely tucked into the Nouvel Hotel (1740 boulevard René-Levesque Ouest, at the corner of rue St-Mathieu; 514–932–6378). Open every night during the Just For Laughs Festival, the Nest has shows at 8:30 and 11:00 P.M.; reserve in advance. The cover charge is $10.

It's a cozy club with linen-covered tables and cane chairs. Seated at stage level, you'll feel close to the stand-up comics who live and die here. The atmosphere in the Comedy Nest hints at the underlying aim of the performers: stardom. Tiny illuminated stars dot the ceiling, and celluloid reels along the walls frame pics of film icons like James Dean and Marilyn Monroe. A romantic evening is a sure thing, particularly if you see a show dedicated to relationships. I saw one here called The Ride. The program notes said: "You meet . . . You obsess . . . You misunderstand . . . You fight . . . You love . . . You take the ride."

Ride it out after the main show. Linger for open-microphone stints by aspiring comics. Under the club's starry canopy, you'll feel like holding each other tight. Or tickling each other. When the show's over, you may want to walk back to your lodging under a genuine starry canopy, retelling the joke that seemed to epitomize your relationship perfectly.

For More Romance

Another alternative to the festival blockbusters is the **Comedyworks** (1238 rue Bishop; 514–398–9661). Like the Comedy Nest, the Comedyworks showcases upcoming talent and also offers special shows related to love and romance during the festival.

Swing and Sway

THE JAZZ FESTIVAL

HIT A HIGH NOTE IN YOUR LOVE RELATIONSHIP at the Montréal International Jazz Festival, where harmony prevails for eleven blissful summer days.

Since 1979, the Jazz Festival has been bringing together luminaries and rising stars for a musical program that embraces blues, salsa, reggae—and all that jazz. Nearly 2,000 musicians from twenty countries perform on the streets and in concert halls—including past headliners like Ray Charles, Nina Simone, Herbie Hancock, and Al Jarreau.

When the concert venues close, the music doesn't end. Without missing a beat, you and your sweetheart will follow the musicians to a hotel for a late-night jam session around the bar, where you'll forge a melodious memory that will linger forever.

PRACTICAL NOTES: The Info-Jazz line (514–871–1881; 888–515–0515) operates year-round, although details about specific performances aren't available until two months before the end-of-June festival. Leave your name and address on the line, and you'll be sent a program free. With more than 400 shows—300 of them free—it helps to plan your schedule before you leave. Tickets to the headliner concerts disappear quickly, so order in advance. Book an early (6:00 P.M.) performance at the Spectrum (514–790–1245). A jazz workshop (see page 188) can also be booked in advance at that same number. Another tip: Purchase a Friends of the Festival card for $5.00, which provides access to a number of concerts and films for free. In addition, *The Gazette* newspaper, Montréal's only English daily, publishes a special Jazz Festival supplement and also lists the hottest acts on a daily basis. One other note: Many of the bars and

*R*omance
AT A GLANCE

♦ Leave your bags at **Château de l'Argoat**
(524 rue Sherbrooke Est; 514–842–2046)
on the edge of the Plateau neighborhood,
where the young and young-at-heart stay.
Then get ready to swing and sway to the free
beat on the street at the Jazz Festival.

♦ See a film about a jazz great at Montréal's oldest movie palace, the
Imperial Cinema (1430 rue Bleury; 514– 848–0300). Recreate a scene from
the movie when you dine on chicken and ribs at **Biddle's Jazz & Ribs** (2060
Alymer; 514–842–8656), a sultry den owned by jazzman Charlie Biddle.

♦ Take a workshop on jazz given by a top performer. Later catch a headliner
perform at the **Spectrum** (316–318 Ste-Catherine Ouest; 514–861–5851).
When night falls, sip a martini (and listen to live jazz) at the **Jello Bar** (151
rue Ontario Est; 514–285–2621), a popular hangout during the Festival.

restaurants frequented by jazz aficionados tend to be smoky. If ciga-
rette smoke annoys you, be forewarned.

DAY ONE: morning/afternoon

The location of your Victorian lodging guarantees a swinging time.
Château de l'Argoat (524 rue Sherbrooke Est; 514–842–2046;
Sherbrooke station; $100, with parking and continental breakfast for
two), sits at the convergence of the Plateau, the Latin Quarter, and
the downtown corridor. It's also across the street from a métro station, near the bus terminal, and within walking distance of every jazz
venue you'll visit. The white Château, with its fanciful turrets and
cornices, is actually two turn-of-the-century mansions combined.
You've requested room No. 6, which has a fireplace (nonworking), a
queen-size antique bed, and a thoroughly modern marble-tiled bath
with Jacuzzi. Before you head for the music, settle into your room
and then have lunch at a lively spot only a stroll away.

LUNCH

Watch the world go by from the outdoor terrasse at **Côté Soleil** (3979
St-Denis; 514–282–8037; inexpensive), billed as the classic urban sidewalk café and tailor-made for people watching. While you indulge in a

grilled vegetable sandwich, salade niçoise, or warm goat cheese and tomatoes served on a baguette, take a moment to notice the fanciful Victorian buildings across the street that used to house the city's French elite. Now they are all occupied by shops. By the way, if you'd rather be away from the hustle and bustle on the street, Côté Soleil offers a lovely solution. At the back of the restaurant is a tiny indoor "patio"—complete with outdoor furniture and umbrella—perfect for lovers.

When you have finished lunch, turn right out of the restaurant and return to rue Sherbrooke, where you'll take another right. Walk to rue St-Urbain and take a left. You're heading toward **Place des Arts**, a complex similar to New York's Lincoln Center in its devotion to the performing arts. During the Jazz Festival, you'll find clowns, jugglers, mimes, and free live outdoor musical performances here as well as inside adjoining Complexe Desjardins, a combination hotel and shopping plaza. Ticketed concerts are also held within a few blocks of Place des Arts. The music begins here at noon and continues until past midnight.

Make Place des Arts your home base this afternoon. Dangle your feet in the pool-sized fountain there, where eight powerful jets of water gush from either side and form arches as you listen to the music wafting from rue Ste-Catherine. Lovers gravitate to the fountain and sway to the languorous sounds of a sax or whirl their legs in the water to an energetic drumbeat.

In the late afternoon, head for the oldest movie theater in Montréal, a cinematic palace. The elegant **Imperial Cinema** (1430 rue Bleury; 514–848–0300; tickets available at the box office; performances at 4:00 and 5:30 P.M.) presents rare films on jazz—or blues—every day during the festival: *Giant Steps, Texas*

All That Jazz

During the Festival and year-round, jazz cognoscenti consider these clubs tops:

* L'Air du Temps (191 rue St-Paul Ouest; 514–842–2003)
* Café Sarajevo (2080 rue Clark; 514–284–5629)
* Biddle's (2060 rue Aylmer; 514–842–8656)
* Club Soda (5240 avenue du Parc; 514–270–7848)
* Upstairs (1254 rue Mackay; 514–931–6808)
* Jello Bar (151 rue Ontario Est; 514–285–2621)

Tenor, *Lush Life*, and *A Great Day in Harlem* are past titles. Hold hands, relax, and catch a classic before dinner.

DAY ONE: evening

DINNER

Two blocks west of the Imperial, you may be able to re-create a scene from a movie you just saw. Walk into **Biddle's Jazz & Ribs** (2060 rue Alymer; 514–842–8656; inexpensive), and you've entered the quintessential jazz club. This sultry den, where the lights are always low, is right out of another era. Bassist Charles Biddle, his drummer, and his piano man have been holding court for years here. Every table is a winner with a prime view of the stage. As you enjoy the music, feast on finger-licking good ribs and chicken wings. During the festival, jazz is served (with dinner) from 5:00 P.M. Just a note: Biddle's has a nonsmoking section, but that may not completely insulate you from the smoky interior.

Let's Party!

According to author John Gilmore, during the Prohibition years (1919–1933), Montréal developed a wide reputation as a party town because it was the only large city in North America that did not totally outlaw the sale and consumption of alcohol. Nightclubs proliferated, prompting songwriter Billy Rose to pen these lyrics: "Speak easy, speak easy, and tell the bunch/ I won't go east, I won't go west, got a different hunch:/ I'll be leaving in the summer, and I won't be back 'till fall,/Good-bye Broadway, Hello Montréal."

When your hunger (for food) has been satisfied, head back to the Place des Arts for a round of free evening performances under the stars. When the main shows end around 11:00 P.M., don't rush back to your lodging. Head instead for the **Hôtel Wyndham Montréal** (4 Complexe Desjardins; 514–285–1450; free admission), festival headquarters and home-away-from-home for most of the musicians. Go straight to the bar, site of impromptu jam sessions that wrap up around four in the morning. Fans have never forgotten spur-of-the-moment performances by George Benson, Wynton Marsalis, and John Scofield. At no charge.

I'll leave you here and say good night—or should I say good morning?

DAY TWO: morning

BREAKFAST

Your first contact with civilization this morning will take place in an adorable breakfast nook at the Château. A tiny room with a tiled floor, this niche is low-lit and intimate—the right ambience for night owls who want to gear up slowly. Juice, toast, croissants, muffins, and coffee will help you get ready for the day—and night—ahead.

Now you're ready to learn a lesson that won't hurt one bit. But before you do, use the morning to explore the Latin Quarter by walking south on rue St-Denis to window-shop (for a list of precise stores, see the "Taste of Québec" itinerary). Take your time as you stroll; at rue Ste-Catherine, take a right and continue west to rue St-Laurent. By calling the number of the Info-Jazz line (514–871–1881; 888–515–0515), you've booked a 1:00 P.M. jazz workshop at **Café des Artistes** in the Monument National (1182 rue St-Laurent; $15). The musicians who lead these workshops do not perform. They talk. They talk about their childhood, about musical influences, about technique. It's a two-hour, behind-the-scenes chat with a star. Questions from the audience complete the session. Diehard fans (and neophytes, too) will be captivated. After the encounter, have a light bite.

DAY TWO: afternoon

LUNCH or SNACK

Boulevard St-Laurent is the international heart of the city, a starting point for waves of immigrants arriving from Asia, Europe, and South America over the past century. You're heading for Chinatown and **Patisserie C. J. Regent** (68 rue de la Gauchetière Ouest; 514–866–1628; inexpensive), where you'll take out a sandwich and pastry and eat on a bench in peaceful Dr. Sun Yat Sen Park across the street. The park has no swings or slides—only a mound of rocks—a symbol of harmony to the Chinese. Feeling harmonious, you'll fit right in.

Spend the rest of the afternoon listening to the free shows near Place des Arts. As evening commences, you'll have a change of venue. You're going to use the tickets you purchased in advance for the early 6:00 P.M. performance at the **Spectrum** (316–318 Ste-Catherine Ouest; 514–861–5851), site of many blockbuster performances and a favorite haunt for jazz fans during the festival. The Spectrum can accommodate a crowd of 1,100 at tables and chairs spread over three levels, but the design of the hall is so intimate that it seems that less than half that number are actually in the audience. Sight lines are excellent. Best bet: Reserve tickets on the mezzanine level, in front, for the most intimate view.

DAY TWO: evening

DINNER

When the music ends, the night has just begun. The best is yet to come, my dears. Walk or take a cab to **Globe Restaurant** (3455 boulevard St-Laurent; 514–284–3823; expensive), where the tin ceiling, palm trees, and spacious banquettes take you to a more elegant time and place. Exceptional dishes are the rule at Globe, and organically grown regional products from Québec are the basis for all the fusion flavors. You'll find six appetizers and six main courses on the ever-changing menu, all done with wild abandon, using color and volume to jazz up the look on the plate—and jazz up your life. Sound off with an asparagus salad laced with hot smoked salmon. Swing into rack of lamb on a bed of sliced mushrooms and potatoes. The food is so delectable and so artfully presented, you'll be rapturous by the time you get to the final note: a bittersweet chocolate tart, perhaps, or maybe almond cake served with homemade vanilla ice cream.

Strike a mellow note as you end the evening not far from your hotel at **Jello Bar** (151 rue Ontario Est; 514–285–2621; $3.00 cover during the festival), where the walls are yellow and mauve and the furniture is retro. Martinis are the specialty of the house—the bar serves more than thirty kinds—and during the jazz festival, the place welcomes hundreds of fans to separate shows held at 10:30 P.M., midnight, and 1:30 A.M. As you lean back and listen to the music, end the evening on a very sweet note. Order a Cherry Blossom martini made with chocolate vodka and Tia Maria. Ooh-la-la. Now you may be ready for more sweetness—in private.

Hot Tip!

Jello Bar owner Yves Dion says his favorite martini is the Jalapeño, made with ice-cold vodka and freshly marinated jalapeño peppers. He calls the marriage of cold and hot "magical."

For More Romance

If your eyes are still open on Evening Two, consider returning to the Spectrum for *Spectacles en Reprise* at 12:30 A.M. With your Friends of the Festival card, you have free access to a reprise of the blues concert held outdoors earlier in the evening. Impelled by the late-night atmosphere at the Spectrum, musicians often perform until 3:00 or 4:00 A.M. This time, I'm really saying goodnight.

Seeing Stars
THE WORLD FILM FESTIVAL

NAME-DROPPING MAY BE GAUCHE, DAHLING, but permit me to indulge. Liv Ullmann. Clint Eastwood. Anthony Hopkins. Claudia Cardinale. Gérard Depardieu. Jane Fonda. Donald Sutherland. Steve Martin. Robert Altman. Nick Nolte. The star power at Montréal's World Film Festival is megawatt year after year. Perhaps this year the two of you can add your own charisma to the glamorous atmosphere.

Movie mavens have been gravitating to Montréal since 1977 to gorge on films (and to stargaze) at North America's only competitive film festival recognized by the International Federation of Film Producers Association—a recognition Montréal shares with Cannes, Berlin, Venice, and Moscow. Montréal's is the best attended festival in the western world: 350,000 film buffs, including 3,500 in the film business, eagerly feast on 400 films—many of them premieres— from sixty countries, and then watch jurors award a trophy (actually a sculpture resembling a piece of film) to the winners.

Fueled by Montréal's powerful java, you and your film junkie companion can live virtually in the dark for days, jockeying among indoor theaters from 9:00 A.M. until midnight. An outdoor venue attracts fans to a movie projected against the side of a building at night. Between films, you can hang out at Complexe Desjardins headquarters to schmooze with actors, directors, producers, writers, and an assortment of wannabes, and attend daily press conferences to which the public is invited.

If the idea of mixing and mingling with the beautiful people is alluring to you both, dahlings, put on your sunglasses and face the bright lights.

*R*omance
AT A GLANCE

◆ Join the star-studded cast registered at the **Hôtel Wyndham Montréal** *(4 Complexe Desjardins; 514–285–1450 or 800–361–8234), your home base for the best-attended film festival in the Western world. Your dilemma, to be contemplated over the best hamburger in town at **La Paryse** (302 rue Ontario Est; 514–842–2040), is choosing which films to view from a selection of more than 250 features and 130 shorts.*

◆ *Attend a premier at the **Imperial Cinema**, the oldest theater in Montréal, and then join the critics at a daily press conference open to the public, where star power radiates. Later follow the stars and the critics to **Jardin de Panos** (521 rue Duluth Est; 514–521–4206), a Greek restaurant and favorite gathering point during the festival where the rule is BYOB (bring your own bottle).*

◆ *See stars of the celestial variety when you view a film at night—outside—at **Le Parc des Festivals**. Before you step into the great outdoors, soak up the atmosphere in a French restaurant where actress Sarah Bernhardt once spent the night. Restaurant **Claude Postel** (443 rue St-Vincent; 514–875–5067) was formerly the Hotel Richelieu.*

PRACTICAL NOTES: Advance planning for your trip is easy because the World Film Festival sets its schedule two years in advance and is held in late August and early September. For information on dates, film screenings, and purchasing tickets, call the Bell Info-Film line at 514–848–3883. Individual tickets to screenings cost $7.00; a book of ten coupons costs $50.00—and is the economical way to proceed if you two intend to catch five films—not a difficult proposition here. Tickets can be purchased during the Festival at any theater venue.

DAY ONE: morning/afternoon

Drop your bags at **Hôtel Wyndham Montréal** (4 Complexe Desjardins, rue Ste-Catherine Ouest between Jeanne-Mance and St-Urbain; 514–285–1450 or 800–361–8234; métro Place des Arts). Well in advance, you've booked a room with a view of the mountain. You've also requested a package that includes a deluxe room, a bottle of champagne, and a full breakfast served in your room (from $169 for two).

As you walk to the elevator, you'll see legions of folks wearing sunglasses indoors—and not just because the hotel's atrium lobby is so bright. Evidence that Hollywood has invaded Montréal, sunglasses are de rigueur in the hotel even at three o'clock in the morning during the Film Festival. You'll likely bump into film stars on the elevator, on the terrace that surrounds the hotel like a big garden, or at the pool, which is visible from the lobby and surrounded by desert cacti that make the Californians feel right at home.

After you've freshened up, familiarize yourself with the hotel layout. Each afternoon during the festival, a thirty-minute press conference—open to the public—is held at the **Complexe Desjardins**, the shopping center in which the hotel is situated. Here is a prime opportunity to see your favorite actor or director and say hello afterward. Check the time for today's press conference (it usually falls between 1:00 and 4:00 P.M.); you will probably want to attend. Then grab a copy of the *World Film Festival Guide* (distributed free), which contains complete timetables and programming information. Pore over your newfound bible at lunch.

LUNCH

The best burger in town (not to mention first-rate homemade fries) can be enjoyed at **La Paryse** (302 rue Ontario Est; 514–842–2040; inexpensive) in the city's bohemian Latin Quarter and a fifteen-minute walk from the hotel. While you're savoring the food, break out your film bible. Your biggest dilemma will be selecting from more than 250 features and 130 shorts. Most films are shown in venues a few steps from the hotel: **Théâtres Maisonneuve** (in Place des Arts, 260 Boulevard de Maisonneuve Ouest; 514–285–4200); **Complexe Desjardins** (rue Ste-Catherine Ouest between Jeanne-Mance and St-Urbain; 514–849–33456), which contains three theaters, and the **Imperial Cinema** (1430 rue de Bleury; 514–848–0330), Montréal's oldest theater. You can expect a wonderful cinema experience in the latter venue. This vintage 1940s theater has a large screen, a mammoth capacity, and a great sound system. **Cinéma Loews**, a ten-minute walk west (954 rue Ste-Catherine Ouest; 514–861–7437; station Peel), houses five theaters and can also be easily accessed by métro.

Decide on a film, but don't dash off to a premiere before sharing a delectable slice of La Paryse carrot cake. And don't forget to pencil in the press conference at Complexe Desjardins. Hold on to that pencil for an autograph.

After lunch, head for the film you've found irresistible. Enjoy the pleasure of sitting in the dark, holding hands, stealing a kiss or two, and watching the movie, of course.

DAY ONE: evening

DINNER

Films from around the world draw participants from around the world. More than sixty countries submit entries to the international festival, which means that the ethnic restaurants off boulevard St-Laurent (mainly above rue Sherbrooke) are the place to go for dinner.

Jardin de Panos (521 rue Duluth Est; 514–521–4206; inexpensive), in an adorable white house with blue shutters, serves simple Greek cuisine, well-prepared, on a street blocked to pedestrian traffic. "Bring your own bottle (*apportez votre vin*)" is the rule at the restaurants on Duluth, so stop at the **Société des Alcools du Québec** (SAQ) at 4053 St-Denis, on the corner of Duluth, before you arrive. Jardin de Panos, by the way, has a pretty garden in back that makes for an enchanting dining spot in summer.

You can see another film tonight or head for **Les Beaux Esprits** (2073 St-Denis; 514–844–0882), which has live music on Friday and Saturday nights. Whatever your choice, enjoy your evening.

DAY TWO: morning

BREAKFAST

When you awaken, enjoy a breakfast in bed. Linger over your eggs and bacon, and savor your café au lait; you've decided to take your time this morning and walk to the Cinéma Loews, where you'll catch a film, break for lunch, then return to the theater for more fun at the movies. When you've devoured the last morsel of your almond croissant, dress comfortably and start walking.

It's only a ten-minute walk west on Ste-Catherine to the theater, but you'll want to absorb the sights and sounds along the way. Ste-Catherine was the hottest street in the city in the 1970s and early eighties; it has been eclipsed these days by St-Denis and St-Laurent as a night spot, but you can still find everything here from classy strip joints that attract New England college boys to the largest bookstore in town (**Chapters**, 1171 rue Ste-Catherine Ouest; 514–849–8825), which provides comfortable chairs for reading magazines and books. Why not take your time exploring the street before the movie?

DAY TWO: afternoon

LUNCH

After the movie, leave the theater in a lovey-dovey mood, and pause for lunch at **Le Commensal** (1204 avenue McGill College; 514–871–1480; inexpensive). Even non-vegetarians adore the vegetarian fare that is sold here by weight, not item. Fill your plate with garden-fresh salads, a yummy array of hot and cold main dishes, and sinful desserts. Don't get too carried away, though. The cashier weighs the plate on a scale to determine the bill. From an ample window seat in this second-floor locale, look down below on a street that is sometimes called the Champs-Élysées of Montréal.

Lights! Camera! Action!

Film crews are a common sight on Montréal streets. The monetary exchange rate makes shooting here a real bargain for Hollywood filmmakers, so much so that Montréal has been dubbed "Hollywood North." Recent films made in Montréal include Universal's remake of The Day of the Jackal *(starring Bruce Willis and Richard Gere);* Afterglow *(produced by Robert Altman), and* In Love and War, *a New Line film on the life of Ernest Hemingway (starring Sandra Bullock).*

Avenue McGill College connects sedate McGill University, founded in the last century, to the contemporary scene on rue Ste-Catherine. It's a spacious tree-lined street with striking art, modern buildings, and a dead-on view of Mont-Royal. After lunch, walk up the avenue for a closer look at Raymond Masson's gripping sculpture, *The Illuminated Crowd*, a showstopper featuring a group of men and women whose facial expressions are cinema in the raw. Thinking about plot and character now, revert to movie mode. Armed with the delicious date squares you've picked up at Le Commensal for later, return to the theater and enjoy the film until the credits roll.

Walk back to the hotel when the movie lets out. You may want to dash into **Maison de la Presse Internationale** (1128 rue Ste-Catherine Ouest), which carries magazines from around the world. Buy a few magazines you've always wanted to read but never had time for. Pile them on the bed at the hotel, prop up the pillows, and read while you snuggle under the covers before dinner. When you're ready, dress up a bit and take a cab to the restaurant.

Do not trifle with love.
— Alfred de Musset

DAY TWO: evening

DINNER

Parisian actress Sarah Bernhardt (1844–1923), one of the best-known figures in the history of the stage, stayed during her international tour in the former Hotel Richelieu, where the restaurant **Claude Postel** (443 rue St-Vincent; 514–875–5067; moderate to expensive) is now situated. Dine on wild game, lamb, or fish in this fine French restaurant, and imagine La Bernhardt, toast of the town, returning to this old, stone building after a performance. In summer, the terrasse at Claude Postel seats fifty. Desserts are homemade, and the restaurant has a take-out chocolate and pastry shop close by (75 rue Notre-Dame Ouest). Stroll over there after dinner, and buy a couple of slices of lemon pie to enjoy back at the hotel after tonight's performance.

For now, tuck your box of sweets under your arm, take your sweetie's hand, and head for Le Parc des Festivals on the corner of rue de Maisonneuve and rue Bleury, where there's an outdoor screening (free) every night. Chairs and bleachers accommodate the crowd. The evening begins between 7:30 and 8:00 P.M. with a concert of taped music from various films. The onset of starry starry night (usually around 8:30) acts as the theater curtain, and the film is projected onto a building nearby. One or two short films precede the feature of the evening. In case of rain, screenings take place just steps away in the Imperial Cinema (1430 rue de Bleury), which can handle a large crowd.

After the films, return to the hotel for more stargazing as the celebrities return to roost. Then, slip away together to the solitude of your room, and savor every last bite of lemon pie. The sunglasses come off tomorrow.

FOR MORE ROMANCE

For a film experience of a different sort, head to the **Imax Theatre** (King Edward Pier, corner boulevard St-Laurent and rue de la Commune). Here you'll find movies shown on a gargantuan seven-story screen from morning until night ($10 a ticket). If you are not bilingual or French-speaking, make certain to attend the English showing (at least two a day), not the French. Sink into cushy seats and transport your body skyward. The three-dimensional technology puts you and your sweetheart in the heart of the action.

Seasonal Sleepovers

⭐ Original Sin
APPLE PICKING IN THE MONTÉRÉGIAN FOOTHILLS

ORBIDDEN FRUIT FLOURISHES JUST TWENTY MINUTES south of Montréal, where apple producers in the Montérégie region seduce you with thirty varieties of the stuff that tripped up Adam and Eve. The seduction process continues as you try apple jam, apple chutney, apple butter, apple syrup, apple pie, and, of course, apple cider—in unexpected incarnations.

On this itinerary, re-create the original sin by biting into a juicy apple plucked by your own hand. Sip prizewinning sparkling cider at the summit of the hill behind an apple orchard, and climb a challenging peak so pristine that part of it was designated a reserve by UNESCO.

Home base for this sinful trip is a Tudor-style *manoir* bordering the Richelieu River, a ribbon of calm surrounded by theatrical colors in fall. In addition to the *manoir,* you'll discover a saucy gingerbread home where the god of chocolate rules—an authentic Belgian chocolate factory where you'll be tempted (yet again) by sweet morsels filled with Grand Marnier, Irish coffee, and peach schnapps.

In fact, temptation beckons every step of the way on this itinerary. Why resist?

PRACTICAL NOTES: Apple-picking season starts at the end of August and continues until mid-October. On weekends, the orchards are packed with families picking apples. Traffic can be a headache. I suggest a Friday arrival so that Day One, which centers on the apple orchards, can be romantic instead of frantic. I also suggest you bring along climbing boots for the more challenging hike on Day Two.

♦ Stow your bags at the elegant **Manoir Rouville-Campbell** (125 chemin des Patriotes Sud; Mont-Saint-Hilaire; 450–446–6060 or 800–267–0525), built in the 1800s and classified a historic monument. Have lunch in **Denis Charbonneau's** apple orchard (576 rang de la Montagne; Mont-St-Gregoire; 450–347–9184), where you'll enjoy refined cuisine on a picnic table under a shade tree.

♦ Learn about the therapeutic uses of apple cider vinegar from producer **Pierre Gingras** (1132 rang Grande-Caroline; Rougemont; 450–469–1895). Sip the nectar of the gods at **Michel Jordoin's** award-winning **Cidrerie** (1130 rang Petite-Caroline; 450–469–2676), where you can climb a gentle trail with your bottle in tow.

♦ Hike up Mont-Saint-Hilaire for a breathtaking view of the Richelieu River; bring binoculars to bird-watch at Canada's first designated biosphere reserve. After a trip to heavenly heights, indulge in a heavenly treat at **La Cabosse d'or** (973 chemin Ozias-Leduc; Otterburn Park; 450–464–6937), a Belgian chocolate factory that also serves ice cream and pastry.

DAY ONE: morning

Less than a half-hour drive from downtown Montréal sits stately **Manoir Rouville-Campbell** (125 chemin des Patriotes Sud; Mont-Saint-Hilaire; 514–446–6060), where you tread back in time immediately upon entering the massive brick gates.

The story of this historic landmark began in 1694, when King Louis XIV granted Jean-Baptiste Hertel a land parcel along the Richelieu River. It wasn't until 1819, though, that a fifth-generation descendant, René Hertel de Rouville, built a modest stone and wood house on the land, only to tear it down fourteen years later and build a manor house more in line with his rank—and better able to accommodate his large family.

Bankruptcy in 1844 forced Hertel to cede all his holdings to a British Army officer, Major Thomas Edmund Campbell, who altered Hertel's home drastically nine years later to look like a manor in his native Scotland. He gave it the Tudor style it retains today—in complete contrast to other grand homes of that era in Québec. When the last owner bearing the name Campbell departed in 1956, the manor remained deserted until 1969, when sculptor Jordi Bonet acquired it and lived there to his death. French Canada's best-loved comedian, Yvon Deschamps, bought the *manoir* in 1996.

When you reserve a room here, request the Chatelain package designed for romantics. In addition to your lovely guest room, the package includes a five-course dinner, breakfast or brunch, and gratuities on the meals and the room. I suggest you choose a so-called "modern" room located in the new wing of the Manoir. You'll have a better view of the river and the gardens than in the original wing, yet the old-world charm still comes through. I recommend either Room No. 256 or Room No. 225 (a "Mezzanine" room that has two floors). I found both airier, brighter, and more cheerful than the older rooms.

Have a walk around the grounds, which include French- and English-style gardens, before you begin your quest for forbidden fruit. The sumptuous location of the Manoir, between a mountain and a river, enhances the sense of grandeur and prepares you for the big sin that awaits.

DAY ONE: afternoon

LUNCH

Once you have settled in and explored a bit, leave the Manoir on a forty-five-minute trip to your luncheon destination. Turn right out of the front gate and follow Route 133 South (chemin des Patriotes) to Iberville. Turn left on Route 104 East until Mont-St-Grégoire. In the village of Mont-St-Grégoire, take rang de la Montagne to **Cidrerie et Verger Denis Charbonneau** (576 rang de la Montagne; Mont-St-Grégoire; 450–347–9184; inexpensive). Here you can choose between a picnic in an old barn in the middle of an apple orchard—or table service on an exterior terrace surrounded by trees. For the most romantic option, call in advance and tell them you'd like to picnic today.

Menu choices range from ordinary to exotic. Why not start with a fresh garden salad, then delve into ostrich meat or pheasant? Le Mousseux du Fermier, a hard cider produced in Charbonneau's cellars, is the perfect accompaniment to the meal. For dessert, indulge in a scoop of vanilla ice cream alongside a slice of Charbonneau's famed fruit pie. It's hard to choose from apple, apple and strawberry, apple and raspberry, apple and blueberry, apple and four fruit—or a wildly popular pie made with maple syrup called "Pets de Soeur"—a comical and mildly irreverent expression in French that means "Farts of a Nun"—something you never expect to happen and never even talk about.

> *Stolen sweets are always sweeter,*
> *Stolen kisses much completer,*
> *Stolen looks are nice in chapels,*
> *Stolen, stolen, be your apples.*
> —Leigh Hunt
> (1784–1859)

After lunch, stroll through the orchard planted by Charbonneau's father. Guides located in the barn will point out specific types of apples on nearby trees—Melba, Jersey Mac, Lobo, Spartan, Empire, Cortland, Vista Bella—which you can pick yourself and take home. A ten-pound sack costs about $4.00. Charbonneau's burgeoning operation is expressed best in a rambling kiosk where local products are showcased. In the tiny boutique on the second floor, you can have a dried flower arrangement made on the spot or pick up fragrant soaps, maple syrup, or a jar of marmalade made by local crafters. Don't pass up the chance to buy some of Charbonneau's apple doughnuts. They'll be wonderful for snacking as you hike later on.

Leave the orchard and turn left on rang de la Montagne, left on rang du Sous-Bois, left on Route 227 North, in the direction of Marieville, and right on Route 112 East to Rougemont, where you'll take the third exit, rang Grande-Caroline. It's a half-hour trip from the Cidrerie to **Vinaigrerie Verger Pierre Gingras** (1132 rang Grande-Caroline; Rougemont; 450–469–4954) where a further incarnation of the mighty apple is introduced—apple cider vinegar, plain or seasoned with herbs and berries. Gingras touts the health-giving effects of this age-old remedy and advises consumers to check for "mother vinegar," a deposit which forms at the bottom of a bottle and ensures that the product is 100 percent pure.

The cider vinegar here is made from natural apple juice, aged in oak barrels under controlled temperatures and touted as a possible remedy for an assortment of problems, including sore throat (gargle with it), muscular aches and pains (rub it on), weight loss (a few tablespoons each day is said to speed up the metabolism), and insomnia (mix a tablespoon with a little honey in a glass of luke-warm water and drink it before bed). Why not buy a bottle and try it later? For now, you have one more stop, just five minutes away.

Turn right on rang Grande-Caroline and left on rang Petite-Caroline, where you'll see **Cidrerie Michel Jodoin** (1130 rang Petite-Caroline; Rougemont; 450–469–2676), a complete contrast to Charbonneau's spread. Jodoin produces cider. Three kinds. That's it; that's all. He has succeeded in perfecting the process to such a degree he's the biggest cider producer in Québec (130,000 bottles a year), and cider artisans from France have traveled here to study Jodoin's "méth-ode champenoise." Cider-making secrets have been in the Jodoin fam-ily for four generations, and deep pride in the product is evident when you speak to the pony-tailed scion who is carrying the tradition for-ward in a picture-perfect orchard at the foot of Mont-Rougemont.

More than 4,500 apple trees on the property bear more than thirty varieties. Only five to seven kinds—McIntosh, Cortland, Empire, and Geneva among them—are chosen to give the cider here its subtle, fruity aroma. Aged in oak casks, the cider gets its rich color and flavor from old-fashioned methods of production—the entire process takes two years from tree to table. For a small fee, you can tour the cider cellars and the production area and have a cider tast-ing. It's wise to call in advance and tell them you're coming. Now what would you like to drink? The sparkling white? The sparkling rosé? The still cider? Jodoin's cider is sold only at this location, so don't let the opportunity pass. Can't decide? I'll help you out. Buy a bottle of Blanc de Pepin flat to enjoy with your apple doughnuts after you climb the lovely hill behind Jodoin's property. This cider outclassed thirteen others in a contest in New York. Then buy a bot-tle of each variety before you leave.

Now alerted to the many properties of apples, chat about your newfound knowledge on the half-hour return trip to the Manoir. Turn right on rang Petite-Caroline. At the crossroads in downtown Rougemont, turn right and follow instructions for Route 229 North. Turn right on Route 227 North in the direction of St-Jean-Baptiste. In St-Jean-Baptiste, turn left on chemin Rouville, which becomes chemin de la Montagne in Mont-St-Hilaire. Turn right on chemin Ozias-Leduc, left on chemin des Trentes, and right on Route 133 North to the Manoir.

Weather permitting, why not take a swim in the outdoor, heated pool—or perhaps you'd enjoy a walk along the river? After your walk or swim, try an apple-based remedy to help you unwind before dinner (see sidebar on opposite page).

DAY ONE: evening

DINNER

Enter the tunnel connecting the elegant reception area in the Manoir to the new wing. Gaze out a panel of windows and watch the sun set over the Richelieu. Now you're ready to enter the dining room for a five-course feast. The meal always begins with *potage*; next is an appetizer, perhaps mousse of duck liver. Next comes a choice of red meat, fish, or chicken, followed by, perhaps, chocolate and raspberry *suprème* with a fruit *coulis* for dessert. After the feast, you might want to walk around the estate before you retire.

DAY TWO: morning

BREAKFAST

The Chatelain package entitles you to a continental breakfast or heartier fare. I suggest you fortify yourself for the climb ahead. The dining room opens at 7:00 A.M. and offers a special called The Rouville and another called The Campbell. The first includes fresh juice, one egg any style, fried potatoes, bacon or ham, and toast. The second, which I suggest, includes two eggs (and fixings) or pancakes or French toast. Eat well. You'll need the energy.

Checkout time is noon, but the Manoir will hold your bags as you explore the village of Mont-Saint-Hilaire after breakfast. Québec's renowned ecclesiastical painter Ozias Leduc (1864-1955) did the frescoes on the walls of **Église de la Paroisse de St-Hilaire-sur-Richelieu** (chemin des Patriotes Nord; 450–467–4434), where visitation is arranged by appointment only. The church is only two minutes from the Manoir (turn left on Route 133 North) and is worth a visit. After a spiritual experience inside, you're ready for a spiritual experience outside—a climb up Mont-Saint-Hilaire, the highest of the eight Montérégian hills that arc across the St-Laurent plain and include Mont-Royal in Montréal. Follow signs to the **Centre de conservation de la nature du Mont-Saint-Hilaire** (422 chemin des Moulins; 450–467–1755; admission $4.00), about a five-minute drive. Part of Mont-St-Hilaire was designated Canada's first biosphere reserve by UNESCO in 1978 and is used for scientific experiments. As such, this portion is inaccessible to the public. No matter. You can hike through 22 kilometers (14 miles) of trail under a shady canopy of towering red oaks and ancient white pine. You'll see dozens of species of moss and flowering plants, and you'll hear the songs of up to 185 bird species. Bring binoculars, not only to bird-watch but to take in the fall colors and a breathtaking view of the Richelieu River, which you will see from the mountain summit.

All your climbing deserves a reward. I know just the place to find one. Return to your car parked at the nature center and follow chemin des Moulins to chemin de la Montagne and turn left on chemin Ozias-Leduc.

Apple Therapy

Put your apple cider vinegar to the test. The product is said to contain a natural therapeutic agent to counter stress and help bring on relaxation. Holistic sources say to pour a half cup in your bath and soak for fifteen minutes. It might help the process if you also bring a glass of hard cider in the bathtub with you—to drink, of course— but that's just my suggestion.

DAY TWO: afternoon

SNACK

La Cabosse d'or (973 chemin Ozias-Leduc; Otterburn Park; 450–464–6937; inexpensive) pays homage to the god of chocolate. In a combination factory, chocolate shop, and eatery, the heavenly product is made by a Belgian couple who moved to Québec to farm in 1981 but sorely missed the taste of the chocolate back home. Martine and

Jean-Paul Crowin returned to Belgium for two years to study chocolate making and then, blessedly, brought their skills back to Québec.

Peek into the factory, where chocolate is melted, molded, chilled, filled, and finally packed away in foil-lined boxes. Then it's time to get serious. Women dressed in gingham aprons and ruffled caps will show you chocolate stuffed with forty kinds of filling. They'll show you eight kinds of truffles, including rum, brandy, Cointreau, and Armagnac. They'll show you chocolate shaped like a wooden shoe, a maple leaf, a teddy bear, a champagne bottle, and, of course, a heart. Sigh. The homemade ice cream here is rich and creamy, and the assortment of French pastry will make your mouth water. Enjoy your indulgence on the terrace, along with a cup of tea or a cappuccino, before you pick up your bags and go home. Few endings are as sweet.

FOR MORE ROMANCE

"Wouldn't you like to fly in my beautiful balloon?" asks the song. If you don't feel like using your own power to get a striking view of the Richelieu River Valley, try climbing sky-high in a hot-air balloon. **Balad'Air** (566 rang de la Montagne; Mont-St-Grégoire; 450–358–9643) will guide your ascent as you fly high enough to ensure the best view and low enough to pick leaves from the trees. The hour-long flight (time aloft) ends with a toast of sparkling wine and costs $140 per person. Mont-St-Grégoire is prime balloon territory: The **Festival de Montgolfières** (514–346–6000), the most prestigious hot-air balloon festival in Canada, is held in neighboring St-Jean-Sur-Richelieu every August.

If you can spend another day here, consider exploring the wine route detailed in the "Clinking Glasses: Wine Lovers Weekend" itinerary.

September Morn
FALL LEAVES AND GOLF AT PINE HILL

I MAGINE A MAN WHO BECOMES INSTANTLY SMITTEN with a woman he sees singing in a choir in Colombia, South America. Imagine a man so intent on courting her that when she refuses to see him unescorted, he flies her entire choir to his hometown in Germany—where he woos and ultimately weds her in a Cinderella ceremony.

Imagine a man so infatuated with children, he supports 5,000 orphans in Colombia and has fifteen of his own kids. Imagine a man so wealthy, he owns twenty-six castles worldwide. Let your imagination take flight, and you've entered the fairy-tale life of real estate mogul Herbert Hillebrand, who developed Hotel du Lac Carling— the only "castle" he's built from scratch—and the place where you'll write your very own fairy tale this weekend.

This hideaway outside Montréal may be the best-kept secret in La Belle Province. Shady hills surround a freshwater lake on the property. A golf course rims the bedrooms. Meals are prepared by a noted chef. And you just might get a peek at the secluded seventy-seven-room villa where Hillebrand and his family stay when they make their yearly visit to Pine Hill around Christmas—and where he keeps a monogrammed snowmobile in the garage for each child.

Pinch yourselves when the weekend's over.

PRACTICAL NOTES: I've dubbed this itinerary September Morn because the brisk fall weather arrives in the Laurentians a week or two earlier than in Montréal, so you'll likely see leaves turning color during your stay. But the itinerary also works nicely at the tail end of August or through mid-October, when fall is either beginning—or

♦ It's hard to leave your sexy room at **Hotel du Lac Carling** (Route 327 Nord in Pine Hill; 800–661–9211), which features a mirrored Jacuzzi just steps from the bed. But there's much more to see in the hotel corridors and the lobby. Feast your eyes on 200 original paintings and tapestries dating as far back as the 1400s.

♦ Indulgence waits in the hotel's sumptuous health center, which offers racquetball, tennis, squash, badminton, and weight-training equipment. After your workout, book a Swedish massage or a mud bath right on the premises.

♦ Walk out your terrace door and onto a golf course where Bing Crosby and Bob Hope swung a club in days gone by. After a day on the links, relax in the hotel dining room, where Québec regional cuisine is highlighted and where a pastry chef whips up luscious confections on the spot.

on its way out. Remember to pack sweaters and even a jacket—and hiking boots if you'd like to climb the hills around the hotel. As well, bring workout clothes for the sports center, which has indoor courts for racquetball, tennis, squash, and badminton, as well as weight-training equipment. It also offers massage and various beauty services.

DAY ONE: morning/afternoon

Have brunch before you leave Montréal. Check-in time at **Hotel du Lac Carling** (Route 327 Nord; Pine Hill; 800–661–9211) is 3:00 P.M., but you are welcome to arrive earlier and explore the grounds—you might even want to wear hiking boots on the drive out so you can climb the hills surrounding Lac Carling, which is on hotel property.

The town of Pine Hill is one hour and fifteen minutes from Montréal, barring heavy traffic. The shortest route is Highway 13 north to Highway 640 west through St-Eustache. Take Highway 640 west to Highway 148 west toward Lachute. The highway ends in Lachute. At the end, turn left and go through Lachute to pick up Highway 327 north through Brownsburg and Pine Hill. About fifteen minutes outside Pine Hill, you'll arrive at the hotel entrance. Check in; you've requested a deluxe room with Jacuzzi; No. 111 has an outdoor patio that fronts the golf course and has a view of the distant, spruce-covered hills. As you walk down the corridor to your bedroom, listen to the sound of a waterfall flowing over the rocks outside.

Hotel du Lac Carling, with one hundred rooms, is run by a husband-and-wife management team handpicked by Hillebrand to supervise the enchanted, castle-like hotel filled with antiques and paintings.

Coral and Wim Steenbakkers—she is an accomplished harpist from San Francisco, he a former world-class sailor from Holland—are your hosts, and their influence has already been felt in an emphasis on the visual and performing arts. There's music in the Great Room adjoining the lobby, where Coral practices harp, and there's live music at dinner on weekends. Coral is in the process of cataloging and identifying two hundred works of art in the hotel so that guests can enjoy the art as if it were exhibited in a gallery.

Your Golf Package ($210 per person) includes a deluxe room with a Jacuzzi steps from your bed, a five-course gourmet dinner, a full breakfast, one round of golf, and all gratuities. Settle into the surroundings—there's so much to see. I suggest heading for the fully equipped sports center. You'll find weight-training equipment, courts for racquetball, squash, badminton or tennis, a pool, a whirlpool, and a sauna. A massage room and a tanning solarium are on the premises as well. Unwind here before dinner.

But before you head off to the sports center, order a bottle of champagne to be brought to your room chilled. Once it's uncorked after your workout, uncork your imagination. The Jacuzzi beckons, and it's surrounded by tastefully mirrored walls and illuminated by recessed spotlights. Need I say more?

DAY ONE: evening

DINNER

The hotel's **Restaurant L'If**, named for the yew tree, has a cathedral ceiling, antique fireplace, a view of Lac Carling, and live music at dinner on weekends. The menu centers on fish and game from Québec —escargots from the Charlevoix region and deer, rabbit, and wild mushrooms found locally. A pastry chef and an assistant make all the luscious desserts, again using local ingredients in their fruit pies, tarts, and cakes. *Délicieux!*

Lap of Luxury

Hillebrand's villa includes a huge indoor swimming pool made of Portuguese marble—surrounded by Persian carpets on which to delicately dry your toes. A Chickering grand piano, a bar, a massive stone fireplace and a bearskin rug distinguish the living room. His office is filled with antiques. A spanking clean garage that hardly resembles yours or mine contains a couple of Mercedes belonging to Hillebrand—and the monogrammed Ski-Doos belonging to his children.

Take a walk after dinner on the grounds. A huge wrought-iron gate leads to Hillebrand's villa less than five minutes away, and even though the sign indicates private property, guests are allowed to walk on the grounds past the home, which sleeps twenty and is now rented out for executive retreats or special events like fashion shows. Bob Hope and Bing Crosby were regular guests here in the early 1970s when the home belonged to woolen mill giant Gilbert Ayers, and they played golf on the Carling course. You can almost hear the conversations that must have taken place in the living room overlooking the lake (see sidebar). A state-of-the-art indoor tennis court was built across the road by Hillebrand, who had it equipped with a stereophonic sound system.

Visions of opulence filling your head, you'll return to your room feeling dreamy. Good thing. You're getting up early.

DAY TWO: morning

BREAKFAST

A continental breakfast buffet (served from 7:00 A.M.) greets you before you take to the golf course. Designed to speed you on your way, the choice is cereal, yogurt, Danish pastry, croissants, fresh juice, fresh fruit, and coffee. For those who wish to linger, eggs, bacon, and toast can be ordered à la carte, at no extra cost.

Built by Howard Watson in 1961, prestigious Carling Lake Golf Club is one of Canada's top eighteen-hole courses and was once Gilbert Ayers' private domain. He owned the course and a thirty-six-hole course in nearby Lachute. He used Carling Lake to entertain the famous. After his death, his family leased the course to a golf pro.

The 6,700-yard course unfolds over rolling countryside as soon as you step off the restaurant terrace. The employees are efficiency plus, directing you onto the mountainous terrain with friendliness and care. Once out there, be alert for hazards—and not just in the form of a challenging layout. The course has some particularities, including a life-sized statue of a man relieving himself on the grounds. Apparently, groundskeepers have to clean the lipstick off the statue every morning—and not always from the lips. Now that will put a little zip in your golf game. When your round is finished, head back to your room to change.

No doubt you'd like to rewind the tape and play another round, but checkout time is noon.

FOR MORE ROMANCE

If time permits on the way back to Montréal, stop at an apple orchard in St-Joseph-du-Lac. (Between Lachute and St-Eustache, you'll see signs along Highway 148 for St-Joseph du Lac. Follow them into town, about ten minutes from the highway.) September is prime apple-picking season in Québec, and the lower Laurentians are second to the Montérégie region when it comes to orchards. **Verger Chez Les Gauthier** (1970 rue Principal; St-Joseph-du-Lac; 450–623–3239; inexpensive) is a cozy place to fill a sack with apples and enjoy a treat—a glass of apple cider and a slice of apple pie.

The Alps (without Jet Lag)

Bavaria on a Budget

OUNTAINS OF FUN. That's how tourism officials aptly describe the Laurentians, a vast and hilly area north of Montréal. The Laurentians embrace 22,000 square kilometers of land and contain 6,000 hotel rooms, making it the biggest tourist region in Québec after Montréal—and a year-round playground where thousands of Québecers maintain second homes.

The Laurentian mountains offer stellar downhill runs and cross-country ski trails from December until mid-April. In summer, verdant and majestic, the very same mountains crawl with bikers and hikers.

This budget-conscious itinerary takes you to the Laurentians in the heart of winter. A thick blanket of snow ensures superb skiing in the village of Val-David, at the foot of a trio of mountains—Césaire, Condor, and King. Lovers' Park—Le Parc des Amoureux—adjoins an Austrian-style B&B where every room is named for a classical composer, and where you two will make your own music when you've left the slopes.

Pack your warmest clothing *tout de suite*. You are off to Switzerland—in Québec.

PRACTICAL NOTES: Maps and general information on the Laurentian region can be obtained by calling 800–561–6673. Those who don't want to bring along cross-country skis can rent them in Val-David at Ski Se Loue; 2444 rue de l'Église; 819–322–5475.

◆ Stay in **La Maison de Bavière** (1470 chemin de la Rivière; Val-David; 819–322–3528), a nonsmoking B&B where the doors, bathtubs, and lamps are hand-painted—and where the rooms are each named after a classical composer. Ski directly from the front door of the B&B onto a historic railway bed that was converted to a cross-country trail in 1991.

◆ Enjoy a hearty breakfast in the decorative dining nook of the B&B, where even the butter is molded into fanciful shapes. Fortify yourself for a day of downhill skiing with baked apples, homemade muesli, and a different egg dish every day. Now you're ready to tackle the slopes; there are a handful of ski centers within minutes of your lodging.

◆ After a full day of skiing, enjoy a romantic dinner in the intimacy of **Edelweiss** (3050 chemin Doncaster; 819–322–7800), an Austrian chalet surrounded by woods. Keep an eye out for deer in the woods behind the restaurant. Head deeper into the woods when you take an old-fashioned sleigh ride, just for two, through the forest at night. Get cozy under a sleigh blanket— and under the stars.

Downhill skis can be rented at the ski center of your choice. If you bring your own gear, however, La Maison de Bavière has a storage cupboard—hand-painted, of course.

DAY ONE: morning

Eat a hearty breakfast before you leave Montréal. If you want to ski before it starts getting dark (as early as 4:00 P.M.), there won't be time for a sit-down lunch today. Bring along some munchies as a snack. **La Maison de Bavière** (1470 chemin de la Rivière; Val-David; 819–322–3528; $75 to $115, breakfast included) is about 55 miles from downtown. Take Autoroute 15 to exit 76 for Val-David. Stay on Autoroute 117 for a few miles until you see a traffic light. Turn right on rue de l'Église, then left on chemin de La Rivière and travel about a half-mile.

You'll be delighted when you leave your car at the edge of Rivière du Nord and see your picturesque lodging right next to the Lovers' Park. The huge rocks in the river, which create a turbulent cascade in summer, are now snow-covered and resemble giant mushrooms.

You'll be welcomed by German-born Ute Schule and her French-Canadian husband, André Lesage. Having met when they were ski instructors at a Club Med in France, they returned to Québec and began to renovate—drastically—the home André already owned, which was actually part of an old sawmill. Ute, who had always been artistically inclined, began painting furniture—a technique called *Bauernmalere* in Germany—as a way to feel more at home in her adopted country. She has carried the artistic vision throughout the house, which contains four guest rooms, three with river views, and all with a private bath. My favorite is named Beethoven; it has a queen-size bed, Dutch shoes on the wall, a painted toilet seat in the bathroom, and a smashing view of the river. Next in line for the award for charm is a pink and green room named for Haydn, which also has a queen-size bed, a river view, and painted panels on the ceiling.

A cozy living room on the bedroom level contains a mini-fridge where you can store a bottle of wine or champagne. Ute likes to deliver it to your room on a platter decked with flowers. But we're jumping the gun here. Weren't you here to ski?

DAY ONE: afternoon

If you're keen to downhill, eighteen ski centers are within a 50-kilometer (32-mile) radius of Val-David. **Vallée Bleue** (1418 chemin Vallée Bleue; 819–322–3427) is just five minutes away. It has sixteen slopes, two chair lifts, a vertical drop of 111 meters (about 420 feet), and well-groomed trails. **Belle Neige** (Route 117; Val-Morin; 819–322–3311), another downhill ski center nearby, has fourteen slopes, a vertical drop of 157 meters (about 660 feet), and two chair lifts. Both centers have dining facilities on the premises, so you can grab a bite if you get hungry. Both close on Saturday at 4:30 P.M.

Cross-country skiers will think they've died and gone to heaven in Val-David. La Maison de Bavière is steps from **P'tit Train du Nord**, a linear park that extends 200 kilometers (120 miles) through the Laurentians, of which 45 kilometers (28 miles) between Val-David and St-Jérôme are reserved exclusively for cross-country skiers. You can literally ski out the front door and onto the trail.

The P'tit Train du Nord was the dream of Antoine Labelle, a priest credited with opening up the province by pushing for a railway link from St-Jérôme to Mont-Laurier in the 1890s. Industry boomed with the link, and in the 1920s tourism officials in the Laurentians promoted the railway as a "snow train" linking Montréal to resort villages like Sainte-Agathe and Mont-Tremblant. Better roads built in the past few decades made the snow train obsolete, however, and the train made its final trip with passengers in 1981 and its final trip with freight in 1989.

That's when tourism officials thought about giving a second life to the corridor. In 1991, a hundred years after construction, the tracks and frames were removed, and the railway line became a linear park —a much-used means of recreation now for bikers, hikers, snowmobilers, and skiers.

Before you strap on your skis and leave the B&B, ask Ute to make you a reservation for a sleigh ride after dinner tonight. **La Ferme Duquette** (1315 Tenth Rang; 819–322–3829; $40 per couple) offers a one-hour ride for coosome twosomes.

DAY ONE: evening

DINNER

After a strenuous day outdoors, you'll want relaxation at night. In keeping with the Alpine theme, dine early at **Edelweiss** (3050 chemin Doncaster; 819–322–7800; reservation requested; inexpensive to moderate), a French restaurant perched on a wooded hill where you might spot a deer or two. The staff here are very welcoming and solicitous in the second-floor restaurant, which features a stone fireplace, Bavarian beer steins on the mantel, an oil lamp on the table, and pink hearts on a wallpaper border along the ceiling. Belgian chef Olivier Sadones oversees the kitchen. The typical table d'hôte begins with *Les Petits Plaisirs*—a tiny appetizer—and continues with two-colored soup (pea and beet, for instance), salad with raspberry vinegar, smoked salmon, and a sampling of three scrumptious cakes for dessert.

After dinner, drive to La Ferme Duquette, where you'll trade your car for a horse-drawn sleigh. Cuddle under an imitation lynx blanket provided by La Ferme and watch the lights of Val-David flicker in the background as you glide through the forest under a velvety canopy.

DAY TWO: morning

BREAKFAST

In her decorative breakfast nook, Ute makes certain you don't leave her house hungry. On the table are four jams, a fruit compote, and a fresh loaf of bread. You'll start with orange juice, then work your way through baked apples stuffed with cranberries, homemade muesli—a mix of oatmeal, fresh fruit, and yogurt—and an egg dish that varies every day. Notice the butter. It's molded into shapes—another of Ute's artistic flourishes.

> ## Snow Job
>
> *The Laurentians may be the birthplace of skiing in North America, but the region offers more than downhill and cross-country to winter tourists. There's snowboarding, snow-shoeing, snowmobiling, dog-sledding, tube-sliding, rafting on snow, or just plain ice skating. You two could also take a simpler and more romantic approach to snow sports. Why not lie down in the snow and make angels?*

Try a new cross-country environment today. Purchase an all-day pass ($8.00) at the **Centre de ski de fond Val-David** (2510 rue de l'Église No. 2) and gain access to twenty-one groomed trails through Val-David and Val-Morin. While yesterday's P'tit Train du Nord linear trail offered ski surfaces that were basically flat, the cross-country trails here are in the woods and include terrain for every skiing ability. Les Deux Vals, for example, is a beginner trail linking the two villages, but far more challenging trails are here for experts as well.

DAY TWO: afternoon

After several hours on the slopes, you've built an appetite. Grab a late lunch before you leave Val-David.

LUNCH

The name **Le Grand Pa** (2481 rue de l'Église; 819–322–3104; inexpensive) plays well in two languages—it roughly translates as "the big step" in French—and, as the proprietors of this restaurant like to say, it's the first step that counts. Ironically, you'll take the last steps of your holiday into this cozy restaurant. Sit near the big woodstove, have pizza from a wood-burning oven, and drink a draft beer or perhaps some hot red wine with a cinnamon stick. Hold hands as you watch the snow fall outside, and make plans for next year.

FOR MORE ROMANCE

If you're willing to stretch your budget, why not shop in the village of Val-David for the remainder of the afternoon and then travel south about 12 miles along Highway 117 (toward Montréal) to the neighboring village of Ste-Adèle. Here, you can enjoy a memorable meal at **L'eau à la Bouche**—it translates as mouth-watering—(3003 boulevard Ste-Adèle; Ste-Adele; 450–229–2991; open daily from 6:00 P.M.; expensive). Restaurant owner Anne Desjardins, Québec female chef of the year in 1996, offers an unforgettable five-course dinner for $57. In winter, the restaurant's tiled floors, beamed ceilings, and assortment of Québec antiques make it a coveted spot for romantic encounters—and gastronomic ones as well.

Saddle Up

WITH THE HORSEY SET IN HUDSON

UIET, WISE, AND GOOD. RESIDENTS OF HUDSON would probably see themselves in Percy Bysshe Shelley's description. They adore their tranquil solitude. They adore their antiques stores, their wools, their plaids, their afternoon tea, the polo matches nearby—and the miles of equestrian trail that run through the surrounding area. They love to socialize with other folks who are quiet, wise, and good at places like the pub in the Willow Place Inn—known locally as the Willow—which just happens to be where you'll be staying.

An English town with a slight French accent, Hudson attracts an upper-class crowd with a passion for the great outdoors. If you're looking for a refined romantic experience in an all-natural setting, Hudson is waiting. Tally-ho.

PRACTICAL NOTES: Finnegan's Market is open every Saturday from May through October, so your stay must include a Saturday for this itinerary to work. As well, the Montréal Polo Club (450–458–0791) in Ste-Marthe has matches every weekend from mid-May to mid-September.

DAY ONE: morning

Leave your bags off early at the **Willow Place Inn** (208 chemin Main; 450–458–7006; $85 double occupancy, including continental breakfast), just forty-five minutes from Montréal (take Highway 40 Ouest to exit 26; then a right on boulevard Bellevue and a left on chemin Main). Even if you can't check into your romantic room just yet—you've requested either Room No. 4, 6, or 9—make your presence known, leave your luggage, then take chemin Main (right turn from

Romance
AT A GLANCE

◆ Drop your bags at the **Willow Place Inn** (208 chemin Main; 450–485–7006), over-looking peaceful Lake of Two Mountains, but don't tarry. Make a beeline for **Finnegan's Market** (775 chemin Main; 450–458–4377), where you'll spend hours combing the merchandise at Québec's biggest open-air antiques bazaar.

◆ Take a ferry across the lake to the oldest monastery in North America, where you can purchase the famous Oka cheese made by the monks. Speaking of deli-cious food, dine that night at the very intimate **Clementine** (398 chemin Main; 450–458–8181), named for the pastry chef's French grand-mère.

◆ Pack a picnic and you're off to watch a polo match in tony company. Hockey Hall-of-Famer Larry Robinson still plays for the **Montréal Polo Club,** and he might be in town the day you catch a match. At half time, join the men in ascots and women in fine hats marching onto the field to fix the divots.

the hotel) about seven kilometers (4 miles) until you see signs for **Finnegan's Market** (775 chemin Main; 450–458–4377). The biggest outdoor antiques market in Québec is a Saturday tradition, attracting folks from the neighboring province of Ontario as well as Québec. Sorry to rush you along, but I'll tell you about the hotel later. It's important now to get to the market, which opens at 9:00 A.M. and wraps up before 3:00 P.M. You don't want to miss out on a find.

Park in the grassy field. The site was once a farm, and you can see remnants of a barn in the sylvan setting. Spend a couple of leisurely hours poking around from stall to stall. You'll see old pine furniture from Québec, art deco lamps and radios, wrought iron fix-tures, carved ducks, antique toys, and some blacksmith implements probably used around these parts years ago. Craft kiosks are here as well—and some stalls offer candy and treats. Save your appetite. You're returning to the hotel for lunch.

DAY ONE: afternoon

LUNCH

The Pub (450–458–7006; inexpensive), located inside the Willow Inn, serves a great roast beef sandwich, steak and kidney pie, a cream of carrot soup that draws raves, and an onion soup that also has legions of fans. Before you eat, sit on the terrace and sip a cold draft beer as you take a few moments to absorb the fascinating history of the hotel.

Originally built in 1820 as a private home for George Mallette and his family, the Willow was bought in 1824 by François Xavier Desjardins, the only French-speaking member of the community. A fervid patriot, he operated the edifice as a store, and it soon became local headquarters for the French patriots intent on overthrowing British rule in the 1830s. So much plotting went on, a scandalized domestic named Mary Kirkbride reported patriot plans to the local head of the British militia.

> *I love tran-*
> *quil solitude*
> *And such society*
> *As is quiet, wise,*
> *and good.*
> —Percy Bysshe
> Shelley
> (1792–1822)

Desjardins, said to be storing munitions in the cellar, fought in the Battle of St-Eustache during the 1837 Patriot Rebellion, survived, and was then imprisoned in Montréal for treason. Since that time, the current owners of the Willow like to say, the establishment has operated peacefully—as a boardinghouse, a residential hotel, and as an inn. Tragedy struck in 1989 when fire completely destroyed the building —but the owners, lifelong Hudson residents, were committed to re-creating it in every detail.

They've done a great job. The inn has nine guest rooms decorated with antiques and romantic touches like brass bedsteads or canopy beds. Each room has a private bath. No televisions or radios are provided—a choice intended to preserve the tranquil solitude.

The white-and-black porch with a sloping roof is extremely inviting, as is the big, backyard terrace on the edge of the Lake of Two Mountains. Linger here over lunch and enjoy the view.

Directly visible across the water is the **Cistercian Abbey of Oka** (1600 chemin d'Oka; 450–479–8361), built before 1890 and the oldest monastery in North America. When your lunch is over, get into your car and take the ten-minute trip across the lake by ferry (450–458–4732), which runs about every twenty minutes. Take a left out of the hotel onto chemin Main, and you'll reach the dock half-a-kilometer away. Stroll through the gardens at the monastery and buy the famous Oka cheese that the monks here have produced for more than a century.

Return to Hudson later in the afternoon and, if time permits, explore the boutiques along the corner of chemin Main and Cameron, just 3 kilometers (less than 2 miles) from the Willow. **Legg & Co.** (422 chemin Main; 450–458–5222), otherwise known as Leggs, is a converted general store that sells upscale casual clothing for men and women—and also houses a tea salon. Pause for a cup of Earl Grey, then it's back to the hotel to get ready for dinner.

DAY ONE: evening

DINNER

The real-life Clémentine was a celebrated cook known for her skill creating wedding cakes, so it's not surprising that pastry chef Louise Beaulne chose her grandmother's name for the restaurant she and husband Michel opened more than two decades ago. **Clémentine** (398 chemin Main; 450–458–8181; moderate; table d'hôte from $18; reservations required; closed Monday and open only for dinner) offers superb regional cuisine at superb prices. The couple tapped into the local products long before the crowd and put a premium on traditional ways—even the bread recipe used in the restaurant comes from Michel's grandmother, a former innkeeper in the Laurentians.

Eighty percent of the products on the menu are regional—rabbit from Oka, and pheasant, quail, and duck from other producers in Québec. A typical Saturday-night, three-course menu offers pheasant leg confit with orange sauce, rack of lamb with fresh thyme, and "Louise's dessert"—a masterful surprise every night.

The cozy restaurant, which seats about one hundred on two floors, achieves an elegant but homey feeling through lace tablecloths, a vast collection of porcelain teapots on display, and Clémentine's Tiffany lamp near the most romantic table on the second floor. As you dine, you can almost feel the presence of Madame Clémentine Léger, whose picture is on the menu (see "Starry-Eyed Lover" sidebar in this chapter).

Starry-Eyed Lover

In October of 1898, Joseph Lalonde, who lived in Oka, wrote this poem to his beloved, Clémentine Léger, who lived across the Lake of Two Mountains in Hudson. After you explore the area, you can understand his wonder.

"Who cannot savour, in pleasant solitude,

the magic spectacle of the stars dancing on the cristalline water?

Even the trees on the shore joined in the enchantment,

admiring their proud silhouettes in the water, taking on fantastic shapes.

Sweet moments of youth when dreams were golden,

evanescent sunfilled hours when each of us floated in our own sky blue ship.

Why do you come so early and leave so soon?"

Return to the Willow. You want to rise early tomorrow for a big day in the great outdoors.

DAY TWO: morning

BREAKFAST

The Willow serves a continental breakfast between 7:00 and 10:00 A.M., a help-yourself affair that is always more elaborate on weekends. In the dining room facing the Lake of Two Mountains, you'll have coffee, juice, croissants, fresh fruit, cereal, scrambled eggs, bacon, and hash browns. Duly fortified, it's time for polo. Don't forget your ascot.

But before you head for the field, stop at **Strudel's Bakery** (429 chemin Main; 450–458–2122; inexpensive), and pick up a sandwich (roast beef, turkey, tuna, or ham) and some luscious pastry. You'll be picnicking at the polo field—not exactly like the Royals—but good enough.

The field is a fifteen-minute ride from here. Take chemin Main to rue St-Charles, which leads to Autoroute 40. Take Autoroute 40 until Exit 17 (Montée Lavigne). Turn left off the exit. Travel about 2 miles until chemin du Parc, the third street on your right.

DAY TWO: afternoon

On Saturdays and Sundays from 11:00 A.M. to 4:00 P.M. from May to October, weather permitting, the Montréal Polo Club stages matches on five polo fields at 756 chemin du Parc in St-Marthe (450–458–0791; no admission charge). In case of rain, or if the fields are muddy from rain the day before, matches are canceled. In addition to the regular weekend schedule, the club sponsors two major tournaments, in mid-July and Labor Day weekend, where participants include higher caliber teams from other provinces and the United States. Hockey Hall of Famer Larry Robinson, who took up the sport when he played for the Montréal Canadiens, still plays for the Montréal Polo Club.

Watching these charging horsemen with mallets in hand is exhilarating, but there's as much action in the paddocks, where patrons rent the space and then stage elaborate picnics on linen tablecloths and fine china. At half-time in the match, men in ascots and women in fancy hats march onto the field, champagne glasses in hand, to fix the divots. Have your picnic on the sidelines and gape at the spectacle. When it's over, you'll be heading for more adventure outdoors on the beautiful grounds of the place where you'll have your dinner—a place that's more than a restaurant.

Leave the polo field and turn right in the direction of Valleyfield. The first road on your right is chemin St-Henri. Stay on it about fifteen minutes until you reach your destination.

DAY TWO: evening

DINNER

Auberge des Gallant (1171 chemin St-Henri in Ste-Marthe; 450–459–4241 or 800–641–4241; moderate; $26 to $40 for a five-course meal) is set on a country estate—400 acres on the southern side of Mont-Rigaud. Dotted with flower gardens, walking paths, cross-country ski trails, and feeders for birds and deer, the estate offers much to explore before your evening meal here. Take a long walk on the marked trails around the auberge, and be sure to circle the trout-stocked pond where beavers build their dams. Birds serenade as you sit on a bench under an apple tree, keeping an eye peeled for deer. They are plentiful in these parts. Owner Linda Gallant likes to invite romantics to come dine with their deer—or dear. So go ahead. Walk with your sweetheart until your appetites draw you back toward the restaurant for dinner. Sip a drink before the fireplace in the auberge as a prelude, then gradually move to a cozy table for two by the window.

The meal is overseen by Linda's husband, Gérard, a former executive chef, whose menu is heavy on regional products and whose delicious three-course table d'hôte might include endive stuffed with salmon smoked on the premises, rack of lamb with fresh herbs, and strawberry mousse cake. Watch the sunset with your dear—and if you can spot a deer on the property as you dine, you'll have an "endearing" memory to take home tomorrow.

FOR MORE ROMANCE

If you'd rather put on an equestrian display than watch one, skip the polo matches on Sunday afternoon and go to **Le Fier Coursier** (416 rang St-Georges in Rigaud; 450–451–4410; half-day rides, $50 per person), where you'll don a riding hat as a safety precaution and take a very romantic horseback ride through heavily wooded trails around Mount Rigaud. Owner Victor Rodriguez, who speaks four languages, loves to cater to couples. He and his French-speaking wife ride with you. After your idyll in the woods, it's time for dinner at the auberge, which is only a mile from the stables.

Forever Loyal
SKIWIPPI IN NORTH HATLEY

NOT EVERYONE IN THE COLONIES APPLAUDED the Declaration of Independence in 1776. Thousands of colonists refused to rebel against the King of England. Some of these so-called Loyalists fled to Canada and settled in a largely unexplored region of southeastern Québec, where they became the first permanent settlers and left an enduring mark.

A British flavor still lingers today in the Eastern Townships, or Estrie, a string of villages just north of the Vermont-Maine border with names like Dunham, Stanstead, Eastman, Roxton Pond, Knowlton, Ayer's Cliff, and North Hatley. Founded by a Loyalist from Connecticut in 1803, North Hatley (population 704) rivals New England for stunning natural beauty, and given the considerable French influence today, has a flair and a gastronomic edge that's hard to match farther south.

Modern-day Loyalists—couples devoted to each other—get a chance to sample three distinct country inns in the heart of Loyalist territory on this romantic getaway, traveling from one to the next on cross-country skis. What lies ahead is a splendid adventure, indoors and outdoors, that will have you swearing loyalty to your partner— forever.

PRACTICAL NOTES: Skiwippi is offered during peak ski season from January to April and is designed for an intermediate ski level, although beginners can do part of the trail. The three-day package is based on a Sunday, Monday, or Tuesday arrival and starts at about $400 per person, depending on choice of room. Bring your own skis and ice

◆ Ski along miles of marked cross-country trail that lie between three distinctly different residences: a French auberge, a Colonial-style mansion, and a British hunting lodge. You'll sleep and eat in each residence on a package called Skiwippi.

◆ Before you take to the trails, explore the village of North Hatley, where colonists loyal to the king of England settled after the Declaration of Independence was signed south of the border. The town still has a British flavor. Order a mammoth hamburger at the **Pilsen Restaurant and Pub** (55 rue Principale; 819–842–2971), then admire fabulous naïf art at **Galerie Jeannine Blais** (100 rue Main; 819–842–2784).

◆ At day's end, warm up with hot mulled wine in your lodging. Relax in thick terry bathrobes and from your bedroom window watch the snow fall on Lake Massawippi. Enjoy a gourmet dinner at every stop.

skates (if you'd like to figure skate); rental equipment is not available either at the inns or in town. For those who don't ski, a wonderful alternative is a gastronomic variation of the package called A Moveable Feast, which is offered year-round. Visitors on this plan move inn to inn as well, but they need not exercise to earn their more elaborate six-course gastronomic dinners.

DAY ONE: morning

North Hatley is about ninety minutes by car from Montréal or from Dorval Airport. Take Autoroute 10 to exit 21 and follow the signs to North Hatley. Tourisme Estrie (800–355–5755) will send you maps and a guide to the region. You won't know where you'll be staying the first night until you reserve; the sequence is predetermined and varies weekly. Check-in time at all the inns is between 3:00 and 4:00 P.M., but you are invited to arrive early, store your bags, change into ski clothes if you'd like—or explore the village.

For our purposes, we'll start the getaway at **Auberge Hatley** (P.O. Box 330; 325 Virgin Road; 819–842–2451), built for a wealthy merchant as a summer estate in 1903. Current owners Liliane and Robert Gagnon decorated the house in country French style, put a premium on fine dining—the inn has won every gastronomic prize in Québec

—and have shown their support of local artists by exhibiting works of art on the premises. Liliane, in fact, used to own a gallery before the couple bought the inn.

Twenty-five bedrooms are here, some with fireplace and whirlpool bath. Since you have arrived before check-in, drop your bags and explore the village, where you'll have lunch.

DAY ONE: afternoon

LUNCH

If you blink, you'll miss the main street in the village of North Hatley, which is only a few blocks from the auberge—and only a few blocks in total. **Pilsen Restaurant and Pub** (55 rue Principale; 819–842–2971; inexpensive) sits alongside the bridge over the Massawippi River. Descend from street level to the pub, order a mammoth hamburger and a locally brewed beer, and gaze out the windows onto the frozen waters that surround you.

Your next stop is just a few steps away. **Galerie Jeannine Blais** (100 rue Main; 819–842–2784) specializes in *art naïf*—all the artists exhibited here have no formal training. The work here is vibrant, dreamy, fantastical—and captivating. So is Blais, a passionate champion of the *naïf* genre, who can tell you stories about every artist. Every fall she holds a five-week exhibition to showcase *naïf* artists from as far as France and the former Yugoslavia. Thousands flock to the gallery to meet the talent—and to purchase an original. You'll almost certainly fall for an oil painting, a painting on glass, a wood sculpture, or a bronze. Take your time. Come back and look again. I'm sure you will find something to remind you of your visit.

> *"There is a pleasure in the pathless woods . . ."*
>
> —*Lord Byron*

In the same building as the gallery, you'll find **Emporium** (100 rue Main; 819–842–4233), which carries porcelain dolls, Canadian antiques, and candy. Browse and perhaps buy a memento or a gift for someone back home.

Now your room should be ready. Walk back to the inn, stoke the fireplace in your room, pull off your cold-weather gear, and relax in your terry bathrobes until it is time to dress for dinner.

DAY ONE: evening

DINNER

In the common rooms at Auberge Hatley, you'll be surrounded by antiques and art. You'll see the work of some of the same artists you saw this afternoon at Jeannine Blais. Sit down on a comfy leather sofa near the old brick fireplace in the living room and have a drink before dinner.

The dining room here is a country French affair with lots of art hanging on the walls. The kitchen is so highly touted, Robert Gagnon says the majority of the guests book a room to sample the food. Gagnon built a hydroponic greenhouse not far from the inn to supply the kitchen with fresh herbs, a variety of greens, and the edible flowers you'll see decorating the plates. Main courses include duck, pheasant, prawns, and lamb. Eating here is a marvelous break from the rest of the world. You'll feel layers of stress melt away as you enjoy the meal and a bottle from the inn's noted wine cellar, which houses more than 8,000 bottles under 650 labels.

You'll be rising early to ski, so leave the dining room after you toast each other with the last drops of wine. Return to your room. Cozy up and turn out the light.

DAY TWO: morning/afternoon

BREAKFAST

Dress for skiing, pack your suitcases, and leave them in your room. Now tank up at the breakfast bar at Auberge Hatley. You'll find a fine selection of juice, fresh fruit, cereal, eggs, bacon, croissants, and muffins. Fill 'er up. You're going to earn the meal.

When you're ready to exit, leave your room keys and your car keys at

Southern Hospitality
Up North

This exercise might take some imagination when snow is on the ground, but try to envision the opulent summer garden parties given by Mr. and Mrs. Henry Atkinson of Atlanta at the couple's residence—which is now Hovey Manor. After the bitter Civil War, wealthy Southerners like the Atkinsons preferred to summer in Québec rather than in the United States. Word is that when the trains carrying Southerners went through New England en route to North Hatley, passengers drew their blinds until they'd bypassed Yankee territory.

the front desk. Your hosts at Hatley will direct you onto the cross-country ski trail and set you in the right direction for your next destination. Then they'll bid you a fond goodbye. Don't worry if you should break a ski or encounter another problem—a ski patrol combs the trail in a Ski-Doo, alert for any problem. While you're on the trail—drawing pleasure from the otherwise pathless woods surrounding the wide path you'll follow—management at Hatley will whisk your bags and your car to **Ripplecove Inn** (P.O. Box 246; 700 Ripplecove Road in Ayer's Cliff; 819–838–4296), where the atmosphere is distinctly British.

Built as a fishing camp in 1945 by innkeeper Jeffrey Stafford's parents, every inch of the lakeside camp has been renovated by Stafford and his wife Debbie. It now has the look of an elegant hunting lodge frequented by the English upper crust. Twenty-six rooms are here, many with a fireplace, a double whirlpool bath, a private balcony—and a television. When you arrive on skis, staff here will show you where to store your gear. After it's tucked away, warm up at the inn's **Nag's Head Pub**, where the wallpaper comes from England and where skiers routinely relax with a glass of hot mulled wine—a combination of red wine, sugar, cloves, and cinnamon. A drink or two and you can retire to your room for a different kind of rest and relaxation before dinner.

DAY TWO: evening

DINNER

In keeping with the hunting lodge theme, the paintings at Ripplecove center on hounds and foxes. At dinnertime, enter the Victorian-style dining room that overlooks the lake, and scan a contemporary French menu that puts a premium on local specialties, such as Brome Lake duck (from a town nearby), rabbit, pheasant, and poached salmon. If you start this itinerary on Tuesday and arrive at Ripplecove on Wednesday, you'll be entertained by a classical piano recital after dinner—a midweek tradition. Enjoy the music, and pretend you're hobnobbing with the Royals.

DAY THREE: morning

BREAKFAST

Like the previous morning, breakfast at Ripplecove includes eggs, cereal, and a range of pastry and bread at the Hunt Buffet. Stoke your fire as you break bread and watch day break over Lake Massawippi.

The Lake is where you'll actually start the trail today, skiing over 5 inches of solid ice to eventually link up with the path. Management will once again send you forth and move your belongings to the next destination, where there's a family connection.

Manoir Hovey (P.O. Box 60; 575 Hovey Road in North Hatley; 819–842–2421) is owned by Steve Stafford, Jeffrey's older brother. Manoir Hovey was built in 1900 by Atlanta industrialist Henry Atkinson, president of Georgia Power, who patterned it upon George Washington's home at Mount Vernon, Virginia. Steve Stafford and his wife Kathy visited Mount Vernon for inspiration after they bought the mansion and, in renovating the home, tried to remain faithful to Atkinson's original intent, leaving untouched the white pillars in front, the stone fireplaces, a book-lined library, and a wood dining table in the taproom. Après ski, you'll want to visit the taproom for a drink, then sink into a couch in the library and pick up a book or magazine. Your guest room is a cheery colonial masterpiece with canopy bed and flowered fabric, so you may also be tempted to get cozy there before dinner.

DAY THREE: evening

DINNER

A colonial feel might pervade the inn, but it doesn't penetrate the kitchen. Québec-born chef Roland Ménard cooks French cuisine with an Asian flair, which means less cream, fewer sauces, and more vegetables and garden greens. The chef here smokes his own salmon, bakes his own bread, and, inspired by one of the Stafford children, even offers a scrumptious vegetarian platter to those who may not eat meat. Pheasant, lamb, and elk are also on the menu. The dimly lit dining room is wonderfully romantic, and the service is attentive and unrushed. Savor your moments here—you'll treasure the memories later.

The wood-burning fireplace in your room is waiting. Cuddle under the blankets and fall asleep as the embers die. You'll have a buffet breakfast in the morning, and, if you have skates, you'll take a few turns around the Manoir's ice-skating rink before you glide home.

FOR MORE ROMANCE

Try ice-fishing, an intimate experience at Manoir Hovey, where the fishing hut has mahogony floorboards, padded seats, and a wood stove. Management provides the fishing lines and will even cook the catch of the day upon request.

Life Is a Carnival
QUÉBEC CITY

UÉBEC CITY'S CARNAVAL is a monumental effort to tame winter. Rio, New Orleans, and Venice may have noteworthy carnivals, but the world's largest winter carnival has a distinction the others don't: Québec City's Carnaval is built around snow, ice, and chilly weather.

And while Québec City may be cold for Carnaval, it doesn't prevent you from having a hot time. Québec City exudes antiquity. It offers the largest collection of seventeenth- and eighteenth-century buildings in North America. It also offers beauty galore. The city shimmers in winter, when the ancient fortifications that surround it sparkle under a regal mantle of white.

Lovers will rejoice in the gorgeous spectacle—and in the absolute necessity to cuddle very close day and night in Québec City (for warmth, of course).

PRACTICAL NOTES: Forget vanity on this trip and go for warmth. Get a pair of lined, thick-soled boots that won't fail you on an icy patch of sidewalk when you're watching the parade or admiring the ice sculptures. The happiest people at Carnaval seem to be those snugly encased in all-in-one ski suits. Bring your skates if you'd like to use the rink at the Frontenac. Make your hotel reservations far in advance. Six months before Carnaval, 90 percent of the Frontenac's rooms are booked. When you call, ask for a room with a river view.

Via Rail (514–989–2626) operates trains to Québec City from Montréal's Gare Centrale several times a day. If you book a first-class seat on Via, it includes a hot meal for breakfast and lunch. You can also

Romance AT A GLANCE

◆ Ride the rails from Montréal to historic **Québec City** for one of the largest parties in the world: Carnaval! Stay in the world-famous **Château Frontenac** (1 rue des Carrières; Québec City; 418–692–3861 or 800–441–1414), where Roosevelt, Stalin, and Churchill convened during World War II and where Alfred Hitchcock made the film I Confess.

◆ Get into a party mood by visiting a palace made from sixteen million pounds of snow, where you'll greet a live snowman standing 7 feet tall. Admire snow sculptures made by artisans around the world, and then visit the home of the late Ti-Père, who collected Carnaval memorabilia. Here you'll trace the earliest days of the celebration and drink a potent brew called caribou.

◆ Pencil in brunch at **Le Champlain** (in the Château Frontenac), where the waiters dress in period costume. After the meal, head for the cobblestone streets in Lower Town, where shops filled with clothing, jewelry, glassware, and fine art line the narrow walkways. When you've reached your credit card limit, drop your purchases at the Frontenac and go skating on an outdoor rink overlooking the St-Lawrence River.

book a combination ticket: a first-class seat (with meal) one way and a coach seat (without meal) the other way. Your choice would depend on what time you want to travel. First-class travel costs about $200 round trip; a combination fare about $150. Both fares, however, drop if you book in advance. Tickets can be mailed to you if booked thirty days ahead, or you can pick them up at the Amtrak station.

You've called ahead to the Carnaval office (418–626–3716; or toll-free from mid-January to the end of Carnaval at 800–363–7777) for a schedule of the seventeen-day event, which is held from the end of January to mid-February (January 28 to February 13 in the year 2000). Festive parades are held on two consecutive Saturdays. Build your weekend around either one. The second Sunday of Carnaval, the famed Course en Canot takes place at 1:30 P.M. Take the event into consideration when you plan your trip. It's a thrill to see five-person teams drag, push, pull, steer, and paddle the 250-pound ice canoes across the partially frozen river from Québec to the town of Lévis—and back—as their ancestors did up until the early 1900s.

DAY ONE: morning

On the three-hour train trip to Québec, founded as New France by Samuel de Champlain in 1608, time passes quickly while you read and relax, enjoying a hot breakfast or maybe an apéritif and a lunch of California corn salad, tuna steak, and Black Forest cake served on a tray table that pulls out from your seat. Before long, you've arrived at the Gare du Palais station in Québec City. It's a five-minute cab ride to your hotel, where check-in time is 3:00 P.M.

DAY ONE: afternoon

The most famous building in Canada may well be **Le Château Frontenac** (1 rue des Carrières; Québec City; 418–692–3861 or 800–441–1414; from $200 per night). Opened in 1893 and named for a French count who ruled New France from the exact site in the late 1600s, it sits on cliffs 200 feet above the St-Lawrence River. Today, it is as much a symbol of the nation as the Royal Canadian Mounted Police.

With its pitched copper roof, chimneys, and Scottish brick exterior, the Victorian structure looks as if it belongs in a fairy tale. Not surprisingly, the 610-room hotel has a fabled and romantic past. Aviator Charles Lindbergh used the hotel's turreted roof as a navigation aid when delivering medicine to a friend. Franklin Roosevelt and Winston Churchill planned the Normandy invasion here in August of 1943. The following September, they again met at the Château, this time to discuss plans for Japan.

When you arrive, check in to your room overlooking the river and take a few moments to absorb the impact of this incredible facility. A $60 million renovation in 1993 for its hundredth birthday gave the hotel a face-lift and added sixty-six rooms, a Greco-Roman-style indoor pool, and a modern health club.

Dress warmly for a short walk to the Grande Allée, the Champs-Élysées of Québec City. Here you'll find perhaps the most impressive spectacle of the Carnaval: a life-sized snow palace erected in front of the Citadelle. The structure has grown more ornate with the years. Made from sixteen million pounds of snow, it is fashioned by more than a dozen artists working for two months.

The palace site is official Carnaval headquarters. It is home to *le bain de neige*, a polar-bear snow bath that attracts people, not bears. The site is also the stamping grounds for Bonhomme, the jovial snowman who first appeared at Carnaval in 1955. The 7-foot mascot, a cross between Santa Claus and the Pillsbury doughboy, can be sighted at the palace every day. He wears a red *toque* (hat) and woven *ceinture fléchée* (belt), typical garb of the Québeçois of yore. You might want to purchase a finely made *fléchée* in one of the boutiques in town and tie it around your waist.

Check out the sculptures created for the International Snow Sculpture Contest by artisans from more than a dozen nations— including those from warm-weather countries who have never even seen snow before they start to carve their designs from massive blocks. Admire Porte St-Louis, the regal gate leading into the walled city. Québec is surrounded by nearly 3 miles of fortifications. Don't leave the site without trying a sweet Québeçois treat: maple syrup candy on a stick—a French-Canadian version of taffy. Roll your own at a sugar shack on-site.

On a narrow residential street not far from the palace, you'll get a genuine feel for the history and tra-

Take the Stairs

The staircase in the lobby of the Château Frontenac is a copy of Marie Antoinette's staircase in the Petit Trianon. It was specially designed to show off the elegant silk gowns worn by the female guests. These ladies climbed the steps slowly, paused on the marble landing, and then made their grand entrance into a ballroom decorated in blue and gold to resemble the Hall of Mirrors at Versailles.

dition of the event on rue Ste-Thérèse, closed to traffic during Carnaval. Since the first modern Carnaval in 1954, residents here have sculpted their own snowy designs right in their front yards. Birds, wolves, and Beluga whales lined the street for years, drawing so much attention that, at one point, Carnaval organizers decided to spiffy up the place by lending a professional sculptor to help the residents with their work.

A few blocks down the street is the 137-year-old home formerly occupied by Ti-Père, otherwise known as Lionel Faucher. Before he died in 1990, Ti-Père, an inveterate collector of Carnaval memorabilia, opened his home to visitors during Carnaval. Some 10,000 sightseers would march through every year. Now his relatives continue his tradition. A caribou bar, established with the blessing of the Québec liquor board, sits in a corner of the basement. If you haven't already purchased your red plastic cane to hold caribou, a blend of wood alcohol and red wine, buy it here.

Now you'll return to the Frontenac, where you'll dine before the parade tonight, which starts at 7:00 P.M.

DAY ONE: evening

DINNER

Café de la Terrasse (moderate) in the Frontenac serves a wonderful hot and cold buffet—everything from pasta salads to carved roast beef—in a dining room overlooking Dufferin Terrace, the 2,200-foot promenade built as a beautification project by Lord Dufferin, governor general of Canada, the Queen's representative. Feast on the bountiful offerings at the buffet and revel in the marvelous setting. After you've sampled the many treats, including an array of pastries for dessert, bundle up and proceed to the parade.

If you are here the first weekend of Carnaval, the parade winds through Lower Town. The second weekend it snakes through downtown, site of the government buildings and stone gates you visited today. Grab your cane—some folks pour out the caribou and fill it with their own special brew. You might want to buy a red plastic bugle as well. When Carnavalers blow their bugles in unison, it sounds like a herd of moose is ready to storm the city gates. Carnaval floats are created in a special workshop by thirty part-time artisans employed by the organizers. The parade features clowns, marching bands, and more than twenty brightly lit floats.

Return to the hotel after the parade, and defrost with a drink at the Bar St-Laurent. There's live music on weekends and a dance floor here. Take your cue.

DAY TWO: morning

You could sleep late this morning, but why not work out in the hotel's modern health club before you indulge in a sinful repast? The centerpiece of the health club is a new indoor lap swimming pool built as part of the $60 million renovation undertaken for the hotel's centennial celebration in 1993. If you are staying at the hotel on the package that includes a massage, this might be a good time to avail yourselves of the pleasure. Afterward, you'll partake in a gustatory pleasure in the hotel's formal dining room.

BRUNCH

Le Champlain room serves a sumptuous Sunday brunch (10:00 A.M. to 2:00 P.M.; expensive). The staff wears garb evocative of *l'ancien regime*. The fabulous menu includes *boeuf* Wellington, lamb, and shrimp. When Alfred Hitchcock made the film *I Confess* with Montgomery Clift and Anne Baxter at the Frontenac in the early 1950s, Baxter used to stun guests in Le Champlain by lighting up a cigar after her evening meal.

After brunch, watch the Course en Canot (if you've decided to schedule it) from the boardwalk at the Frontenac. The ice canoe used to be the only form of local winter transport. Boats were carved from the trunk of a huge pine tree. While the canoes in today's race are made of fiberglass, the elements in the mighty St-Lawrence have not changed. Teams still battle the current while darting around ice floes and avoiding slushy traps that might plunge them into freezing waters. The winners usually make the round trip in under a half hour.

DAY TWO: afternoon

After the race, take a cab or the Funicular ($1.00) outside the hotel to Lower Town to shop away the afternoon at the boutiques and galleries along narrow, cobblestone streets. The city of Québec (*kebec* is an Algonquin Indian word meaning "place where the river narrows") is divided into two parts—Upper and

Lower Town. Upper Town was the traditional domain of the military and the government. Lower Town was where merchants traded and bartered within easy reach of the port. Today, commercial activity keeps going strong, thanks to tourism.

Le Quartier Petit-Champlain off Place Royale (the original habitation of Samuel de Champlain) is a good place to start shopping. Boutiques here offer clothing, glassware, pottery, and jewelry. Antiques shops dot rue St-Paul, and on rue du Trésor, near Place d'Armes, local artists sell watercolors, sketches, and prints.

When your arms are heavy with packages, return to the hotel, store your purchases, and be a little daring. Take the toboggan run on Dufferin Terrace ($1.00). Even the faint-hearted will enjoy the descent. Then, if you'd like, go skating on a rink near the slide. While you glide over the ice, a waltz plays in the background. When you've circled the rink, hand in hand, to your hearts' content, return to the hotel and dress for dinner at one of the trendiest restaurants in Lower Town.

DAY TWO: evening

DINNER

Chef Daniel Vezina and his wife Suzanne Gagnon named their restaurant **Laurie Raphaël** after their two children, but there's nothing childish about this sophisticated little spot (117 rue Dalhousie; 418–692–4555; reservations required; open every night; expensive). The food is a throwback to the past with a forward-looking approach. The decor is deco and very romantic. The menu changes every three weeks here, but favorites include grilled rabbit flavored with honey and Labrador caribou cooked with raisins—fine examples of Québec regional cuisine with a modern twist. Vezina hosts a cooking show and is a well-known TV personality in Québec.

After dinner, return to the hotel, where you'll walk, glove in glove, along Dufferin Terrace in the still of the night. The gazebos dotting the boardwalk are graced with snow. Stop for a moment and look across the frozen river, where the competitors in the canoe race struggled so valiantly earlier in the day. In the stillness, notice the patchwork quilt of irregular-shaped roofs on the buildings in Lower Town. Engrave the memories in your mind. You and your sweetie will revive them often when you return home.

For More Romance

If you choose instead to visit Québec City in summer, when the city is equally romantic, replace the first day of this itinerary with a fabulous daylong whale-watching cruise up the St-Lawrence River to the Saguenay Fjord. Operated with precision by the renowned cruise ship organization **Famille Dufour** (418–827–8836; 800–463–5250; $139, includes two meals and a snack) and led by a bilingual tour guide, the white catamaran leaves from the pier in Québec City at 7:30 A.M. and covers almost 400 miles by the time it docks around 7:00 P.M. Start the day aboard ship with a hearty breakfast while you listen to live music provided by a keyboardist and singer. Between traditional Québec folk tunes (and pop numbers later on), your guide provides trenchant commentary on the sites. You'll pass Grosse Île, where Irish immigrants to Canada were quarantined in the last century, and La Petite Rivière de St-François, one-time home of celebrated French-Canadian author Gabrielle Roy. Ahead lies Tadoussac, the whale-watching mecca, and Famille Dufour almost guarantees a sighting. I saw three minke whales on the cruise. You'll also see the village of Pointe-au-Pic, where President William Taft summered and where he swore that the air was "like champagne." Finally, you'll arrive at the Saguenay Fjord, where a glacier existed more than 10,000 years ago. High above, a huge statue of the Virgin Mary looms. How it got to its mountaintop perch is a fascinating story; you'll hear the tale as you both toss coins into the sea (for luck) and listen to the strains of "Ave Maria" wafting from the boat. It's a quiet moment you'll recall again and again long after your visit.

Special Indexes
ROMANTIC RESTAURANTS

Restaurant price categories in this index, represented by one to three dollar signs, designate the cost of an appetizer, an entree, and dessert for one person. The approximate price for each category is indicated in the following key:

Inexpensive ($): Less than $20
Moderate ($$): $20 to $40
Expensive ($$$): $40 and above

Asian

Chez Caroline ($), 1844 rue Amherst, 115

Chez Chine ($$), Hotel Jardin Sinomonde, 145

L'Orchidées de Chine ($$), 2017 rue Peel, 49

Sushi Maki ($$) 1240 rue Crescent, 146

Zen ($$), 1050 rue Sherbrooke Ouest, 134

Breakfast/Brunch

Beauty's ($), 93 rue Mont-Royal Ouest, 167

Casual/Cafes

Biddle's Jazz & Ribs ($), 2060 rue Alymer, 187

Bistro On The Avenue ($), 1362 avenue Greene, 135

Cafe Bicicletta ($), 1251 rue Rachel Est, 55

Café Cherrier ($), 3635 rue St-Denis, 38

Café Le Petit Flore ($), 1145 rue Fleury Est, 82

Café Romy ($), 1307 rue Ste-Catherine Ouest, 30

Café Terrasse Fleur de l'Île ($), Jardin des Floralies, Île Notre-Dame, 50

Frite Alors ($), 433 rue Rachel, 46

Galaxie Diner ($), 4801 rue St-Denis, 127

l'Avenue ($), 922 avenue Mont-Royal Est, 16

L'eau Vive ($), Biosphere, 61

La Boîte à Café ($), 1112 boulevard de Maisonneuve Est, 117

La Paryse ($), 302 rue Ontario Est, 193

La Rotonde ($), 185 Ste-Catherine Ouest, 37

Le Grand Pa ($), 2481 rue de L'église, Val-David, 218

Ovation Resto-bar ($), Centre Molson, 74

Patisserie de Gascogne ($), 4825 rue Sherbrooke, 69

Patisserie L'Opéra ($), 1185 rue Fleury Est, 85

Petite Europa ($), 1616 rue Ste-Catherine Ouest, 41

Pilsen Restaurant and Pub ($), 55 rue Principal, North Hatley, 229

Première Moisson ($), Marche Atwater, 57

Schwartz's Delicatessen ($), 3895 boulevard St-Laurent, 169

Second Cup ($), 1551 rue St-Denis, 21

Stash's Cafe ($), 200 rue St-Paul Ouest, 10

Toi, Moi & Café ($), 244 avenue Laurier Ouest, 128

Van Houtte ($), 1538 rue Sherbrooke, 65

Dessert

Le Daphne ($), 3803 rue St-Denis, 125

Patisserie Bruxelloise ($), 860 avenue Mont-Royal Est, 16

Patisserie C.J. Regent ($), 68 rue de la Gauchetière Ouest, 188

Patisserie L'Opéra ($), 1185 rue Fleury Est, 85

Strudel's Bakery ($), 429 chemin Main, Hudson, 224

Eclectic

Ambiance Tea Room ($), 1874 rue Notre-Dame Ouest, 119

Exotika ($$-$$$), 400 avenue Laurier Ouest, 128

Globe ($$$), 3455 St-Laurent, 189

Le 9e ($), Eaton's ninth floor, 108

Steak

Gibby's ($$), 298 Place d'Youville, 11

Vegetarian

Le Commensal ($), 1204 McGill
College, 195

ROMANTIC LODGINGS

Indulgent

Auberge du Vieux Port, 56
Auberge Hatley, 228
Château Frontenac, 236
Hotel Vogue, 99
Maison Pierre du Calvet, 4
Manoir Hovey, 232
Marriott Château Champlain, 72
Omni Montréal, 130
Reine Elizabeth, 106
Ripplecove Inn, 231
Ritz-Carlton Kempinski, 23

Moderate

B&B on the Park, 44
Château de l'Argoat, 185

Hotel Wyndham Montréal, 214
Hotel de La Montagne, 28
Hotel du Lac Carling, 210
Hotel Jardin Sinomonde, 145
Hotel President Laval, 81
Manoir Rouville-Campbell, 202

Inexpensive

Angelica Blue B&B, 179
Auberge Les Passants du Sans Soucy, 91
Auberge St-Denis-sur-Richelieu, 153
Aux Portes de la nuit, 36
Château Versailles, 63
Jardin d'Antoine, 14
Maison de Bavière, 215
Roy d'Carreau, 114
Willow Place Inn, 220

EVENING DIVERSIONS

Bars

Hurley's Irish Pub, 78
Jello Bar, 189
Sir Winston Churchill Pub, 137

Comedy Clubs

Club Soda, 186
Comedy Nest, 182
Comedyworks, 183

Dancing

Cactus, 19
Deux Pierrots, 150
Le 727, 109
Spectrum, 189

Sir Winston Churchill Pub, 137
Tango Libre, 22
Thursday's, 97

Jazz and Blues Clubs

Biddle's Jazz & Ribs, 187
Café Sarajevo, 186
Club Soda, 186
Exotika, 128
Hotel de La Montagne, 28
Jello Bar, 189
L'Air du Temps, 8, 121, 186
Le Sofa Bar-Porto, 126
Les Beaux Esprits, 194
Upstairs, 186

Geographical Index

VIEUX MONTRÉAL:

EASTERN TOWNSHIPS:

Activities

Attractions

Lodging

Restaurants

General Index

A

Alexander Calder's *Man*, 95
Altitude, 20
Ambiance Tea Room, 119
Amelis, 128
Amphitheatre Bell, 76, 112
Angelica Blue B&B, 179
Antiquaire Joyal, 116
Antiqués Alley, 113
Antiqués Puces-Libre, 125
Antiquités Claude Blain, 120
Antiquités Curiosités, 116
Antiquités Michelle Parent, 120
Antiquités Pednault, 116
Aqua Cité, 127
Arboretum, 146
Archambault Musique, 21
Arthur Quentin, 125
Atwater Market, 57, 91
Auberge de La Fontaine, 123
Auberge des Gallant, 225
Auberge du Vieux Port, 56
Auberge Hatley, 228
Auberge Les Passants du Sans
    Soucy, 91
Auberge St-Denis-sur-Richelieu, 153
Aux Baisers Volés, 19
Aux Deux Pierrots, 150
Aux Portes de la nuit, 36
Aventurier, 20
Avenue Greene, 135
Avenue Laurier Ouest, 128
Avenue Mont-Royal, 15
Azimut, 20

B

Bagel Factory, 170
Balad'Air, 208
Balloon Festival, 208
Bank of Montréal, 119
Baumgarten House, 26
B&B on the Park, 44
Beauty's (restaurant), 167
Beaver Club (restaurant), 31
Belle Neige, 216
Benaiah Gibb Pavilion, 30
Benson & Hedges International
    Fireworks Competition, 179
Bersons Monuments, 169
Beth Shlomo, 169
Bibliothèque Nationale du
    Québec, 21
Biddle's Jazz & Ribs, 187
Bijouterie J. Omer Roy & Fils, 17
Biodome, 46
Biosphere Reserve, 207
Biosphere, 60
Birger Christensen fur salon, 132
Bistro à Champlain, 105
Bistro On The Avenue, 135
Bonsecours Market, 148, 180
Botanical Garden, 47, 145
Boulevard, 69
Boulevard St-Laurent, 167
Boutique des Canadiens, 74

C

Cactus, 19
Café Bicicletta, 55
Café Cherrier, 38
Café de la Terrasse, 238
Café de Paris, 25
Café des Artistes, 188
Café Le Petit Flore, 82
Café Romy, 30
Café Sarajevo, 186
Café Terrasse Fleur de l'Île, 50
Camille Brets, 85

About the Author

LINDA KAY, A FORMER SPORTS COLUMNIST for the *Chicago Tribune*, moved to Quebec for love. Her columns and opinion pieces have since appeared in the *Globe and Mail*, *Montreal Gazette*, and *London Free Press*, and her magazine credits include *Chatelaine*, *Newsweek*, and *Inside Sports*. Kay currently teaches journalism at Concordia University in Montréal and resides just outside of the city with her French-Canadian husband and bilingual daughter.